HOUSE OF YES

The story of Truck of Love

By Susan Fullerton
Illustrated by Pete Fullerton

Dedication

This book is dedicated to:

Pete

Our children: Tim, Julie, Ian, Peter, and Andy
And their families: Rob, Gregory, Kayleigh, Timothy,
Samantha, Anthony, Katrine, Alissa, Ethan, Ella, Audra,
Hugo, and Fiona

Gordon Stewart and Father Elias Galvez

Sister Patrice, Sister Anne, Sister Carla,
Cathy and Nancy

Julie, Michael, and Susan

Ken and Sal

The countless people who are and have been
Truck of Love

Thank you

Acknowledgements

This story could not have been properly told if it were not for the many people who have encouraged us and reminded us of memories long forgotten, names in the shadows of our lives, and events jumbled in our fading recollections.

It could not have been told without the permission of our children who were often caught up in the chaos of the life we chose, who suffered because of it; but who each triumphed with the wisdom and knowledge they gained from our collective experiences. Though we were often distracted, you are the most important people in our lives.

Thank you to everyone who answered our plea for stories. I have tried to be true to what you wrote.

A special thanks to Nancy for reading and re-reading and giving such valuable suggestions.

Thank you to Andy, Rob, and Kayleigh for your insights and counsel about writing and formatting.

Please forgive any discrepancies with dates, events, and details. It is impossible to recall every fact over these past fifty years. When I did not have good notes or journals, I tried to be true to the spirit of the people and experiences.

As you read, remember that *Truck of Love* has always been about relationships. That is why there are so many stories about the people we have encountered. We are eternally grateful for each of you who have graced our lives with your presence.

Foreword

Driving down a country road in the early hours of a South Carolina February morning, my parents were taking me to the airport after a short visit from New York City. My mom - you know her as Sue - had knee surgery about a month beforehand, and I wanted to come check on the folks to make sure their gutters were staying clean. I was expecting some sort of doomsday scenario: dishes piled up, cobwebs covering the ceiling, mushrooms in the bathtub. As it turned out, they couldn't have been doing better, and I realized I had come down more for myself than for them. A fitting tribute to my upbringing and the selfishness of altruism.

When we get together the conversation is always lively, and that drive was no different. We spoke of the beginnings of the *Truck of Love*, about how I and my four siblings, remembered and coped with it, and we started brainstorming titles for the manuscript you're about to dive into. When it was said out loud, "House of Yes" seemed fitting, and it still does. If you ever want a master class in how to banish the word "no" from your vocabulary, look no further than Pete and Sue. Sure, as we were growing up there were plenty of "No, you can't put that paperclip in the electrical socket," or "No, you can't have that sugary cereal," or "No, you may not punch your brother in the face repeatedly." The title refers not to the banalities of life in the Fullerton household, but to the broader spectrum of a family being led by parents who never faltered in the choice they made almost four decades ago to live their faith rather than talk about how they wished they could.

There were plenty of obstacles that could have, and many people would argue, should have stopped them from saying "yes." Can we afford this with five kids? Do we care what others think of this decision? What happens if a homeless person asks to use our bathroom? What if we need a new couch? How will we afford groceries?

Well, much of our diet after the transition was rice and beans, and as it turned out, a bunch of homeless people showed up to use our bathroom. And our phone. And sleep in our van. And on that van, in huge block letters, was written *Truck of Love* with our phone number prominently displayed underneath. Pause to infer the phone calls we got at all hours of the night...eh hem.

Imagine finally convincing a girl to come watch a movie at your house, and a schizophrenic woman named Jo-Jo coming through the front door asking to "call his Lordship in British Colombia." What adolescent gets to experience that? Yes. *Gets* to. Who else can claim to have been dropped off at school dances in a fifteen-seater bearing the title *Truck of Love*? In case you're wondering, no, the van did not do well with the ladies. Christopher Marlowe was right, "Money can't buy love, but it improves your bargaining position."

Yet, through all the late night door knocks, Guatemalan refugees, teenagers with no place else to go, homeless folks crashing our holiday celebrations, phone calls from women who were suicidal because they were unable to escape domestic abuse - you name it - none of these pitfalls were the concern. The heart of the decision lay with the true feeling my parents had of being called to the work by God. And it won't surprise you to hear that they've never wavered in the decision.

Imagine your home. It shouldn't take too long. There's a good chance you're reading this perched on your couch. Now imagine your home being 1,200 square feet and housing eighteen people at a time. Not necessarily the same eighteen people, but a revolving door of friends of the family in your shed, a relief worker who biked to your Northern California house from Tijuana (yes, biked the entire way and still showed up with a bouquet of flowers before crashing his bike on the front lawn), distant cousins who weren't able to cope with home life, Native American students, friends of friends, and friends of their friends - and, of course, Jo-Jo out in the van.

Take a look at the cover of the book. I'll wait. That's our childhood house. Notice how the door is open? That is not allegorical. That was life. There was a policy in our house to never lock the door.

Some of you may be wondering how the kids in the family fared through all of this. If not, please skip the next few paragraphs.

After long talks and years to ponder, my siblings and I wouldn't change how we grew up. Not even if a time machine were invented and we could all go back to that fateful day we sat around the table and our folks asked us one by one if Dad could quit his job and work on TOL full-time. Well, perhaps knowing the full extent of sacrifice we were agreeing to would have made us pause. Maybe we'd opt for a simpler, normal life: video games, soccer leagues, and the occasional European vacation. But how could we change what was, without a doubt, the most impacting event in our lives?

That having been said, growing up Fullerton did come with certain challenges. My brothers, sister, and I always felt we were on the fringe. Never quite a part of the affluent community we grew up in, but never far from it. Some of the students that went on the Tijuana or Arizona trips with TOL came back complaining of culture shock. Understandable, as the visitations were to extremely poor communities: families living in garbage dumps, Mexican prisons, distressed communities on Native American Reservations. To us, it was simply where we spent summer, winter, and spring breaks. It was a chance to road trip with our dad and visit Disneyland on the way home. It was our family.

But fringe living is far more challenging in the adolescent years. There are tantrums, and arguments, and questions of why we couldn't have everything that everyone we knew had. The toys, the gadgets, the cars. Why did Art (another homeless follower) have to stink up our couch? Why weren't our parents judgmental about the people they helped? Some of them, such as Art, were in their state by choice, after all. Always the same answer: It's not our job to judge. We vowed to help those who asked, and help we will. I'm paraphrasing, but this comes from a hundred conversations.

All of the five kids, at one point or another, felt that the people our parents were helping were prioritized above what we needed in the moment. It was a forced independence. A shoving into the world, perhaps before we were ready. But having so many people around all the time was an opportunity to cultivate multitudes of relationships. Many of them so impactful it shaped who we've become today.

The steadfast approach of my parent's faith was the foundation for our entire lives. Clearly, it has reverberated over the years and gained quite the following. But, that comes with its own pitfalls as a child in the house. The deifying of our very human parents. Everyone thinking they knew us because of what our parents had accomplished. The long cast shadow of the saints raising the five children. Everyone saying how lucky we were to have such amazing parents. How they wished they could do something like what Pete and Sue had done. Etc. etc. etc.

Don't get me wrong. All of my siblings and I know exactly how blessed we were, and are, to have Pete and Sue as our parents. But, deifying is not only an unfair assumption of the human parents we had, it is to create an unattainable prospect. It's an excuse. I know if there's anything my parents would want to impart on the world, it's that anyone and everyone can do what they've done. Moreover, they patently have disproven the skeptics. A single person can make a difference in the world. A big one. Actually, an enormous, gigantically massive difference. Pete and Sue are living proof that everyone in the history of the world who has ever said the words, "I can't do that," is patently wrong. The impact they've had is incalculable. It is so ubiquitous that there is no possible way to quantify how the lives of so many have changed because they said "yes."

It's difficult not to eulogize when speaking of Pete and Sue Fullerton. They are, without a doubt, the most deserving people of praise that I've ever known. To call them Mom and Dad is a privilege; and if altruism is an act of selfishness, then my parents are the most selfish people I know.

Andrew Fullerton
5/1/16
Brooklyn, NY

Introduction

Over the many years we have been involved with the poor, we have had innumerable encounters with people who ask us how we got started. We repeatedly tell our story of being two young people in love with each other who also had a heart for people in need.

One of my early experiences with Pete - in the first two weeks of our relationship - was a day he met me after classes at the University of San Francisco, where I was a nursing student, and he told me that he had given his last dollar to a homeless man panhandling on the streets of San Francisco. I'm not sure if I should have been scared away at that point, but I chose to embrace this loving, innocent, generous, unguarded boy of nineteen.

The rest, as they say, is history. He was a musician when we met and married. He was part of a folk-rock group called "We Five" that had a number one hit in 1965. He travelled a lot and when we finally settled down to be a family in the '70's, it was tragedy that caused us to rethink our life with our growing brood.

We realized we could do more and be more. Opportunities were all around us, but we were led to Pete's god-father, Gordon Stewart, who had begun a small project he called *Truck of Love*. He was transporting food, clothing, medicine, and household items to a Franciscan priest who was working with desperately poor people in the desert of Arizona outside Phoenix.

Meeting people who had so little, who struggled for survival each day, and whose faith in God kept them alive was the beginning of a new life for us and for our children. One isolated trip morphed into two trips each year with Gordon.

Pete and I were hooked.

Eventually the pull of helping people who fall through the cracks of society led Pete to quit his lucrative paying job and jump into full-time ministry with the poor. We gave up the prospect of material success as we answered what we perceived to be a call from God to do this work.

There were people who criticized us, saying we ought to take care of our own family, that we were teaching our children the wrong things about life by giving up profitable jobs to help people who ought to be helping themselves.

Once our children were old enough to work, they each found jobs that provided school books, clothing, entertainment, and transportation. We gave them a roof over their heads and food on the table.

We certainly had some lean and difficult times, but we would not change our life's trajectory. Our children are now grown with children of their own. Each of them has developed into the person they are meant to be. We could not be more proud of the way they lead their lives.

Though this story is primarily about our journey with *Truck of Love*, it is inextricably linked to our lives as family: how this work has formed each of us from the people we were into the people we are today.

This life is not yet over but we are at a place, where in looking back, we can see how good it has been and continues to be.

We pray that we continue to say "yes" to the opportunities that God puts before us.

Susan Fullerton
2/6/2016

"Love your neighbor as yourself.
There is no commandment greater...."
(Mark 12:31 New International Version)

AUGUST 2013

I was stopped by two Sheriffs' cars this morning. They drew up in front of and in back of me, lights flashing as I drove in my blue Toyota truck along the deserted, heavily wooded, rural road leading to the community of people living in the woods. I pulled over and retrieved my registration, license, and proof of insurance while they approached me.

One officer demanded, "Let me see your papers."

The other officer asked, "Do you know why we pulled you over?"

Dumbfounded, I replied, "I don't have a clue." I hadn't run any stops signs, I wasn't speeding, and my registration was up-to-date.

The first officer directed, "Get out of the truck. Put your hands on the hood."

He frisked me and found sixty cents in my pocket.

I joked, "If you'd just waited, I would have been at the Goodwill buying kids school clothes."

He was not amused. He pulled out handcuffs and snapped them around my wrists. He took my keys out of the ignition. I remained silent.

"Get in the back of the car."

Once I was seated and the patrol car door was closed, he got into the driver's seat and pulled out onto the road. He drove and I sat in silence. The other patrol car drove out behind us.

After about ten minutes of aimless driving, both cars stopped on the side of an isolated road.

The officer opened my door. "Get out."

I clumsily climbed out, still handcuffed, and he pushed me against the trunk of the patrol car. Then he took off the handcuffs.

"Get back in the rear seat." I followed his direction. He closed the door behind me.

The two officers stayed by the side of the car discussing something I could not hear. Finishing their conversation, they both got back into their driver's seats. One car took off, leaving me alone with the other officer.

He said, "I want you to know, Mr. Fullerton that we are not going to call in your vehicle. We stopped you because the Sheriff is real curious about you and what you're doing' here."

Astonished, I asked, "What's going to happen then?"

He replied, "We're ordered to cuff all riders in the back seat. I'm gonna take you back to your truck. I'm gonna tell the dispatcher I did my due diligence and questioned you, but nothing came up on you and you're free to go. I know all about the people in the woods and what you've been doing' and I don't care. So long as they don't steal or cause a ruckus me and my friends will look the other way."

He went on to say something surprising to me: "You need to be careful. You've been targeted by our department. We've all been directed to be on the lookout for a blue Toyota truck with Truck of Love on it. Ever since you called in those two boys being beaten up, I've been interested in you and your work. We're told to scare the heck out of people we see along the road so they'll go on their way, but you seem to be ok."

We arrived back at my truck. As he let me go he said, "Don't call the County Station, we don't need publicity."

PART

I

"For I was hungry and you gave me something to eat, I was thirsty and you gave me something to drink, I was a stranger and you invited me in, I needed clothes and you clothed me, I was sick and you looked after me, I was in prison and you came to visit me." (Matthew 25:35-37)

1966 - 1973

Father Elias and Gordon Stewart

What we call *Truck of Love* began with a friendship between two men: Gordon Stewart and Father Elias Galvez, O.F.M. They met in a Catholic parish in Union City, California when Father Elias was a new priest and Gordon was a new Catholic. Gordon answered the door at the priest's rectory where he heard people's stories of terrible suffering. He would enlist Father Elias and together they could often be found "borrowing" items from the St. Vincent de Paul collections to help these people in need.

They worked this way for several years until Father Elias felt called to be with the poorest of the poor. He requested, and was granted, a transfer away from the San Francisco Bay Area. The Franciscans assigned him to their Mission Apostolate, a 900 square mile area of desert near Harquahala, Arizona.

15

For Father Elias, this wilderness was populated with some of the poorest people he had ever encountered. He reveled in meeting the spiritual needs of the people who called this area home.

Regularly he sent audio tapes to Gordon describing his new life.

He told Gordon about a day he chanced upon a whole family sitting in the dust along the side of the road. They were huddled together as if afraid. When he stopped his car and got out with water for them, they could see his Roman Catholic priest's collar and they visibly relaxed. The father stood up while the mother and son sat side-by-side on the barren ground.

The father explained in broken English: "My boss bring us here. I sick. I no can work."

Father Elias didn't hesitate. "Get in the car."

He took them to the parish house where they stayed until he found suitable lodgings, work, and medical care for them.

As Father Elias shared these kinds of stories in his audio tapes; Gordon thought about how he might be able to help. The result was a collection of food and clothing that Gordon and his friends accumulated over a period of about six months; so in December of 1969, Gordon and some friends packed their goods into a pickup truck and trailer and took off to surprise Father Elias for Christmas.

Returning from that trip Gordon kept getting phone calls from friends asking when he was going back to Arizona. As he reflected on the hungry children he had seen he made the decision to return with another truckload at Easter. He kept going for almost ten years.

We met Gordon on a married couples' retreat in the summer of 1966, shortly after our wedding. We knew what he was doing with these trucks because we received letters asking for donations.

We'd get Gordon's letters in the mail and say to each other, "How wonderful." Then we would file the letters in the garbage and go back to the daily chaos of family life and work.

We started married life in Mill Valley, a small tranquil community nestled in the hills across the Golden Gate Bridge from San Francisco. We lived in a rented house high on a hill overlooking Richardson Bay. We could not afford furniture on our meager income, so we had only the new bed we had bought on "time," meaning we made payments of $10.00 each month. Pete was a scavenger at heart and proudly brought home an old rickety kitchen table that he discovered on the side of the road accompanied by two broken chairs which we happily installed in our living area that happened to have an astoundingly beautiful view, over the tops of trees, of the glimmering blue bay in the distance. It was into this home that we welcomed our first son. It was here that Pete decided he wanted to become a Catholic, like me, so we could share this most important part of our lives with common beliefs and practices.

Pete was a musician in a group called We Five. They recorded a hit song, *You Were on My Mind*, in 1965 and entered an intense period of traveling around the United States doing concerts, radio shows, television, and even the Coca Cola commercial for the first Super Bowl.

Before we married, we were never together for more than three days in a row. He and the group toured the U.S. for up to six weeks at a time and returned home for a few days only to be in the recording studio or rehearsing for the next gig. When we married the schedule remained unchanged. He was home and we were blissfully happy for a few days and then I would be in tears as I once again said goodbye, knowing I wouldn't see him for weeks, our only communication being a few short expensive phone calls and long letters written daily.

The absences were torture for both of us. We were kids. Pete was nineteen when we met, just twenty when we married. I was two years older and his actual legal guardian for the first year of wedded life.

We Five was composed of Pete and five other kids. They were each in the process of discovering the big world of music and the excitement of life as recording stars, but as the months went by it was apparent that Pete's musical desires were not compatible with those of the other members of the group. Shortly after our first son, Tim, was born, Pete resigned from the group and settled into to getting reacquainted with his family.

We weren't out of music very long. We Five had dissolved, but two of Pete's friends asked him to play bass with them and soon we were back into the routine of rehearsals and gigs in local clubs. However the music scene in Marin County was not great and the lure of Southern California beckoned.

In pursuit of an agent and a new recording contract, we moved to Pomona, thirty miles east of Los Angeles. We lived there long enough to welcome three more babies before returning to the San Francisco Bay Area and settling in Los Altos.

About the time our fourth child was born we'd had enough of the constant travel and long separations and once again, Pete resigned from the group so he could spend more time with all of us.

In the first seven years of marriage we'd had five children. One child, a daughter, had died at birth.

We were ready to be a family living together.

I had been raised in the Santa Clara Valley just south of San Francisco where, during many months of each year, we watched the shadowy fog crawling over the Santa Cruz Mountains. We settled in Los Altos in a tiny three bedroom house with one bathroom. Our four children, three boys and one girl, shared bedrooms and toys and the boys shared clothes.

Pete got a job working for a local building supply company in Menlo Park and I managed the household with four children under the age of six. It was a challenging time. The transition from the glitz and glamour of life in the spotlight on stage to being a full-time employee, husband, and father seemed simple on the surface, but it was a huge adjustment. We had formed a routine in our early years with Pete's travel schedule that got turned upside down. Now that he was home every day I had to form new habits that included him in the daily mix. We had to work at growing into the family we imagined.

We became part of a wonderful Catholic parish community, St. Nicholas, which also happened to be the parish in which I was raised. Our oldest son was in the first grade at St. Nicholas School and our only daughter was in Kindergarten. The baby was five months old.

It was then that a life-changing experience occurred, an experience that had its beginnings in our college days.

Pete and I were introduced to each other in 1965 by my best friend, Julie, when Pete was a budding musician and she and I were nursing students at the University of San Francisco. Pete's music group was spending a week performing and auditioning for an agent at a San Francisco institution: the Hungry I. The year before, Julie had sung with some of the guys in the group when they were all students at USF and they invited her to their last performance one Saturday night.

Julie spent time with the group throughout the week, whenever she was free from classes. She met Pete, who was new to the group.

Returning each night to our dorm room she would say, "You've got to meet this new guy, Pete. He's really nice."

I was busy with my school work and would brush her off, "I can't today."

"Then how about Saturday? Pete and I are going to the DeYoung Museum. He's an art major. We can meet you for lunch in the hospital cafeteria."

"Okay."

I arrived at the cafeteria at the appointed time and waited and waited; Julie was notoriously late for everything. Finally hunger overcame me and I walked inside, went up the elevator to the cafeteria and ate lunch. Leaving the lunch room and strolling out of the hospital entrance onto Grove Street, I looked toward Golden Gate Park, wondering if I would see Julie and Pete coming from the museum.

Sure enough there they were lazily sauntering, deep in conversation. As they got near I noticed he was tall and blond. On closer inspection I saw he had big blue eyes, and a huge smile that seemingly went from ear to ear.

Julie introduced us and we politely shook hands, but they were going up the stairs and I was going down. As I descended I turned around to take a second look at this guy. Something about him was very attractive. When I turned to look, he was doing the same. Pete and I like to say it was love at first sight. We were married eighteen months later.

Love was in the air and Julie married another of our friends, Michael, later that year. The four of us spent lots of time together. We shared a love of faith, family, and food. The men loved to eat, Julie and I loved to cook, and we had endless hours of fun together.

Julie and I shared similarities in our backgrounds. She was raised on a farm and I had been raised in a rural area where my father had a small orchard, some chickens, and a vegetable garden. We understood each other, frequently without words. We were so close that often we didn't need to finish a sentence to communicate our thoughts.

When we were pregnant with our second child, Julie and Michael were expecting their first. Our daughter was born in April and Pete chose the name Julie Ann.

Julie and Michael's baby, also a girl, was born in May and Michael chose the name Susan Ann. Julie and Michael were godparents for our two children and we were godparents for Susan. We joyously looked forward to a long life of family activities with each other.

When our third child, a daughter, died at birth, Julie came to stay with us for a week. It was late one night when Julie and I were having one of our heart-to-heart discussions and Julie said to me, "I really want another baby. I don't want Susan to be an only child."

She loved children and was what we referred to as a "child magnet." She had a loving, playful presence that attracted any child in a room. But this night she continued, "I don't know why, but I have this feeling that I'm not going to have any more babies."

A few short years later we were to understand. One Thursday night in March 1973, Julie and Michael went out to an annual dinner with some of his insurance clients. She called me that morning and we discussed every detail of what she was wearing and where they were going. I hung up the phone with strict instructions: "Call me in the morning. I want to hear all about your night."

I lived vicariously through her as I sat at home nursing our youngest son.

That night Michael was the driver on the steep San Francisco hills. They were laughing with the couple in the back seat as they entered an intersection with the green light. It was at that moment that a drunk driver ran the red light and plowed into the side of their car hard enough to push it through the brick wall of a nearby restaurant.

About 2 a.m. our phone rang. I staggered out of bed and picked up the receiver. Michael's sister, hysterically screamed into my ear, "Julie and Michael have been in an accident and Julie's been killed!"

The days following that accident were some of the toughest we've ever encountered. It felt as if the light illuminating our lives had gone out. We got up each day because the children needed to be cared for and Pete had to go to his job, but we lived inside a dark cloud of sorrow.

We brought Susan to stay with us while Michael was in the hospital. She was almost five and thought she was having a fun vacation with her pseudo-cousins. It was their unending energy and joy in life that got us up each day.

Pete sat at the hospital with Michael who insisted, "Don't say anything to Susan about her mother until I can tell her."

We went to Julie's funeral. She came from Patterson, a small town in the San Joaquin Valley. The tiny church was overflowing with friends, neighbors, and relatives. It was the same church where, just a few years before, we had celebrated her marriage to Michael.

After the Mass the long procession of cars to the cemetery wended its way down expanses of bucolic farm roads to an isolated area filled with headstones. We walked in silence through the wire fence to the gravesite where her casket sat beside the open hole. After the prescribed Catholic prayers, I watched in my own personal agony as her coffin was slowly lowered into the ground. I was devastated when I had to walk away - and leave her behind.

When Michael was dismissed from the hospital he came to stay with us so we could care for his injuries. He had come close to losing his own life. Susan was all he had left.

They were with us until he could manage on his own. We each went through the motions of living, but there was not any joy in our existence.

Pete and I began frequent discussions about life. We wanted to do something more with our lives.

Then one day about a month after Julie's death, everything changed for me. I was driving Pete to work in our only car during the brutal first hours of the morning. The sun was just coming over the foothills and I felt the warmth of the light breathing new life into me.

In subsequent weeks, we continued the long dialogues about existence and its purpose. At the time we didn't realize it was God calling us forth out of our darkness into life.

We turned toward what we knew: Gordon's little project that his daughter had named *Truck of Love*.

Pete called, "Gordon, is there any way you can dedicate your next truck to our friend Julie? We want to do something in her memory, something that will help others."

Gordon was receptive to this and, being the smart person he was, he said, "If we dedicate this truck to Julie, you're gonna to need to help collect food and clothing."

Happily, we sent out about fifty letters to our friends and relatives asking for their good used clothing, any non-perishable food, and medical supplies. Our parish, St. Nicholas Church in Los Altos, helped us by having the children bring donations to school.

Julie was a loving, welcoming, and wonderful friend to many. Our small community of friends and family wanted to do something to honor her and they succeeded. By the time of departure, we completely filled a twenty foot rented Ryder truck, the largest truck of any that Gordon had taken. With the money we received, we paid for the truck rental, gas, and had money left over to give to Father Elias. This had never happened before. Gordon always made up the additional monies out of his own pocket.

So in the dark, and chilly early hours of Thanksgiving 1973, Pete and Gordon took off in the bright yellow truck filled with warm clothing, food, and medical supplies that had been loaded by friends, relatives, and neighbors in Union City.

They drove the seventeen hours to get to Father Elias where, since 1969 he had been living with the Yaqui Indians in Guadalupe, Arizona.

Nearing the town Pete could see two huge white churches standing side by sided overshadowing the tiny houses scattered about the desert sand.

Father Elias and the Franciscan priests in Guadalupe ministered to the people through the Catholic Church and the Yaquis held their own ceremonies in the Yaqui church.

That day after Thanksgiving, when Pete and Gordon arrived in Guadalupe, Father Elias and the people were waiting. Many people had travelled from miles around when they heard Gordon was coming.

Pulling into the dirt area in front of the churches, stopping the truck, Pete got out and raised the tailgate at the back of the truck. The load had shifted and some cases of cookies had opened up. As the door was raised, the cookies spilled onto the dirt. Several children who were standing nearby ran over and began to stuff the cookies into their mouths and pockets.

Pete watched as the children with their swollen bellies and skinny legs grabbed for the last crumbs. He was told that some of the most desperate people had not eaten in three days. He had never witnessed anything like this before. We didn't know this kind of poverty existed in our beautiful country.

Pete came home with stories of his trip. He and I talked through what he had seen until he finally declared, "I want to go back with Gordon when he takes the next truck."

We spoke with our friends in our home parish of St. Nicholas. People wanted to hear Pete's stories. They wanted to help.

Pete asked Gordon, "Can I go with you at Easter?"

"You sure can."

1974 - 1978

In the spring, Gordon and Pete drove a truck loaded to capacity and arrived on Holy Saturday with thousands of pounds of food and other items for the 2,500 residents. The joy in Guadalupe that Easter was both spiritual and physical. People had new clothes and full bellies as they celebrated the Resurrection.

However that night the Catholic Church caught fire and burned down. The candles used as prayer offerings had been too close to the statues that were reverently dressed in fabric.

Immediately the Yaqui leaders met with the priests and offered their Yaqui Church as a place to celebrate the Catholic Mass until the church could be rebuilt. The Yaquis and the Franciscans shared a mutual respect that valued each tradition.

As it became apparent that Pete would be making the twice a year trip with Gordon to serve the people of the desert, it also became apparent that Pete would miss every Easter and Thanksgiving with the family. He would be taking his vacation days to make these trips and there would be no family vacation experiences, so he got permission from Gordon to bring one of our children with him each time.

We loved hearing their perspective on what they saw during these excursions. Tim, our oldest child, remembered standing in the Catholic Church in Guadalupe with a young Yaqui boy who asked him if he was rich.

Tim's reply: "Not where I come from."

At that time we were blessed to live in Los Altos, California. It was a sleepy little town nestled among the apricot orchards of the Santa Clara Valley. We lived in a small rented house owned by a delightful family friend who charged us $175.00 a month. The low rent enabled us to manage our growing family and have a comfortable life on Pete's modest salary. We had everything we needed, but our neighborhood and town were filled with families who enjoyed a prosperity that was well beyond our meager earnings. We were surrounded by million dollar homes and our children went to a school where the other students had opportunities that we could never provide for our family. Their friends had everything they wanted.

As our children grew up, they each had some difficulty with the reality of not being able to do all the things their friends did or have the clothes or toys that they saw when they went into other homes. However, our children gained a perspective of life from these trips that no amount of money or privilege could buy.

Our third son, Peter, went on his initial trip when he was in the first grade. I can still see the endearing image of him, a little round-faced boy clutching his stuffed animal; wearing his hat and sunglasses as he climbed into the truck.

Upon his return to school he was asked by his teacher to tell the other children in the class about his experience.

His teacher later told us what he said to his classmates about the way the people lived, "These Indians don't live in tepees. They live in small houses made of mud and they don't have refrigerators and swimming pools like you have."

Today as we drive along Highway 10 through Phoenix and Tempe, it is hard to see the town of Guadalupe with its two tall churches side-by-side. It is surrounded by freeway walls and has been all but swallowed by the urban sprawl that is around it. The one square mile is still their land. The people are still there. The small ramshackle homes and the dusty streets are still there. We remember the years that Father Elias enjoyed with this community and the many trucks filled with gifts of love that we helped unload.

Pete made these trips with Gordon until 1978 when Gordon died. Every year we did a little more. Soon there were two 20 foot trucks being loaded each time, one in Union City and one in Los Altos. St. Nicholas School and parish became huge supporters of our work. We were invited to talk to various parish groups and the checks and donations came pouring in. Friends shared what we were doing with their friends and gradually our mailing list increased. By the time of Gordon's death, *Truck of Love* was a major part of our life. With his death we realized that we wanted this work to continue.

With the help of his widow, Rose, and the dedicated group who were our helpers we sent the twenty-third truck to Father Elias in memory of Gordon in November 1978. The outpouring of love for Gordon was so great that all the donations could not fit into the Thanksgiving truck and that year Pete took another truck on December 27. The monetary donations enabled us to send a monthly check to Father Elias for food and medical emergencies.

1979-1984

Gordon had been our mentor. He showed us the way. He helped us see the bigger world, the world beyond family, a world in which people had tremendous needs. He helped us say "yes" to that nagging voice of God, the one that doesn't give up on us until we see it His way. Those years after Gordon's death were a time of tremendous growth for *Truck of Love* and for us.

Father Elias was transferred to Cashion, Arizona, but he requested that we continue our deliveries to Guadalupe. We decided we could also help him in Cashion, a poor farming community about twenty miles west of Phoenix populated by mostly seasonal Mexican farm labor.

Cashion wasn't much of a town, just a bunch of small houses, a couple of convenience stores, and a church nestled among miles and miles of agricultural land in the midst of the desert. The people of Cashion were dirt poor. Many people lived in rundown shacks lacking running water and electricity. They worked the local cotton farms when there was work. Because they did not have regular employment, they needed help with food and clothing.

Father Elias introduced us to a terrific woman, Olga, who received the donations we brought and made sure they were distributed to people in need. Her husband had a good job on a sod farm. They squeezed their large family into a humble mobile home, but whenever Pete brought a truck, they made room for him and, as a result, he became good friends with Olga, Luis, and their five children.

Olga and a few of the women from her parish church unloaded each truck into a tiendita (little store) on the church grounds. We sent Olga some money each month with which she would purchase bread and milk. Then each Tuesday, Olga and the ladies opened the tiendita and the people were given enough food to supplement whatever their inadequate incomes allowed. The clothing and other items were given as needed. Each week people were fed and clothed.

I was privileged to stay with Olga and Luis a couple of times. It was during these visits I learned about Olga's life.

"My father was a migrant farm worker. He worked the farms from the northern U.S. border to the south of Texas. I was the oldest child in my family and I had to leave school to work with my father so that my brothers and sisters could stay in school."

We formed a warm bond with Olga and her family over the many years we visited Cashion. As her children grew, she became restless. She didn't like the fact that they were learning things in school that she had never learned. She went back to school and graduated from college about the same time as her oldest daughter.

There were so many little connections that were being made. One day I answered our home phone and a sweet, soft voice quietly asked, "Is Mr. Fullerton at home?"

"No," I replied," May I help you?"

The voice belonged to a Poor Clare Sister who lived in the convent in Los Altos Hills. I knew of the Poor Clare Sisters because my mother had taken me to visit them when I was very young. They live within the walls of the convent and never go out; they are cloistered, contemplative nuns who live a life of prayer, community, simplicity, and joy.

This day the sister introduced herself and explained, "We need some things transported to the sisters in Illinois. One of our friends thought Mr. Fullerton might be able to help us."

This began a tradition of many years during which Pete would load up his van with treasures made by the sisters in Los Altos and deliver them to Roswell, New Mexico; Chicago, Illinois; and even Richmond, Virginia. Pete became one of the army of people who help the Poor Clare sisters.

Mother Colette wrote about this connection in her book "And No One Saw His Footprints":

> *But Mr. Fullerton also gave us another priceless gift and that was the inspiration of his own self-sacrifice, his eagerness to pour out himself for others, and his great love and concern for the poor. We began to find ways to assist him by pooling our talents and resources to make items he could give to the poor. We set aside "Truck of Love days" for this labor of love; Valentine's Day, the celebration of love; and Thanksgiving Day, the expression of loving gratitude. We even had a "Truck of Love room" where we would put extra supplies, things we did not need or things we could do without. We made Christmas stockings and Easter baskets for him to distribute to the needy. In all of this we were only trying to follow the inspiration he had awakened in our hearts by his own example.*

When I heard one of those sweet voices calling on our phone, it transported me out of our commotion and filled me with peace. Thirty plus years later, the sisters still send us boxes of homemade quilts, pillows, and stuffed animals. We give these to the people we now serve in South Carolina.

Another day some of our local friends asked us to help a family of Laotian refugees who arrived in the Bay area with only the clothes on their backs. They had escaped the terrible conflict in their homeland and after many months in refugee camps in Cambodia they landed in the Bay area.

We met a man named Bounsy who was the first of hundreds of Laotians we came to know as friends. He had worked for the United States government in Laos during the war. He and his family were forced to flee. It was a journey of six months between Laos and America. Bounsy, his wife La, and their three children were sponsored by a church in Menlo Park. They were supplied with the basic necessities to set up housekeeping and helped to find jobs. Then they began to assist other Laotian refugees. At the time we met them, they had three families living in their rented home.

Bounsy was the leader for the Laotian community. Each time a new family came into town he would call us and say, "I have new family. They have no food. Need clothes and beds."

One day Pete delivered two beds and a chair to an address in Mountain View. A tiny Laotian woman opened the door and bowed, inviting him inside. There were ten people living in the apartment. One bed in the corner had several children on it and he saw one bag of rice on the kitchen counter. The woman could not understand English, but her smiles and bows expressed her thanks.

We supported their growing community for many years with food, clothing, furniture, and monthly cash donations. We are blessed to have been invited to many Laotian gatherings where our friends shared their food and culture with us. We learned to appreciate their music and dances. We know them as a community of people who care deeply for family and for this country which has given them new opportunities.

We became aware of an Orthodox Bishop in Juarez, Mexico. His name was Bishop Theodore and Pete was introduced to him in Juarez, where he lived and ministered among the poor. Pete began to make regular trips in our van to bring food and clothing to Bishop Theodore, one of the most unique people Pete ever encountered. He regaled Pete with stories of his early years in Russia escaping the Communist regime by walking across Siberia and his miraculous life of encountering the people who could help him with just what he needed.

Pete witnessed his subsistence living in Juarez, where he slept on a cot with a mattress comprised of crumpled clothing that rested outside on a dusty hillside in front of a simple house that belonged to a friend. He ate very little and prayed constantly. He cared for the physical and spiritual needs of the people in the tiny village where he lived and he traveled by foot to neighboring areas where they still used animals and carts to carry their goods. He loved his God and all of God's creation.

Our lives were a whirlwind of activity. We had five growing children. Pete was in and out of several jobs. Nothing seemed to fit.

At one point he went back into music as a way to support our family. He drove to San Francisco to play his guitar and sing on the streets, bringing home enough money to keep a roof over our heads and food on our table. He also played in local clubs and bars. We lived on the edge of financial catastrophe.

On Super Bowl Sunday in 1980 I took all the children to a grammar school basketball game at St. Nicholas School and Pete stayed at home to fix a fence post. When I returned from the basketball game I was surprised to see one of our neighbors coming out of our house. He said there had been an accident. Pete had hurt his hand and the ambulance had taken him to the local hospital. He didn't tell me exactly what had happened, just that I should go and he would take care of the kids.

I hopped into our Volkswagen van and took off, my mind racing, not having a clue what to expect. My heart sinking and a feeling of dread engulfing me, I got to the emergency room and was ushered into where Pete lay on a gurney. As I approached him I began to shake with nervous energy. He looked ok, but there was a piece of white gauze draped over one hand.

He said, "I hurt my fingers."

"Can I take a look?"

He nodded.

I lifted the gauze and saw three red stumps where his fingertips had been. From somewhere a sense of calm came over me.

I looked at him and said, "Okay, what's next?"

I was painfully aware that his days of supporting our family by playing the guitar were over.

About a month into Pete's recovery period, he got a job caring for a retired priest from our parish who was terminally ill with cancer and was living in his deceased parents' vacant house. Pete could be present to him and keep him company even with the huge bandage on his left hand. The priest lived around the corner from our home and Pete walked to work.

During that same time period, I cared for an elderly lady who had been my Catechism teacher when I was a child in St. Nicholas Parish. I walked to her home each morning to make sure she had her breakfast and that her abode was clean. She was a gentle woman who swept the sidewalk in front of her home until she turned 102 years old, at which point she started to slow down.

Each day I opened her front door and she would smile up at me, a tiny figure dwarfed in a huge easy chair, wearing Coke-bottle thick glasses.

She would say, "Good Morning! Isn't it a lovely day?"

I dusted, vacuumed, did the few dishes, and each week I'd help her bathe.

These two jobs kept the rent paid and food on the table for our family of seven.

About the time Pete was healed enough to work full-time, a friend called and told him he ought to apply at Lockheed in Sunnyvale. There were a couple of people we knew in St. Nicholas Parish who worked at Lockheed. It seemed someone put in a good word for him and soon Pete was a tool coordinator for the Hubble Space Telescope.

He was employed, but his creative spirit was sorely injured. Pete was determined he would play guitar again. He tried several ideas that friends proposed, but in the end he had to tough it out and, over the course of several years, build new calluses on his stumps of fingers.

Those first years after Gordon's death and Pete's accident were constantly filled with new encounters and transforming experiences. One of our local TV channels, KRON, came to interview us. There had been some newspaper articles about the work of *Truck of Love*, but that particular Thanksgiving our donations were way down. Three days before Thanksgiving we had only four small boxes of food for the annual November truck to Arizona. We anguished over what to do. We had no money to buy food and it seemed like a huge waste to send a truck that was only partially filled with clothing.

After the TV spot aired people began to arrive at our front door with bags and boxes of non-perishable food, clothing, and cash donations. By the time to load we had so much food that we were hesitant to put it all on the truck. At risk of being terribly overloaded we packed everything into each crevice of the truck and delivered every last can and box to Father Elias in Cashion.

Pete continued to work at Lockheed. It was not what he wanted to do with his life, but it paid the bills. He worked his way up the ladder into being a salaried employee and earned more than we ever thought we would have. I supplemented our income by babysitting and working in people's homes, cleaning, cooking, or caring for the elderly. These were skills I had from being a wife and mother and from my very short time in nursing school.

Our lives were full, but we were restless. We still had a persistent dialogue going on about wanting to do more.

Late at night we went back and forth, "Wouldn't it be great to do *Truck of Love* full time?"

"Yeah, but how would we support the kids?"

Time passed and our older children grew into teenagers. We were involved with the youth ministry in our parish and had Monday night dinners at our home for the teens who were part of the parish youth group. These were pot-luck meals feeding anywhere from ten to forty kids who showed up on our doorstep about 5:30 p.m. I made sure there was a big pot of spaghetti with sauce and some garlic bread and salad. Sometimes the kids brought drinks or desserts. Mostly we ate whatever there was and everyone was happy. After our shared meal we all got into cars and drove to the church hall for the meetings.

Because we loaded trucks each Thanksgiving and Easter, the kids from the youth group got involved. They were great workers and could load a truck in a fraction of the time it had taken us. They also got involved in trick-or-treating for *Truck of Love*. All kids love to go trick-or-treating and our youth group kids took pre-printed lists of non-perishable food items with them. When they knocked on doors, they presented the list and told the homeowners about *Truck of Love* and the need for food. They returned to our home with hundreds of pounds of food that was then used to feed hungry people wherever we encountered them.

Occasionally Pete was stopped and told by concerned people, "This is a cheap trick. You shouldn't send kids out to beg for food."

PART

II

"He has shown you, O mortal, what is good.
And what does the Lord require of you?
To act justly and to love mercy
And to walk humbly with your God." (Micah 6:8)

1985 - 1986

Early in 1985 Pete decided he could no longer keep his salaried position at Lockheed. He had been promoted because he was a good worker and could speak well in meetings, but he felt ill-suited for the position. We both felt the additional money wasn't worth the stress it created in his personal life. We determined that in order for him to go back to an hourly position, I needed to find a job that would bring in $900 each month. At the time I worked a few evenings each week at our parish rectory cooking for the priests.

We talked about what kind of job I needed to have. I dreamed of a job with a school, so I could have vacations off. Our youngest was just eight and I couldn't imagine being gone during all those long days of vacations.

One night in early February, I went to a back-to-school night at Saint Francis High School where our two oldest children were enrolled. They were on the work program to pay their tuition, and our daughter was assigned to the Dean of Students. She was very happy working in an office instead of the job she'd had during the summer of scraping gum off the undersides of desks. I had never met the Dean and that night I went to introduce myself to him. I wanted to thank him for how wonderfully he was treating our daughter in her work situation.

I began, "Hi, my name is Sue Fullerton..."

As soon as I said my name he interrupted, "I was going to call you. A mutual friend told me you would be a good candidate for a position that is opening as the attendance clerk."

The next morning I interviewed with the principal of the school, and the following Monday I began full time work that brought home exactly the needed $900 each month. Because the school paid the tuition of all employees' children, our two oldest no longer had to be on the work program. They now got jobs that paid real money that they saved or used for life's necessities.

Work for me at St. Francis High School was an adventure. It started that first day I left home at 6:30 a.m. Our youngest son, Andy, was only eight and I had always been home in the mornings to get him ready to go to school. He and his brothers walked the mile or so up the road to St. Nicholas school, but they didn't leave until near 8 a.m. The first morning I left for my new job I kissed the boys goodbye, made sure they understood all my instructions, and walked down the path to get into the car.

Then Andy came running after me crying, "Who's going to zip up my coat?"

My heart melted. I desperately wanted to turn around and forget that this income was so necessary.

I started working at St. Francis with the intention that I would quit when all of our children graduated. I figured I'd give them about ten years of my life. Little did I know what was ahead and that it would be more than 25 years before I said goodbye to the people and place that became part of the very fabric of my life and the life of *Truck of Love*.

I finished out the school year at St. Francis and to my great surprise, when I had a meeting with the principal to go over my contract for the following year, he had bumped me up a couple of slots on the salary scale. He said he was rewarding me for good work, but I think he just wanted to encourage me to stay in a job no one wanted.

There was little time to celebrate my good fortune because a couple of months after I began work at St. Francis, our youth minister, Greg, mentioned that he had read a flier from an organization called Children of the Americas. They were looking for groups who wanted to work in Tijuana, Mexico. Greg thought he might get a few of the youth group kids to go. I said I wanted to go too. For some time I had been thinking I wanted to work in a foreign country, but I never quite knew how to go about it.

Greg did all the organizing for the trip. He had seven youth group kids who wanted to make the journey. Several were St. Francis students.

Following the months of preparations that included collecting food and clothing, we were on our way. We left home in the pre-dawn hours of a July Saturday. By the time we stopped for breakfast in San Ardo on Highway 5 in the San Joaquin Valley, the sleeping teens were about ready to wake up. We drove south through Los Angeles and San Diego and went a bit east near to the Otay Mesa border crossing into Mexico. Our destination was Brown Airfield, an old military complex that was being used as a detention facility for illegal immigrants who were picked up by the Border Patrol. Paul Weiss, who headed Children of the Americas, rented a dilapidated, vacant two story barracks that had 44 rooms. It cost him $1,100 per month and was used as the base camp for the groups he shepherded into Tijuana.

We brought a trailer full of food and clothes and Paul was immediately impressed that, when we unloaded everything, we filled his storage room.

He explained to us, "You won't have any trouble getting the clothes through the border, but the food will be harder. You're gonna have to put a layer of food on the bottom of the van and have everyone sitting on it when you cross."

That first night we met Paul's helper, Martin, who turned out to be our constant guide and educator during the week. A recent college graduate, he was on fire about issues relating to social justice. As we got to know him, we all marveled at Martin's unlimited energy and enthusiasm.

Living together at Brown Airfield was part of the whole experience. Because we were across from the Border Patrol Headquarters, we heard and saw things that had never been on our radar. Helicopters took off at all hours. Vans arrived to unload their cargo of "illegals." Officers hurried the men, women, and children into the holding cells. Sirens blared every few minutes, signaling they were pursuing yet another escapee from the facility.

One night I was sitting at the window of our barracks looking out at the Border Patrol van pulling up. The doors opened and people began to tumble out. A young woman hopped down and following her was a small child clutching a stuffed animal and dragging a blanket. As I sat staring, tears running down my cheeks, the woman and child walked hand-in-hand into the building.

We were invited to take a tour of the facility. The Border Patrol guards were happy and proud to show us what they did. They explained how they picked up the people crossing from Tijuana. We saw the holding cells: benches surrounded by chain link fencing. After documenting the people (getting names and country of origin) they loaded them in buses and took them many miles down the road to Arizona where they crossed the border in order to let them go in the Mexican desert. They said this made it harder for them to cross back into the U.S.

We started our daily trips into Tijuana on Sunday after Mass at Christ the King Catholic Church in San Diego where, in front of the church, there was a statue of Jesus with no hands. The strong message from this church was that we are the hands of Christ in our world.

Our first crossing into Tijuana was nerve wracking. Terrified, the teens spread themselves on top of the food we were smuggling. The Mexican border guards were known for stopping Americans and searching their vehicles, but this first time through they just waved and smiled and we sailed into Tijuana.

We were on the main road that skirted the border on our way to the old garbage dump when we came upon a police blockade consisting of some patrol cars with flashing lights and a pile of dirt across the road to discourage traffic. This detour forced us up a steep, rutted, dirt road and over a hill to our destination. There were houses on the sides of the mountains that were built on top of foundations of old tires. An indefinable smell engulfed us: a mixture of burning plastics and rubber tires mixed with an overlay of rotting garbage that thickened the air.

Finally we traversed another bumpy dirt road that led up a hill to a community of tiny houses. We pulled in front of one such home and piled out of the van.

We didn't stay long, just unloaded the food at this home of the woman who ran a food co-op for about thirty of the poorest families. There was a very fat baby crawling around in the dirt sucking on a rusty potato peeler. His legs were caked with black dust, the result of living on top of an old garbage dump where years of burning trash had been compacted to provide the foundation for the building of the homes.

I learned that most developing countries have communities that survive in the garbage dumps. After the incoming garbage is burned, workers dig through it with their hands to extract the metals and glass for recycling. They carry large burlap bags back and forth over the smoldering earth to a truck where they unload their cargo and get paid pennies for their labors. The man they sell to pays them one tenth of what he earns.

Being in Tijuana that week in July was transformative for me. I had read about the poor in other countries. I had a lot of information. But when I met other mothers who cared for their families just like I cared for my own, I saw the world differently. I was privileged to live in a place where I was the recipient of a good education. I had health care and a safe comfortable home. These mothers struggled each day to survive and to provide for and protect their children.

I met a woman whose husband had been killed one month before we were there. She was raising her own children and three children from another family. Her oldest son had been moved into one half of the pig pen because there was no room for him in the family's small house. They lived in the old garbage dump that had now become a tract of rickety houses built of pallets, bedsprings, old wood, tarpaper, and anything that could form walls.

The people used timeworn rusty fifty gallon metal barrels to contain the water that was delivered a couple of times a week by the water truck. Tiny children played in the green water of the puddles that collected under the water barrels.

We drove through and around Tijuana, following Martin in his truck. By mid-week the standard joke was Martin's driving. He'd speed into the round-about intersections in downtown Tijuana, career around the circles, weaving in and out of cars, buses, and other trucks and spit himself out in the direction we needed to go. We followed behind in our van dodging all the other vehicles as we managed to stay behind him and not get lost in the maze of streets and the throngs of people. This was all before the advent of cell phones, so if we got lost we were doomed to a fate we did not want to suffer.

The days were long and we were exhausted. We shared the cooking and cleanup duties, but not all the kids had experience cooking. One night we ate what we dubbed "Spaghetti Blocks" because our very hungry teenage cook did not wait for the water to boil before adding the noodles. As a result the pasta clung together in huge clumps.

Food was an important learning tool. In solidarity with the people we were meeting in Tijuana, we ate simply: no meat. There was plenty of food, but no frills. There were no snack foods or soft drinks. We ate what was put before us.

We visited an orphanage, Casa de Cuna, where we did craft projects, played with the little children and fed the babies. At lunchtime, there was a row of a dozen high chairs with toddlers sitting in them. As the person chosen to do the feeding, I had one bowl and one spoon and started at one end of the row. I delivered the spoon full of food into the first gaping mouth and then moved on to the next child to give him or her a mouthful. If a child was sleeping, I passed over them. I moved from child to child as quickly as possible, repeating the process until the bowl of food was empty. The runny noses and drool passing from one child to the next ensured that any cold or cough was shared by all.

This dance of feeding didn't take long because each child who was awake was eager for their next taste of whatever mystery food was squashed into the bowl. I'm not sure their hunger was ever satisfied, but they each received a somewhat equal portion.

It was here during play time one afternoon that I sat exhausted in a corner while the teens ran around with the little kids. I noticed one boy who looked like he was about three years old who was also sitting off to the side and not joining in the fun. I motioned to him and he quietly got up and toddled over to me and curled up in my lap. We sat together for about an hour just watching the excitement.

One of the caretaker women passed by me and made a circle around the side of her head with her hand and said, "Loco."

I took that to mean that they assumed this child was not right in the head. He seemed a little slow to me, but he was so sweet just sitting in my lap. He gave me a huge hug when I left him.

One day we took the children from the old garbage dump to the beach. We stuffed 33 children into the van with us. I had a very small boy sitting on my lap for the cramped ride and the smell of urine was suffocating. There were very few diapers in this community. When we got to the beach the children ran into the ocean with all their clothes on. We did too. There was just enough time to throw off our shoes as the children pulled us into the waves. After our somewhat refreshing swim, we gave them snacks of watermelon and cookies.

The ride back was smelly in a different way as we sat in our sandy wet attire. Two of our teen boys joined in with the little kids who were singing "Gua, gua, gua..." to the tune of "It's a Small World" (from Disney). They later reflected on the irony and pervasive influence of the U.S. culture in children raised in this Tijuana neighborhood.

Something that surprised all of us were the TV's we saw, even in extremely humble homes in the garbage dump. The people were incredibly resourceful and industrious. They used car batteries to power the TV's; thus the children had a view into the wider world, including their nearest neighbor, the United States.

Another day we went to the location of the new working dump. There before us was a colossal mountain of garbage, smoke rising from several areas of burning refuse. People were silently bending and sorting, stuffing recyclables into their brown burlap bags. Almost everything was the same dull brown dirty smoke color, including the people. There was the constant, quiet, everlasting work and the cacophony of the garbage trucks opening their dumpsters and releasing their effluent into the already festering space. The undulating clouds of scavenging screeching seagulls circling and diving. The overpowering smells stunned us, but I was almost used to it. It was the smell of Tijuana.

We walked from the dump across the compacted trash through the cemetery to where homes were built. The cemetery in the dump was a unique experience. It was huge, filled with row after row of simple white crosses. Occasionally we had to navigate around several deep pre-dug holes that were open and waiting for the next person who would fall victim to disease or accident. Interspersed among the white crosses and other markers were full size infant cribs straddling the ground around a child's grave that would be fully decorated with dusty artificial flowers.

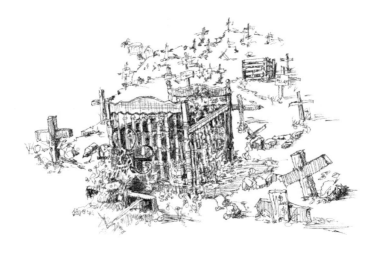

Infant crib in dump cemetery

I discovered it was easy to sit down on top of the garbage as we listened to a man named Dionysio and his wife, Maria. They had seven children all being raised in their home located at the edge of the mounds of the active garbage dump and the cemetery. It was a small shack hardly big enough for the nine of them to occupy at one time. The dirt floor was swept clean. The fence outside was made of old bedsprings tied to-gether. Attached to one spring was an exquisite flowered tea-cup; a lonely, stunningly beautiful decoration. There was a couch in the middle of the one room. They told us that when the roof leaked they all piled onto the couch because that was the one dry place inside. It was humble, but it was home. Maria showed us where she cooked outside on the open fire. They got their firewood from the dump.

Dionysio was a middleman. He drove a truck from the dump to the recycler. When he worked, he earned $9 a day. They were proud to share their home with us and tell us their story. This was an area of the dump that had previously been active, but by the time of our visit it was packed down and ready for neighborhood growth. They told us that at night it was very dark and no one went outside because they felt it was too dangerous. Subsequently we have come to under-stand how violence and poverty live side-by-side in so many communities.

Paul and Martin did a great job immersing us into the lives and culture of the poor of Tijuana. As we sat on the final night in our barracks at Brown airfield we shared our thoughts and feelings about the week. Hearing the teens wonder out loud about what good was done if we came for a few days and then left caused me to recall an event in my early life that had remained dormant all these years:

My parents were alcoholics, and when I was four years old my two brothers and I were removed from our home by social services. A strange woman came into our house and dragged me kicking and screaming into a car. We drove away from my home and my mother. We went to the school to pick up my brothers who angrily got into the car. I didn't see them after that.

Very frightened, I was delivered to a place where the beds were all lined up in a room. There was an enclosed concrete play yard where I could ride a tricycle. Other children were playing around me as I rode the tricycle in my bare feet. I recall what must have been a sense of loneliness.

Without warning my toes got caught in the spokes of the wheel and I screamed out in pain. I cried and cried until a very large, soft woman scooped me up in her arms. She held me close comforting me as she took me inside where she placed me in a large sink to wash the blood off my injured foot. She tenderly bandaged it and got me calmed so I could go back to playing in the yard. I have no idea who she was. As I think of her, I know that one small kindness made a difference in my life.

It was very difficult for me to return to Los Altos after this trip to Tijuana. I was angry and frustrated. I had a hard time justifying my life of luxury with what I had just experienced. I had been with people who struggled for each day's existence. They were thankful for everything they had. Many of them found the energy to help others in their small communities. They prayed and they really knew the God who gave them the strength to survive. Yes, they had lots of problems. Many were alcoholics and drug addicts. Some of the men abandoned their families. But they kept getting up each day with new resolve. I had seen with my own eyes and I could not ever again be blind. It gnawed at my soul.

I returned to my loving family. We lived in a beautiful place. My children went to the finest schools. We had absolutely everything we needed. I feared taking all this for granted. I hadn't really understood it before. I knew people were poor, but I had no concept of what that meant. Now I had a tiny measure of experience and knowledge. I felt such an obligation to act on what I had learned. I knew the poor were not just in Mexico, but I had met these people and to a small degree, I knew them. I also knew that poverty wasn't confined to material poverty. I lived in a country that had a great poverty of spirit. I kept thinking about the children in the orphanage who let go of us so easily. No one ever stayed; there was always someone different to play with. I thought how hungry for touch they were and how simple it is to meet those needs.

Pete and I shared our thoughts a lot over the following days and weeks. I thought that my experience in Tijuana must have been a lot like his first experience in Guadalupe, Arizona, with that first truck load of food and clothing and the children picking up the cookies off the ground and stuffing them in their mouths. We reflected on the beauty of the people we were meeting in each of these places and how wrong it is for them to have such suffering. We knew that we had the education, knowledge, and power to do something about the poverty we were seeing. We kept coming back to the same fact: if we really love God, then we must oppose the oppression of people and adopt for ourselves a simple life that enables us to be open to hear what God wants of us.

I had returned to the new school year at St. Francis and, as the attendance clerk, I was struggling to see equal value in writing late slips and experiencing Jesus in the poor.

Daily Pete and I re-evaluated our lives. We knew we wanted to keep our home open to all who wanted to enter. We also knew that we wanted to keep having the youth group dinners at our home. The teen years were so challenging. We felt honored that the youth group kids liked to be in our modest home.

In October we did a thirty hour fast with Greg and the St. Nicholas/St. Williams Youth Group. The priest who talked with us at the end of the fast spoke about Christ feeding us with bread in the Eucharist and how basic and right that is, because we are hungry not just for food, but hungry for love. It made sense because our empty stomachs were churning and growling. I thought how good it was that *Truck of Love* fed people, sharing in the beauty of Christ feeding us.

I wanted Pete to experience Tijuana and I was very excited when an opportunity arose that was exactly what I hoped for. Two days after Christmas Pete and Greg took a group of 15 teens and adults to build a house. Paul had written to us about a family that had just lost their one month old baby to pneumonia. He wanted to get them out of the mud. Greg answered the request by putting out a call for volunteers. The response was immediate and the group took a load of food and clothes to Paul and spent the week constructing a sturdy one room home.

In January Paul wrote and asked us to become part of his organization, Children of the Americas. We weren't sure what that would mean for us, so we told Paul we would discuss it at Easter. We had already decided that during our children's Easter vacation we were going to make a trip to Tijuana and Arizona with our three youngest sons. We also knew that Pete had made a commitment to himself that he would no longer be working at Lockheed by the end of 1986.We had no idea where we were going in life, but we knew God was guiding us. All we had to do was say "yes." That was the hard part, to say yes and trust in God.

This was a chaotic time of mental turmoil and soul searching discernment. We had five children ranging in age from nineteen to ten. My 88 year old Aunt Griffie, my father's sister, was living with us. She took up one of our three bedrooms so we bought a small trailer and put it in our backyard for two of the boys to use as a bedroom. I had a full time job that took me away from home for about 50 hours each week. We were deeply involved with our parish youth ministry and hosted the Monday night dinners before youth group meetings. Our home was the place where the youth group leadership meetings took place.

In the midst of this mayhem, it was my Aunt Griffie who took much of my energy. She had come to live in our home the previous year. She was forgetting things and needed more regular supervision. Having been single all her life, she adapted surprisingly well to our busy household. She loved our children, especially our youngest son, Andy, because she was with us through my pregnancy and she had known him since he was three days old.

When I had returned from Tijuana the previous summer, Aunt Griffie greeted me with an exceedingly cold reception. She listened intently to our conversations about *Truck of Love* and Paul Weiss' invitation. She worried out loud about us possibly moving south to join Paul. We kept telling her that no decisions had been made; we were just considering what we wanted to do with our lives.

Easter vacation arrived and we took off for our trip to Arizona and Tijuana. We loaded two trucks, one for each location. We took our three youngest sons, Ian, Peter, and Andy. Pete drove one truck and I drove the other. The kids alternated between the trucks.

Our two oldest children, Tim and Julie, stayed at home. Tim was in his first year of college at Foothill Community College, and Julie was in rehearsals for "The Sound of Music" at St. Francis. They were in charge of making sure Aunt Griffie was well cared for.

Our first stop on the trip was the Mojave Desert home of our youth minister Greg's parents. There we added Greg and his fiancée Kate to our entourage heading south and east. They followed the trucks in their car across the vast expanse of desert to our next stop, Cashion, Arizona. Olga received much of what was in one of the trucks. She had expanded her ministry to three communities. Her husband, Luis, had built a shed on their lot that was used for storage and distribution. They and their children all shifted beds to make a space for us. We had a great evening laughing, singing, and eating homemade tacos.

The next day we took the very beautiful drive away from Phoenix deep into the desert. It was spring and the desert was an artist's paint palette, alive with every color of wild-flower. Pete pleaded for us to stop and take pictures, but I wanted to get to Father Elias. Mistakenly, I figured we could take pictures the next year. It's been more than thirty years and I've never seen the desert like it was that year.

Father Elias had been transferred to a place we knew as the Papago Reservation. Driving onto reservation land we noticed signs saying "Now entering the Tohono O'odham Reservation." Subsequently we learned that the word Papago meant "bean eaters." It had been the slang term affixed to the O'odham by the Spanish missionaries. The proper name was Tohono O'odham meaning desert people. Unknown to us, this was a time in the history of the people when they were trying to reclaim their identity.

Pete had been splitting his truckloads between Olga in Cashion and Father Elias in PisinMo'o on the Tohono O'odham Reservation for a few years, but this was my first trip to Arizona. We drove what seemed like endless two lane paved roads flanked by a desert filled with a variety of bushes and cacti until we finally arrived at the sign directing us to PisinMo'o. We were about two and a half hours outside of Tucson and hadn't seen more than a handful of small houses scattered along the way.

We turned left onto a road that had definitely seen better days. Partly paved, partly dirt, with pavement and earth tumbled together in the low spots they called washes. These were the natural places in the desert where the water ran when it rained. The water moved with such force that it destroyed the old roadway and lifted it into mounds that we now had to navigate. We delicately navigated that road that seemed to lead to nowhere for eleven miles, until we saw some buildings off to the right.

When we arrived, it was difficult to see that this was a village of almost three hundred people. A few homes dotted the terrain among the mesquite and greasewood trees and there was a chain link fenced and gated building that was the trading post.

We pulled up to a tiny thick walled adobe house that sat in the shadow of a fairly large church, identifiable by its bell tower. A very tall man stood outside. Pete knew him and introduced us to Johnson Jose, one of the tribal members and a friend of Father Elias. Father Elias came out to greet us and I was struck by how tiny he was next to this massive man.

It was a trip of firsts for me. I had not previously met Father Elias. I had heard stories about him from both Gordon and Pete, and I quickly fell in love with this soft spoken, joy filled, peaceful priest. He directed us to unload our truck into the storage area. We were introduced to the three Franciscan sisters who lived nearby in a mobile home. With Father Elias, they ministered to the spiritual needs of the people in the three southern and most remote districts of the reservation. They were the ones who would see to the distribution of the food and clothes we brought. Then we were given a tour of the area and the church.

Mission San Jose Church, PisinMo'o

When I commented to Father Elias how much I liked his church, he kindly corrected me saying, "It is the people's church."

This became one of those moments in my life where I began to understand "church" in a new way. Having been raised in a very hierarchical church where the priest was the leader to whom we all looked for guidance, I started my evolutionary journey into the church of the people where we share equally in our common faith.

After the tour Father Elias ushered us back to his tiny dwelling for dinner. He had cooked a small pot of beans and reverently served each of us a few beans with lots of bean juice over a piece of white bread. Our boys were polite and ate what was put in front of them. I think later we may have supplemented their dinner with some of the sandwiches and fruit we'd brought with us on the trip. (Ian tells me now that Father Elias made the best beans! On a previous trip Father Elias had told Ian that if there aren't enough beans, you just add more water.)

Dinner over, we went outside to walk around and saw some of the boys from the village were playing basketball. Ian and Peter stood on the sidelines until they were invited into the game. They had a great time with the village boys until dusk when we were treated to the first of many memorable sunsets that we savored over the years. We stayed outside in the warm evening air, the sun disappearing behind clouds that reflected a myriad of vibrant colors while the horses wandered past us through the village.

Soon it was time to sleep. Father Elias' house was pretty small and after he'd told us stories of herding the cockroaches by turning off the lights in one of the rooms, none of us was too eager to sleep on his floor. We unrolled our sleeping bags in the back of the empty truck and tried to get some rest; but cows moaned all night, bats swooshed around the trees, and the moonlight got all over everything. We were exhausted when it was time to greet the new day.

I loved PisinMo'o, Father Elias, the sisters, and the O'odham we had met. I wanted to return again and again. But I had obligations at home and I knew it would be hard for me to do what I wanted to do. Reluctantly, I said goodbye to the sisters and Father Elias. I did not know when I would see them again.

We spent the day driving through more astonishing desert land, across Highway 8 to the Tijuana crossing. Getting two trucks across the border involved being sent to secondary where the Mexican guards grudgingly let us go, emphatically saying that next time we had to have a letter from the organization receiving the items.

Pete smiled and waved goodbye and we careened into the Tijuana traffic. It was easy to get lost and after several attempts our caravan found the road that led to the beach (the Periferico). We were staying at a hotel on the coast, El Jardin; and as we pulled into the parking lot we sighed with relief that we had gotten this far.

Our rooms were adequate and cheap. We cleaned up and then ventured out to walk along the beach. There had been a bad storm and some of the buildings on the bluff were damaged. One had slipped down the side of the hill and sat at an angle resting on the beach below and the sidewalk next to the road above. There were broken off sewer pipes spewing waste water near the path that we had to navigate to get down onto the sand.

We showed the boys the fence that separated the border between Mexico and the United States. In those days, the fence was just chain link. It extended along the whole border by Tijuana and ended at the water's edge; bisecting a monument dedicated to the friendship between Mexico and the United States. It was low tide when we escorted the boys to the end of the fence where there was some compacted wet sand we could traverse.

Monument to friendship

We walked from Mexico to the United States and back again – several times – laughing and giggling more each time.

Strolling along the sidewalk near the border we encountered a dog that was lying very still on a pile of rags. The kids stopped to engage him and then they saw that the dog's whole back end was being eaten by maggots.

Andy, our youngest, cried, "Why did they leave the dog here? Can't we help him? Do something, Mom."

I unsatisfactorily explained, "The dog is dying. There's nothing we can do."

I ushered the kids away from the dog and we continued our walk along the road next to the ocean.

Our hotel was adjacent to a vacant lot where a basketball court had been roughly constructed on the dirt and rocks. We could see it from our hotel room. Through our window Peter watched the kids playing ball and asked if he could go join them. We gave him permission to go out and witnessed from the window as he approached the boys and positioned himself to be invited into the game. Soon he was running and blocking and shooting with them. He never said much about the trip, but I always thought he engaged through his language: the commonality of sports.

In Tijuana, we emptied our trucks into the co-op Paul had set up in the colonia. Then we had a long conversation about joining his organization. Soon it was time to head north.

We arrived home from our trip at 4:00 a.m. on Sunday, April 6, Ian's fifteenth birthday. It was a strange, tired day. Each of us had to be at work and at school the next day.

Aunt Griffie was giving us the cold silent treatment, so she didn't join us for our youth group dinner that Monday night. We plodded through the week and finally on Thursday night most of us were home for dinner. It was a fun time, with lots of laughter and good food. Aunt Griffie was happy because we told her we would not be moving south to join Paul Weiss. We had decided he was too interested in working in Central America and that was not where our hearts were leading us.

We finished dinner and Aunt Griffie collected all the scraps to take outside to the dog. A short while later we heard her calling for us, and Andy went to see what was going on.

She had fallen and broken her hip.

This began a month of daily trips to visit her in the hospital in Palo Alto.

I was in a complete daze. Our daughter was playing Maria in *The Sound of Music* at school, Aunt Griffie had surgery and was in serious condition in the hospital, and we still had our other children, the obligations of managing a home, youth group, and *Truck of Love* that all needed attention.

I had prayed really hard during our trip to Arizona for God to open the way for us to do our ministry with *Truck of Love*. I knew one of the huge obstacles to this was Aunt Griffie. She really didn't like it when I was gone. She had done whatever she could to discourage our deeper involvement with this work.

Two weeks after her hip replacement, on a Friday afternoon, the doctors decided to take out the breathing tube that had prevented her speaking with us. They were not sure if she would breathe on her own, but we all thought it was time to give it a try.

As soon as the airway was gone, she cried out, "I want to live!" followed by "Where's Andy?" and "I love you all."

The next day the doctors gave us the bad news: due to complications from a lifetime of health problems, she had only days to live.

On Sunday I brought all the family to see her. They stayed in the waiting area while I ushered them one at a time to her room. First was our daughter, Julie. We took the walk down the long hallway to the entrance of Aunt Griffie's room. I stood in the doorway with Julie so she could see all the equipment attached to her. When Julie was ready we walked in and stood next to the bed. Aunt Griffie immediately brightened up. She was too weak to talk much, but she managed to say what was most important, "I love you so much."

I made the walk with each of our children and family members and she was able to get out the same words, "I love you so much."

The following day I spent the whole day at her bedside. She talked non-stop for twelve hours. It was very hard to understand her, but I got in close and listened really carefully. Each person who came into the room that day would say, "I'll see you later."

She would reply, "No," and in halting phrases she would utter words that made it clear she knew she would soon be in heaven.

I asked her if this was alright. She said, "Yes!"

She talked about how she had seen Andy the day before and how he was crying. She knew she was dying and she was at peace.

This was a woman who had been afraid of life and terrified of death. She had never married and never seemed very happy. She would often tell me that she did not want to die alone.

Two weeks later the doctor called me to come, because the end was near. It was a blessing for me to sit with her, holding her hand and praying, "Yes, Lord. Take her. She is yours. Yes, Lord."

Gradually her breathing slowed until she stopped.

It was May 1986, and we were all exhausted. I was emotionally drained. Our daughter was about to graduate from high school. We were laying the groundwork for *Truck of Love* becoming a non-profit organization. We'd had a generous offer from a lawyer friend to draw up the papers with no cost to us.

Greg, our youth minister, moved in to Aunt Griffie's room. He was about to leave for the east coast because he was getting married the following year.

Julie had saved her money from various jobs and was leaving on a graduation trip to England. Ian was graduating from eighth grade. Tim had told us he was taking a year off from college. Pete had given notice at Lockheed and his last day of work would be July 31.

We'd had a family meeting and explained to the kids that we felt called to do full time ministry with the poor. We told them that if Pete quit his job we would be living on my salary which at the time was $12,000 a year. That meant that each of them would be responsible for their own books for school, their transportation, and their entertainment. We said we could provide a roof over their heads and food on the table. My recollection is that they said a resounding "Yes." They now tell me that they agreed because they figured we were going to do it anyway.

These months were incredibly full for all of us. I alternated between feeling enormous excitement for the opportunities we were being given and paralyzing fear of our anticipated financial situation.

I had learned from Martin that he did food drives at the supermarkets in his hometown of Santa Barbara, so we did our first food drive in Los Altos. We printed up slips of paper with a list of non-perishable foods and our *Truck of Love* information. The food was going to go to Children of the Americas to feed many of the poor we had met in Tijuana.

Andy and Peter were stars. All day they stood with other kids from the youth group at the door to Midtown Market handing out lists and telling people they were collecting food for the poor children. By the end of the day we had over 500 pounds of food and $125.

In mid-July we loaded a fifteen foot truck destined for Tijuana. Fourteen of us, adults and teens, were on our way to join Martin and Children of the Americas for a week of working in the garbage dump and orphanages.

During that week we met Jose, a boy of about twelve years. His clothes were dirty, his hands were cut and rough from working in the garbage dump. His teeth were decaying, but his smile and generosity filled me with love and gratitude. We brought lunch to him one hot day as he was working, digging through the mounds of refuse looking for bottles and cans to fill his burlap bag. He ate his tortilla and beans, drank his water, ate a nectarine; and when he was finished he disappeared over the hill of refuse only to return to give each of us a gift of love, a small cheap plastic toy.

We also met Margarita, mother of seven children. She was a huge woman with an immense heart. She laughed as she led us into her home: a two room shack built atop the decay of the dump, a home with no running water or electricity. She cooked outside on a metal barrel, turned upside down, in which she built a fire. Her husband worked in the garbage dump, but the person who bought his bottles and cans had not paid him for the previous month. Margarita told us she was borrowing food from the neighbors to feed her huge family. She was very proud of her tiny flower garden. When I asked why she did not grow vegetables, she simply said they don't grow. Being a gardener myself, I understood that the soil was devoid of the nutrients necessary for vegetables to develop.

Working with Paul on this trip, we learned that he didn't want to host teenagers any more. He was more interested in the young adults. By now we had seen the amazing effect of the trips on our teens and we were reluctant to give this up. We talked with Martin about how we might continue to work with the teens.

Martin had promised Paul one year of service. He was done with that year and was very interested in what we were doing. We invited him to come stay with us to help us out.

Martin was an avid bike rider and had organized fund-raising bike rides from Santa Barbara to Tijuana. He now told us he would ride his bike from Santa Barbara to our house in Los Altos.

We were expecting him one afternoon in late July and he arrived with a flourish. He was towing a bike trailer loaded with his personal belongings. Having ridden a great distance in a few days and just conquering the Santa Cruz Mountains, he came flying through the gate into our yard on his bike carrying a bouquet of flowers, caught his back trailer wheel on the gate and fell over onto our front grass! He popped up, flowers still clutched in his hand as we welcomed him with open arms. He knew the three younger boys and soon became good friends with Tim and Julie.

Pete ended his job with Lockheed on July 31, 1986. Receiving that last paycheck occasioned a feeling of great uncertainty in the core of my being. How would we survive? I was good at budgeting, but this was terrifying. We were jumping off a cliff with God as our safety net, but what if God wanted us to do something else? I had to believe this was going to work.

Lockheed gave Pete an unpaid leave of absence for one year, telling him that they thought he would want to return. His bosses believed it was a noble idea he had, but they never imagined he could succeed.

There was no time for self-doubt. On August fourth the adult leadership of our youth group left Los Altos in four cars destined for the Nevada Desert Experience. Organized by the Franciscan Friars of California, it would be an experience of prayer, reflection, and non-violent demonstration against nuclear testing and for peace.

Greg invited all of us to join him because this was the first stop on his cross country venture to live near his fiancée, Kate. This is where we would say our goodbyes.

There were ten of us and we had no idea what to expect. We each had our own reasons for coming. We shared two hotel rooms in Las Vegas and ate in the excessive, cheap, buffets. The contrast between the glamour and extravagance of the city and the mission we were on was striking and absurdly disconcerting. We drank gallons of water and sweated in days above 100 degrees.

We spent the fifth of August in non-violent training sessions with members of the Franciscan Order of priests and brothers and the more than 200 participants from all over the world. It was a revolutionary time for me because I had always been a person who followed the rules. But this day they challenged us to see the difference in man's laws and God's laws. They had us think and pray about the events that would occur the following day.

People would be walking through the desert to the line that marked the entrance into the Nevada Test Site, an outdoor laboratory of 1,350 square miles of the Nevada desert where nuclear weapons were tested.

Some would choose to cross the line to be arrested. This was in protest of the continuing tests of nuclear weapons. We discussed the principles of non-violence, including not antagonizing the "opponent." In this case the opponents were the men and women of the police and military security forces who were present to prevent trespassers from entering the test site area.

For twelve hours we prepared and discussed how best to calmly make public our desire for peace and an end to nuclear testing. I was struck by how the people in my small group valued the fight for peace. We came with different perspectives: some were concerned about man's inhumanity to man. The Christians in the group shared a common belief in Christ's command to love one another.

There were two military veterans with us who had been stationed years before at the test site. One was returning for the first time in thirty-two years. He had been in a group of men who were placed in bunkers one-half mile from ground zero during the test of an atomic weapon. His arm and leg were torn open by the explosion. He was part of a group of other veterans fighting to stop what he called "this insanity."

The day of the demonstration, we rose at 4 a.m. and went to an address we had been given where we picked up four people who were planning to be arrested. They didn't want to leave their cars at the site because they assumed they would soon be in jail, possibly for up to a month of incarceration. In the dark we sped out into the desert; driving through the sunrise until we came to a spot on the side of the road to park, an hour out of Las Vegas, in the heart of the barren desert.

The Nevada Desert Experience people had been busy. We were greeted and directed to walk to a cattle guard to pick up a piece of paper on which were written the names of two nuclear tests. We read these and reflected and prayed about them and all the people affected by them as we hiked the two miles to the demonstration area. As I walked I turned around and saw a seemingly infinite line of people moving silently down the left side of the road. It took us about thirty minutes to complete our peaceful journey, stopping for water along the way.

We were in the demonstration area by 6:30 a.m. where we prayed as a community with music and a Eucharistic service that was a universal expression of our unity of purpose. We met with our small group to commission the three who had chosen to be arrested. One woman was in tears as the reality of arrest and jail caved in on her. People lined both sides of the road as we marched with those who would be detained. I was shaking with nervousness and fear as I made this very public statement.

Silent questions bombarded me: "Why be arrested? What good does it do? What will people think?"

At that moment I understood that the only value in this whole experience was the effect it was having on me. This was between me and my God. I saw so many people watching us with cameras clicking. I knew somewhere there would be an FBI file on me, but I realized that none of that mattered. I could not influence what anyone else said or did. I could only choose what I would say and do.

By the time I was at the Nevada Desert Experience, there was a weight of perfection that was pushing down on me. I'd been raised in an Irish Catholic family that made rules, guilt, and expectations the way of life. I was the good child. I didn't make waves. I did what I was told. I had a desperate need to do what was right and be right, but all of a sudden I began to see that my world of being right was very small and confining. As I met people who were different, I also came to see how wonderful they could be. I learned that it was okay to disagree and that it was possible to still like and respect someone who had another way of thinking, feeling, or behaving. I also discovered that some of my long held truisms were not so true. There was a whole big world out there and I had to make some adjustments.

That morning in the desert we watched as our new friends were taken away in plastic zip-tie handcuffs and a part of me wished I had the courage and freedom to join them.

I could see how the events since my first trip to Tijuana were connected. The work in Tijuana, Cashion, PisinMo'o, Las Vegas, and the Bay Area were all about me seeking the will of God for me. I was beginning to lose my fear of what was happening. The walk back to where our cars were parked in the desert was filled with thoughts about how this was all playing out in my life.

Returning to the parking lot, it was time to say goodbye to Greg. He was going east to live near his fiancée, Kate. We were happy for them, but we knew we would miss him. He was a huge force in helping our youth group grow. He was and is a person of deep spirituality who drew in the kids. He provided fun as well as thoughtful experiences for the teens and he had become a treasured friend.

In our car, we followed Greg down the road for a while and then waved goodbye as he headed toward New York and we veered south to Arizona. Pete and I, with Martin, were on our way to the Tohono O'odham Reservation to introduce Martin to Father Elias and show him the Arizona component of *Truck of Love*.

As we drew near PisinMo'o, we came upon a man who was walking along the side of the road. It was burning hot in the sun as he plodded along; looking, with each step, as if he might collapse. We stopped and asked if he wanted a ride. Getting into the car he told us his name was Chester. The heat of the afternoon sun radiated off his dry clothing and parched skin. He was sucking on a small pebble saying this helped his thirst by keeping his mouth moist. He'd walked the six miles into the village of PisinMo'o to use the phone to call the water district to tell them that the solar water pump in his village of Santa Cruz was out. The village had no water.

We gave him a ride back to Santa Cruz where his three children were waiting patiently for him in the shade of the village chapel.

On our return to PisinMo'o we gave Martin a tour. The sisters cooked lunch for us that day- a feast of chicken and biscuits with all the trimmings. The sisters were gracious hosts and made us feel like we were part of the family.

That evening we were again visited by Johnson Jose, who wanted to share his story with us. We stood outside Father Elias' adobe in the dark with the hot wind blowing and lightening flashing all around us. With the rumbling of thunder, the shadows of the buildings, trees, and saguaro cactus illuminated by the flashes of light; there was an eerie feeling to our experience. An enormous presence, Johnson stood before us and told us the story of how he had been an alcoholic for years. He was single and drinking all the time until he ended up in a hospital. That changed his life and now he spent his time trying to help other O'odham overcome the lure of drugs and alcohol and find their way to a sober life. He talked to us about the teenagers and how they had nothing to do. The rate of unemployment on the reservation was at seventy percent. At one time he had worked at a home for recovering alcoholics, but he was currently running the Wednesday night AA meetings in the village.

We knew that a portion of the money we sent each month to Father Elias helped with the AA program. We were now even more committed to seeing it succeed.

This was a quick introductory trip for Martin and we left early the next morning to make the seventeen hour trip back to Los Altos, California.

I struggled with the desire to be in Mexico and Arizona, and the knowledge that I had a home and family in Los Altos. I spent a lot of time being angry: angry that people were so desperately poor and angry that I lived among the rich. It was an anger that persistently boiled under the surface.

One Sunday at the end of that summer I was in church, praying silently after Mass, when I clearly heard a voice speak to me.

The message was: "You have met the Christ in Tijuana. You must bring Him home to these people who either cannot or do not choose to go."

I didn't really understand the idea of being "called" to a particular job or mission. Part of me thought that because I felt so strongly about the people I was meeting in these faraway places that everyone ought to feel the same commitment. It took me some time to accept that we are each called in different ways.

Our lives were on fast forward. We had just signed the papers for the 501(c)3 tax exempt status that made us a not-for-profit public benefit corporation. Pete was free from his forty hour a week job. Daily he was going out into the streets and stopping each time he saw someone with a sign that read "Will work for food" or "Homeless, need work," or a person who just looked down on his luck. He was coming home with lots of stories, among them that of a man who said he was Michael the Archangel, several women who were prostitutes, a woman who heard voices in her head, and a man who died his beard green for St. Patrick's Day. Some people were homeless, others had places to stay. Each person had unique needs.

Michael was standing on Castro Street in Mountain View and as Pete drove by, their eyes met. Pete thought, "This man must want something," so he parked his van and walked to where Michael seemed to be waiting for him. Curiously, he greeted Pete by name though Pete had no memory of meeting him. Pete asked him if he needed anything and Michael said he would appreciate a ride. They talked as they rode and Pete discovered they had a common interest in music. Michael said he was playing in a local club and invited Pete to come hear him. Then he continued, asking Pete if he remembered him.

Pete said: "Have we met before?" (Pete was thinking that perhaps they had met in his We Five days.)

Michael responded, "Oh, yes, many times."

Pete told him he was sorry, but he did not recall meeting him before. Michael sighed and reiterated that they had met many times. He then gave Pete his card that said "Michael, Archangel." Pete took the card, which had small pictures of several angels on it. They arrived at their destination and Michael said goodbye and got out of the van. Pete drove away wondering what had just happened.

Joanne, the woman who heard voices, soon became part of our everyday lives. She wanted to work, so we paid her to sort the food and clothing that were now being delivered to our home every day by very generous people. She was a huge woman, well over six feet with a contrived, high-pitched voice. She always wore one of two wigs that were very full bouffant hair styles. She had thick makeup covering her face and painted her eyebrows and lips in exaggerated style. There was a cloud of sickly sweet perfume that enveloped her, but could not mask her lack of personal hygiene.

As she talked to us she would pause in the midst of a sentence, cock her head and say, "Not now." or "I told you not to interrupt." or some other innocuous statement that led us to believe she had a visitor inside her head.

We learned that she was completely harmless, but as much as she wanted to get a real job, it was apparent to us that no one would hire her. Thus she spent long hours working in our back yard sorting all the donations we received. She was incapable of telling us about herself though she did make reference to her mother living in a convalescent hospital. What we saw was what we got.

She had a yellow Dodge Dart that she drove around town. Andy, our youngest son, recalls her occasionally driving up to our house with a small elderly lady sitting in the passenger seat. In the early years of our relationship with Joanne, she lived in a small mobile home. Later, she became homeless and no longer had the car. She walked to our home pushing her belongings in a small cart and on cold nights she slept in one of our vans.

A few years into our friendship with Joanne, she disappeared for a while, and then we received a phone call from a hospital in the East Bay. Joanne was dying and she had given the hospital our phone number. We told them we were not related and we had no knowledge of any family or friends who could take responsibility for her.

Shortly after she died our home phone rang and Andy answered. It was a man asking to speak with Joanne. Andy told him how sorry he was, but that she had died. The man seemed genuinely sad about this and explained that he was a county sheriff and had known Joanne when they were young. He was calling because of a series of phone messages she had left for him some weeks before. He then proceeded to tell Andy some of her story. She had been born to an affluent family in Southern California. Her childhood was relatively normal. She had a horse and loved to ride, until one day she fell off her horse and hit her head.

This Sheriff had dated her when they were in high school. He said she was a beautiful girl. After high school she became engaged to another man who subsequently died. Apparently, after that, she was never the same. Slowly she drifted north to where, many years later, we met her on the streets of Mountain View.

As sad as we were that Joanne had died alone, we were pleased to know that someone cared that she was gone.

The man with the seasonally festive green beard, Art, sometimes slept on our living room couch. He did this for several months until our children began to complain about how bad he smelled. We asked him to sleep in our van instead, and many days I had to wake him up so he could get out and I could drive to work. Those chilly winter mornings he exited the van with his clothes stuffed with newspaper that kept the cold away. Many mornings I drove to work in the frigid winter air with the windows rolled down and the heat cranked at full blast afraid that the stench of his unwashed body would permeate my clothing before I could get to school.

Art sleeping on park bench

Art shared his story in bits and pieces. He was a veteran who became a teacher, husband, and father. But when he and his wife divorced the alimony and child support payments took most of his paycheck. Frustrated, he dropped out of mainstream of society and became homeless.

By the time we met him he was well over retirement age. Pete helped him apply for and get his Social Security check. One day he received a check for back payments of $24,000.00. He put it among the newspapers and other things he carried in his cart. Months later he still had not deposited the check, saying he had it in his rented storage unit.

Packrat would describe Art. His storage unit was filled to the brim with old newspapers and bags upon bags of used clothing and small knickknacks he had collected. The check was never deposited.

The prostitutes that Pete befriended were living on the brink of constant danger. One day Pete was driving along El Camino Real in Mountain View when he stopped to pick up an attractive young woman who was hitchhiking.

As was his habit, he asked, "Would you like something to eat?"

When she tried to get friendly with him, he reiterated, "No, I don't want anything from you. I'm only interested in how I might be of help."

It was then that the young woman revealed she was an undercover police person. "We are investigating some beatings of prostitutes in the area. You are not doing anything wrong, but you need to be careful."

Now that Pete was not working at a paying job, we felt the need to meet with our pastor. We didn't know how we were going to pay the tuition for the two children still in school at St. Nicholas. Father Pritchard knew us quite well, and knew what we were doing with *Truck of Love*, and he told us we no longer needed to pay tuition. Father Pritchard also told us we could use the church mailing list one time for an introductory letter about *Truck of Love*. We met with Father Sullivan at our neighboring parish, St. Williams, and he also agreed to let us use his mailing list. I typed up the letter we were going to send out.

The response to that first bulk mailing was tremendous. The people of Los Altos were and are among the most generous people we have known. They got us started and many are still on our list thirty years later.

1987 - 1998

We were surrounded by love and support from all corners. And then we were gifted with yet another great blessing from God. Our first grandson, Gregory David Fullerton, was born. Our daughter, Julie, became a single parent at the age of nineteen.

There were some tumultuous months preceding Gregory's birth, but Julie was a determined, devoted mother.

We told Julie we wanted her to be free to take care of Gregory for the first six months. After that we expected her to get a job and we would care for him while she worked. She was a loving mother and he was a sweet tempered, good baby. It was a joy to come home from long hours at work and simply sit down and hold him.

The rest of our life was out of our control. *Truck of Love* was going strong. Pete was thriving. We were exposed to new thoughts from many great people of our time. I was reading some pieces by Elizabeth O'Connor from the Church of Our Savior in Washington DC. She wrote extensively about creating church communities that helped people become strong individuals while serving God and others. Her message resonated with me as I struggled to maintain my own direction in the midst of the commotion that was our life.

During this time Pete made monthly trips in our van filled with food and clothing to Tijuana and Juarez, Mexico. He was also out and about meeting people who worked for local agencies. He got involved with the Mountain View Soup

Kitchen by picking up food and helping move things with his van. He made connections with the Moneta Davis Senior Center in East Palo Alto. He met a dynamo of a woman, Oneida Branch, who lived in East Palo Alto and worked in her community with the very poor.

The name *Truck of Love* and our phone number was emblazoned on the side of the van and we got phone calls at all hours. A young woman, Linda, called; she was living in her car. Her daughter had been taken away from her because she had nowhere permanent to live. She was a simple, proud person and we gave her food and some clean clothes. We fixed the latch on the trunk of her vehicle and helped her wash the car. As Julie vacuumed the inside of the auto she was shocked to see there were maggots crawling around under the upholstery in the ragged seats. Julie valiantly made a solution of bleach and water and scrubbed the maggots away.

Linda was embarrassed because the car looked as though someone lived in it; she didn't like the stares she got. We sent her on her way in a cleaner, neater vehicle with a few dollars and the phone numbers of local agencies who might be able to help her further.

We often got stopped by people who asked, "What is *Truck of Love?*"

A scruffy, long haired man approached Pete in San Francisco asking that question. Pete explained we were a private organization set up to help the poor, all the time expecting the man to ask for money. Instead he listened to Pete's story and handed him a dollar for our work.

I was spending long days at St. Francis High School. Peter was in the eighth grade at St. Nicholas, getting ready to graduate. Our television broke, the portable dishwasher was leaking, and the washing machine was making strange noises. Money was very tight.

Martin was living with us and his favorite meal to cook for our hungry hoard was a huge pan of baked potatoes. Many nights we ate just potatoes or beans. Meat was in scarce supply on our new budget.

We'd formed a Board of Directors for *Truck of Love* and when we had our first meeting, they insisted that Pete take a salary. We were adamant that we did not want to take any money from the poor people we were serving. The members of the Board persisted and we settled at the grand sum of $500 each month, so the combination of Pete's salary and mine kept our heads just above water.

In spite of the stresses we were happy in our work and the possibilities for the future. During Easter Vacation we again took a trip to Tijuana and Arizona which turned out to be a decisive trip for all of us.

Our caravan consisted of three twelve-foot rented Ryder trucks filled with food and clothing followed by our new (to us) fifteen passenger van recently purchased at cost from a friend who was in the car business.

Truck of Love van

We arrived in Tijuana on Holy Saturday and after getting settled in our hotel near the beach we went down the hill and had an Easter prayer on the sand. Our trip was filled to the brim with activity. There were thirteen of us including our three youngest sons, Ian, Peter, and Andy. We unloaded the clothes and food at Pan Americana, the old garbage dump. We sat with Juana and talked about the co-op she coordinated that helped distribute the food and clothing. She gave us a tour of the pig project which was the result of a gift from Heifer International. We held baby pigs and marveled at how cute they were. We bought belts from Lupe's husband, belts he wove from the colored wires he extracted after burning the outer sheath off electrical wire dumped with the garbage. We admired the piñatas made by another resident of the dump community.

We went to the active dump with a large box full of gloves. I was brought to tears as I once again saw how hard the people worked for so little. Their hands were rough, black with dirt, scored with cuts, and streaked with dried blood from the ever present wounds that resulted from digging through the garbage with bare hands.

That day our lunch consisted of fresh tortillas and cokes in the van on the way to Santa Teresita, an orphanage for older girls. There we met with Madre Rosario who gave us a tour of the facility and showed us work that needed to be done.

In reality we were on a fact finding mission to see what we could do in the upcoming summer time when we planned to bring a group of teens to Tijuana for a week. We rode from place to place in our new van, all of us in one vehicle laughing, talking, and singing our way around town. On Easter Sunday night we took Juana, Lupe, her husband, and several of their children to dinner. They were like little kids, laughing uproariously at Pete and his shenanigans.

We had gotten up late that morning and rushed to get to Easter Sunday Mass. On our way we watched as a dog got hit by a car on the highway and then run over by another car. The cars did not even slow down. I thought how cheap life is in this place. The kids were traumatized, but there was no explanation we could give that justified what we had witnessed. By the time we got to the church there was no room to even get close, so we left the colonia and drove across town to La Mesa Prison. Martin wanted us to see it and he wanted us to think about bringing groups there in the summer.

The prison sat beyond a vast barren dusty field. We looked at four solid concrete walls topped by guard shacks. There was one very small chain link gate where a line of people stood, waiting to get in to visit loved ones.

The stark outside belied what lay inside those walls. Martin explained to us that fourteen hundred inmates lived in shacks built throughout the inner space. Inmates with no place to sleep crouched in the corner where the garbage was burned. Spouses and children lived with those who were incarcerated. Everyone roamed freely with no bars to restrain them. If an inmate had no family to bring food or no money to purchase food, then that inmate would be fed a thin soup that they said made them sick. Small businesses were everywhere on the inside and anything could be had for a price.

Feeling an intense coldness of spirit after seeing this place, we then paid a visit to Casa de Cuna, the orphanage for small children. This was the place where I had sat in the corner with the little boy who did not speak. He was still there and this time he had a friend, a little girl. She was a pretty child with a welcoming smile, but all that was overshadowed by a tumor the size of a volleyball protruding from the right side of her head. We were told there was no medical help available for this sweet child.

The sisters didn't have much time for us, but we talked about what we might do in the summer.

Our two days in Tijuana generated lots of discussion as we dreamed of all the work to be done and experiences we might be able to provide for our teens as well as for the people in Tijuana. The next day we talked and spawned ideas all the way across Arizona to Cashion. We unloaded the second truck into Olga's tiendita. She and Luis and their family were thrilled to see us arrive and excited to see what we had brought.

We left the Cashion area on Tuesday to go to PisinMo'o. The sisters and Father Elias were gracious hosts. The third truck was for them. After unloading and sharing in the sisters' feast that they had prepared for us, we collapsed exhausted into the trucks where we were going to have a peaceful night's sleep. Of course that was the night that the cows were feeling frisky. We listened to the moans and groans of cows all night and got up in the morning feeling like we'd been run over by the truck.

As we said goodbye to the sisters that morning I casually remarked to Sister Patrice, "Is there anything else we can do for you?"

She didn't even pause as she responded, "Well, yes, the boarding schools have closed and the children will all be home this summer. We were thinking about having a camp. Do you think you could help?"

Unaware of the history of the schools, or the history of the O'odham themselves, I innocently said to Sister Patrice, "You know I've been cooking at a small camp in California and we work with the youth group in our parish. Yes, I think we can help."

The next adventure began. Our drive back to California was animated by our conversation about this camp and what we could do and how we could help make it happen. It was already the end of April and we told the sisters we would come back for camp in July, before our trip to Tijuana. We had some work ahead of us.

We had no idea what we were doing. Neither Pete nor I had been to camp as children. I was a cook for a Russian Orthodox camp run by a close friend. We didn't really know much about the O'odham, but we did know that there were tremendous problems with alcohol and drug abuse on the reservation.

Eventually we got six volunteers: some high school and college students, one retired teacher, Pete and I, and finally we recruited our oldest son, Tim, who happened to be available.

There were nine of us who made the two day drive to PisinMo'o. We left at dawn on Friday, July 10th, drove south on Highway 5, then east on Highway 10, and arrived on Saturday. That gave us Sunday to get ready for camp.

We pulled into the church compound in the middle of the afternoon. We were aware that it would be hot, but nothing prepared us for the scorching heat of the mid-summer desert. Climbing out of the van we felt the burning hard hot desert sand through the soles of our shoes. The intensity of the sun pounded down on us as we looked around at the space that would be home for the next week.

One of our group queried, "Where are we going to put all our stuff?"

We had pulled a trailer with our sleeping bags, suitcases, and assorted materials for camp: sports equipment, art supplies, and miscellaneous items we had thought might be of use. The sisters came to meet us, eager to be introduced to each person in the group. They graciously escorted us to the adobe building next to their trailer where we unloaded our personal items. The materials for camp we carried to the multi-purpose building. For our personal needs, we had the use of the village public bathrooms and showers that stood between the priest's house and the sister's home. There were also several outhouses behind the cafeteria.

The multi-purpose building had two fairly good sized rooms divided by an entry way. Each room had a swamp cooler that sometimes worked. The rooms could be closed off so that a different activity could go on in each space. There were an assortment of folding chairs, some shelves, and some tables. The sisters prepared food for us and we used one of the rooms to set up a buffet table. Everyone was excited to be there. A few village kids began to appear and hang out at a safe distance.

Cafeteria

After eating we took some time to show the group around the compound. Individually we were trying to imagine how we could make camp work in these facilities. The two school rooms, the one side of the cafeteria, and the ramada (an open area shaded by a roof of ocotillo cactus ribs) gave us four areas where we could be shielded from the sun during camp hours.

The plan was to divide the children into three groups: grades three to five, grades six to eight, and grades nine to twelve.

The sisters had been visiting the villages in the three districts around PisinMo'o since Easter telling the families that we would be having a camp.

Many of the O'odham asked, "What's camp?"

The sisters explained we were coming and there would be sports, games, and art projects. The sisters would also be doing some religious activities.

Sister Patrice clarified: "We have been taking sign-ups for camp and so far we have twenty-five, but we think there might be as many as thirty-five. So plan for that."

We slept in the cafeteria. It was an old long low adobe building with a concrete floor that was divided into a meeting space and a kitchen.

The people we brought with us from California had lots of positive energy. As we discussed what we would do each day and tried to complete our preparations, they took on their responsibilities with high spirits. We were navigating unfamiliar territory. We completed our preparations by Sunday evening and tried to sleep. It was hot and we were tired, but excited to begin camp. Sleep was elusive in these new surroundings.

It was a challenge to get the kids to camp. Few families had cars and most people in the outer villages relied on district vans for transportation to school or the doctor. The sisters told us we were responsible for transporting the kids into PisinMo'o. They had two vans and we had one van. Early Monday morning we sent the vehicles out in three directions. The farthest villages were fifty miles away. The few of us left behind did the final preparations for our first assembly with all the campers. We set up twenty five chairs in the cafeteria. Some of us helped the sisters with lunch preparation.

The morning air was beginning to warm – by 9 a.m. it was probably 85 degrees. Slowly some of the PisinMo'o village children started to appear. We tried to engage them, but they just stood looking at us. They talked with each other, found shady places and sat down in the dust, all the time silently watching us and whispering among themselves. When all the vans had finally returned and we gathered the children under the wato (ramada), we counted heads and saw we had fifty-five children. The sisters frantically began to increase what they were serving for lunch while we tried to divide the children into workable groups.

The biggest surprise was that the youngest child was three, not in third grade. That was when "flexibility" became our banner. The plans we had carefully crafted had to be altered immediately. The age groups were modified to fit our situation and we began our activities.

Somehow we got through our first day and Pete and the other drivers climbed into the vans to take the children back to their villages. Those of us left behind did the clean-up and tried to prepare for the second day of camp. It was nearly dark when the drivers returned and we all sat to discuss what had transpired during the day. This is when we attempted to make more adjustments. Universally we were stumped because the children were so elusive.

Our conversation was scattered. "It's almost impossible to get the kids to say anything."

"They just sit by themselves and laugh at us."

"I can't get them to do the activities I had planned."

"It took me the whole time just to try to learn their names and I'm not even sure the names they gave me were their own."

"At snack time, the kids just threw their Otter Pop wrappers on the ground. We spent a full hour after camp cleaning up the mess they left."

We soon realized that the idea of beginning camp at 9 a.m. and ending at 4 p.m. was overambitious for a number of reasons. Many of the children came to camp hungry and lunch wasn't until after noon. The little children could not cope with the long day and so we immediately instituted a rest time in the afternoon when we read stories to the youngest ones. The monsoons fired up around 4 p.m. and so the van drivers needed a second person to help in the event of flash flooding. But perhaps the best argument against the seven hour camp day was the amount of energy it took to corral and entertain the large number of unruly children who knew we were novices at what we were doing.

The second day we instituted a half hour clean-up time of the camp grounds before everyone went home, but we were locked in to the seven hour camp day for this year.

By Wednesday of that first week of camp I was exhausted in a dragged out lifeless way I had never before felt, but I managed to get up earlier than usual to have some quiet alone time. As the sun rose I walked across the basketball court agonizing over what was happening and not happening at camp. The kids were not responding, and the leadership group was drained by the long days and nights of constant preparation. I was at the end of my energy trying to keep up everyone's spirits. We didn't even know if the kids wanted us there. It was impossible to read their body language. We were in unknown territory and we had three more days. I was beginning to question my sanity and the fact that I had so casually said yes to this fiasco. I wanted to go home, get out of the oppressive heat, and sleep in my own soft bed.

That morning, as I slowly walked toward the church I looked up and saw in the distance a figure coming across the village in my direction. I paused and as the person got closer I could see it was one of the girls, Elisa, who was the most overtly cooperative in my group of teens. Soon she was in front of me. Without a word, she reached out and placed a small crumpled piece of paper in the palm of my hand and then she ran off into the desert. I stood there and slowly opened up the folds of the paper and saw that something was written on it. Elisa had written a poem that unfortunately has been misplaced over the years, which stated something akin to:

"Who are these people who come seven hundred miles to be with us in the desert?

They come here because they love us."

All of a sudden my exhaustion didn't matter. I saw that what was on the surface with the children was not at all an indication of what they were feeling inside.

The rest of that first week was filled with learning about the O'odham and ourselves. We were loud and quick to act. The O'odham were soft spoken and thoughtful. Though the O'odham spoke English, they spoke with a slow unfamiliar clipped cadence, breathing in as words came out. It was a mixture of their native language and English. We began the long process of learning how to wait and listen before speaking.

By the last day of camp that year we had seventy-five children. The California volunteers created a musical finale that we presented in the cafeteria.

When we were done, Elisa came to me and declared, "Keep the counselors inside until I tell you to come out."

As we sat, sweat pouring down our bodies under the sputtering swamp cooler, Elisa corralled the children and took them outside.

We looked at each other in the sudden quiet and wondered, with some measure of apprehension, "What is going on?"

A few minutes passed and Elisa came in to tell us we needed to exit the cafeteria one by one. Individually we walked through the cafeteria door into the blinding sun where we encountered all seventy-five of the children lined up ready to shake the hand of each of us.

We were in ecstasy! The vans got loaded up with their now precious cargo and took off for the final drive out to the villages. The rest of us began the huge clean-up of the compound and the packing up of the supplies that would go back to California. We were leaving in the morning and we had lots of work to do. We didn't know much, but we did know we would return.

The ride home to California was two days of recuperating from one of the hardest and best weeks of our collective lives.

The sisters were already anticipating next year. We were excited about what had just occurred in PisinMo'o.

The group talked all the way home.

"How can we make this better next year?"

"What if we change the schedule and have stations where the groups with their counselors can come to do art, sports, movies, or whatever?"

"We're gonna need more help. How do we get more volunteers?"

"We need to serve breakfast."

The questions and ideas poured out.

We arrived home on the evening of July 19, unpacked the van, and bid goodbye to each person who had spent the week with us in PisinMo'o, a week none of us would ever forget.

The next morning Pete and I rose at 5 a.m. to pack up and greet the group that we were shepherding to Tijuana. Martin was already in Mexico and had the first of our two Tijuana summer trips underway.

Martin was the organizer of these early trips. He made arrangements for us to live in a small colonia called Tenochtitlan that sat high on a hill outside of downtown. We met lots of local families, worked in the orphanages and garbage dump, took trips to the beach, and had a great time.

We met the Orozco and the Jarero families, who became a huge part of what we did in Tijuana. Maria Felix was a sober, soft-spoken woman who was mother to thirteen children. She hosted dinners in her home for our groups. Juanita was the energetic smiling mom of nine who always wanted to practice her English. She was known for her tamales. Each woman was active in the local Catholic parish church.

Martin had arranged for us to live in what was called the salon, the meeting hall, at the local Catholic parish. It was a large room attached to a small kitchen with a bathroom at the end. The kitchen had no sink, so we got water from the spigot outside the back door and we washed dishes on the back step and threw the dishwater out into the dirt road where the moisture helped keep down some of the dust. Washing dishes in this way helped us meet many local kids who hung out around the church.

As we met the neighborhood kids, we also invited them to accompany us wherever we might be going. Madre Victor and Madre Ancila, the Catholic Sisters who lived in a house attached to the salon, also came with us to several of the places we visited. We built wonderful relationships with the local people.

Lovingly dubbed the Rug-Rats

At night we came back to the salon where that day's dinner crew cooked while the others played games with the locals or slept off some of their exhaustion. We always cooked enough of what we were eating to feed the kids that hung around.

There was one group of boys we eventually and lovingly dubbed the "Rug Rats." They were dirty and ragged, and had no concept of being part of a family or community. They ranged in age from six to eleven years old. They were skinny, small in stature, with eyes that drilled into us. I'm not sure what they expected of us, but they kept coming back.

We built a tradition of getting into a circle, holding hands, and offering a thank you prayer before we ate. It took us several years before we could get these boys to join hands with us. When they sat at the table to eat it was apparent they had rarely, if ever, sat at any table to eat. Eventually they also became a huge asset to us in our life in the Colonia.

One year we had a terrible problem with our vans being damaged. They were parked on the dirt street behind the salon where we lived and we locked them up each night only to find broken windows in the morning and anything of value missing. We began to roll the windows down (we got tired of replacing them) and then our batteries were missing in the dawn.

Our vandalism problem ended when one of the boys volunteered to sleep in the van if we let him have access to the stack of children's books we used for our school. At night he took the stack of books into the van and "read" by the light of the street lamp.

Several of Maria Felix' children, Laura, Fermin, and Francisco, went with us on our daily excursions. These kids were a huge help with many of the projects we attempted. One summer Fermin spent many days in a hole we were digging for an outhouse for the lady across the street from the church. She had never had an outhouse and had used a fetid bucket for many years. She was excited and proud that this project was happening in her yard.

This particular summer we had our own pastor from Los Altos with us, Father Gary. He worked in that woman's yard making a concrete path for her from the street past her house and to the outhouse. Father Gary was a great sport and got sweaty and dirty along with the rest of us.

His introduction to Tenochtitlan was a crash course in how to celebrate liturgy in Spanish. We had arrived on a Saturday afternoon and the sisters immediately came to tell us that there was no priest for the evening Mass.

They knew we were bringing our priest and without delay Madre Victor approached him. "Father, can you say Mass for us this afternoon?"

Fr. Gary generously stepped up, but requested that Sister deliver the reflection on the readings.

The summer of 1987 was a decisive time for *Truck of Love.* We had taken over the responsibility of the group trips to Tijuana and begun our commitment to the O'odham and the camp in PisinMo'o. We had no idea where this was taking us. We really had no idea how to do any of this. We asked a lot of questions and made a lot of mistakes. We had no formal education in working with children or teens.

Something we were learning as *Truck of Love* evolved was that if God asked something of us, we needed to say "yes." We discovered that what we required to complete any task would be made available to us. We gradually formulated what has become a guiding principal for us: if we are doing what God wants us to do, then we will have what we need.

Pete finished his first full year of ministry with *Truck of Love.* We took a moment to look at how far we had come. It was awesome.

His boss at Lockheed called him at the one-year mark and asked, "Pete, when are you coming back to work?"

"I'm not coming back," was his reply.

Pete was happier than at any time in his life. He was doing what he wanted to do. He was a born helper and we loved our new life with all its complexities.

In Los Altos, shortly before Thanksgiving, three neighborhood kids came to our door carrying several bags of groceries.

We asked, "How did you get this food?"

Their answer surprised us. "We went around to people's houses and asked if they would give food for the poor people."

They vividly reminded us that this is what we were trying to do, "to act." In the first year of full time ministry with *Truck of Love,* Pete reached out to everyone he met. If a person needed help, he tried to find out how he could help: it might be food, clothing, or a place to live. He constantly got calls from generous people who had items to donate. Then he delivered those items to the individuals and families who could use them. People were getting involved. It became an amazing circle of faith in action.

The poor were no longer unknown. We put a face with the stories, and as we talked about the people we were meeting, others responded. The local work took up part of every day. The phone rang incessantly. There were knocks on the door, food and clothing appeared on our front porch.

Our neighbors never complained when day after day, our porch was covered to the ceiling with boxes and bags that obliterated any view out our front window. Sometimes when I came home from work I had to move sacks before I could get into the house.

Near the first of every month an envelope appeared under our doormat. We would open it to find a short note: "This is for you, Fullertons." In the envelope was a fifty dollar bill.

After much sleuthing we discovered it was a wonderfully generous woman we knew from our parish who was widowed, retired, and earned extra money by babysitting. She shared what she could with our family. Some months that $50 made the difference in what we ate.

The thoughtfulness and kindness of people kept us going. Just when we were so tired that we could hardly think, some person would say or do something that lifted our spirits and gave us energy to continue.

There was another side to being so public about this work. The area papers had done a few human interest articles about our local activities and the trips to Arizona and Mexico with teens.

People would yell things at Pete when they saw what he was doing. "Who do you think you are?" or "I'm calling the police to have you stopped!"

One night we got a call from an anonymous woman who lambasted our son, Tim, who had innocently answered the phone. "How can you possibly live in Los Altos without your father working? I know he's smuggling drugs from Mexico."

Tim did his best to deflect her accusations and then hung up. A few nights later she called again. This was an almost nightly occurrence for several months.

A few weeks into this routine, our anonymous accuser began calling our parish, the school where I worked, local TV stations, radio stations, and any other place she thought might pay attention. The parish secretary, the school secretary, and others let us know that someone was trying to defame us. We couldn't understand why this was happening, but we knew that we were trusted by those who knew us and that this poor woman obviously needed help.

It all ended after several months, with a final call to the parish secretary. She was a good friend of ours and was so fed up with this woman's frequent tirades that she had reached her limit of kindness and understanding. She let loose with her own defensive explosion that silenced the woman once and for all time. To our knowledge there were no more anonymous calls after that day.

This helping mission could get pretty discouraging. The barrage of encountering desperate people and attempting to direct them toward some kind of help was exhausting. It was dispiriting to realize that not everyone wants to be helped.

We had a huge learning curve as we delved deeper into working with God's poor. One thing was loud and clear to us. The "poor" were not all lazy. In so many cases, they worked incredibly hard to simply survive. We learned there are so many factors that cause a person to live on the street or to be homeless. Some people have a run of bad luck such as losing a job, getting sick, or having an accident. Some are abusers of alcohol and other drugs, some are ex-offenders, and some have mental illnesses that go untreated.

If a person has no income, no home, and no hope, they have often worn out the welcome of their families who cannot or will not help them anymore. They are on their own with no safety net. They have exhausted their financial resources and are surviving day to day in any way they can: part time work, waiting at designated spots for day labor, prostituting themselves, or panhandling. The longer they are on the street, the harder it is to get a job and get ahead. They get dirtier and dirtier with no way to shower or wash clothes. The little money they earn goes to food and lodging. Living in motels costs every cent they might get each day. They cannot save for their own place and it's all but impossible to get a job

Other people on the street have a deep distrust of "the system." Sometimes a soothing word or a listening ear was the only personal connection some of them might have in a day. Many of the people we encountered had no place they were ever expected to be and no one ever waiting for them. They experienced a kind of aloneness we could not imagine; if they got sick or died, no one would ever know or care.

Many of the homeless were once contributing members of our society. They went to school, had loving families, got good jobs, and then disaster struck. If they had no savings, or illness cost them everything, then they ended up on the street. During this time in California we encountered many individuals who had been let out of the state psychiatric hospitals when they were converted to facilities for the developmentally disabled.

Homelessness can cause other problems. Alcohol and other drugs soften the hardships a person experiences when they have nothing else; addictions surface. The mistreatment a person receives from the public drives people away from civilization. The cruelty exhibited toward the poor baffled us. When a person is perceived as powerless there are multitudes of others who take advantage of them in horrendous ways.

We learned there are many people who try very hard to help. There was a man, Gilberto, who Pete first noticed when Gil was urinating on the wall of a Seven Eleven store in downtown San Jose. He was surrounded by police. We later encountered him at a local church that housed homeless individuals and families. He was a small man with a vacant stare, a scraggly grey beard, long tangled hair, and filthy ragged clothes. He stood or sat on the steps outside the church meeting room. He rarely engaged anyone unless it was to bum a cigarette. It was difficult to understand his garbled speech – mostly, we guessed what he might want.

Gilberto

The people who ran the shelter at the church tried to get him to come inside to sleep, but he preferred the bushes outside at night. He refused to come indoors for food, so they handed him his plates and he would sit on the grass. Occasionally, when he got too dirty and smelly, the church members coerced him inside where they helped him shower and shave. He was the silent sentinel. Mostly people kept as far away from him as possible.

Pete sat near him and tried to engage him in conversation. Eventually he began talking and we discovered through his incoherent ramblings a story that rang true. Gilberto said he was raised in the Santa Clara Valley. He mentioned his father and a prune farm and work that involved picking the fruit. He also mentioned that this father beat him when he didn't do things right. At some point he was admitted to Agnews State Hospital which, at that time, cared for the insane. He stayed there for many years and recalled it as being a happy, peaceful time for him until he was abruptly released in the 1970's when Agnews was converted to a hospital for people who are developmentally disabled. Spending a short time in a residential community, he then migrated to the streets of San Jose where, by the time we met, he had lived for over thirty years.

He told Pete he recalled the initial fear he felt at being on the streets, but he gradually built a routine and adjusted to his new life. He was one of the many mentally ill people we encountered on the streets, each with a story, each a child of God, and each alone in their own world.

Our life resembled a ping-pong game with balls flying everywhere. We went from working with the poor to caring for our family, to giving talks, to working with the teens in our youth group.

The high school students in our youth group were very involved with *Truck of Love*. After our first summer of camp one of the teens, Julie M, approached us about bringing some of the Tohono O'odham teens to California for leadership training at Hidden Villa, a multi-cultural summer camp in Los Altos Hills. Julie had a connection with Hidden Villa and introduced us to the camp director, Susan, who was excited by the prospect of having Native American children at the camp. Julie and the youth group spent weeks organizing a fundraising dinner to help subsidize the teens who would be chosen to come.

When we drove to the reservation in the spring to deliver the regular truck full of food and clothing, we were accompanied by one of the Hidden Villa staff members. The sisters chose the five teens who were to come.

In PisinMo'o the sisters arranged for the teens and their parents to meet us and talk about what they might look forward to on their trip to California. Evonne was from PisinMo'o, Wilma was from Gunsight, Brian and Gary were from Charco, and Alton was from GoVa. The sisters drove out to the villages to bring the families to us and we met one afternoon in the multipurpose building. The parents and teens entered the room in their normal quiet fashion. We sat in a circle and tried to introduce ourselves and I was reminded of how difficult it is to get the kids to participate, to even say their names.

We proceeded to outline what they had to look forward to. "You will be flying to California and driving back to PisinMo'o with us and the rest of the group of this year's camp counselors. We want you to be counselors here in PisinMo'o for summer camp."

They looked down at the floor in silence.

We addressed the parents. "We'll take care of your children. They'll stay with us until we get them to Hidden Villa. It's a great place and the staff is very happy to welcome them."

It was impossible to gauge the thoughts of the teens because they were all so reserved. The parents had few questions, but smiled a lot. We had to assume that since no one said we could not do this, that it was going to happen. We wanted more O'odham involvement at the camp. We encouraged the parents to come volunteer in the summer and we hoped for the best.

The five O'odham teens arrived at the San Jose airport on June 18. They were silently observant as we drove the few miles to our home in Los Altos. Some of our local youth group kids were there to greet them and I believe they were disappointed because the O'odham were so quiet. It took us a while to realize that as long as we were talking, the O'odham felt no need to speak. They are people of very few words who listen with an intensity that comes from living in the desert; far, far away from the hubbub of city life. They were very comfortable watching and listening. Once we relaxed and stopped trying to entertain them, they began to participate and share a little bit of themselves.

The O'odham clung together, but by the time we dropped them at Hidden Villa they had started to warm up to us. The leadership training was a two week program, so we would not see them until the end of that. We drove away from Hidden Villa feeling some apprehension at how they would respond to this new experience.

Three weeks later Bryan, Gary, Evonne, Alton, and Wilma finished at Hidden Villa and we headed out in vans for the Arizona desert. This second year, we had twenty counselors: the five O'odham, twelve Californians, and three from New York. There were ninety-five kids who participated in camp.

The summer of '88 brought the late afternoon monsoons: a phenomenon that cannot be imagined until it is experienced. The wind roared across the desert. We watched as the sand was picked up and the brown clouds got bigger and bigger. The day became night as the soil hit like tiny hot pins pricking at the skin. Everyone screamed through the wailing wind and ran for cover as the thunder blasted and lightning flashed. Then came the rain, pounding the ground into rivers that ran in every low spot. It was spectacular!

Unless you are the one driving the bus to get the kids home to their villages.

This summer Pete drove what he called the "bus from Hell." We had so many campers from the outlying villages that we needed more space than a van offered. The sisters negotiated with the district to use an old school bus that was sitting at the district yard; however, the bus had a few problems. My nephew Tom, who was stationed at a nearby Air Force base, had come to camp for a couple of days. He could fix almost anything. He, Pete, and Paul, a science teacher from St. Francis, went to look at the bus to see if it could be used. There was a bullet hole in the middle of the windshield, a rag stuffed into the chasm left by the missing gas cap, and no air filter. Pete's expertise with wire coat hangers and duct tape, combined with the knowledge of an engineer and a science teacher proved to do the trick. Together they managed to get it roadworthy and off Pete went to the villages.

In case of emergency, he always took one of the O'odham teens and a shovel. Several nights that year, the monsoons started while they were in the bus delivering kids to the villages after a long day of camp. One night Pete got to the wash - a low spot in the road - just outside of the village of Managers Dam. This village was fifty miles from PisinMo'o and the last stop on a long, weary ride with a lot of very noisy kids. Pete sat in the idling bus staring at the wash where the rain water runoff had become a raging river.

Gary, his O'odham companion, said: "We need to wait till the water goes down. It's too deep to go through"

Pete could think only of spending several more hours with this bus load of rowdy children. After a short time waiting in front of the torrent, he decided, "I'm going for it."

Backing up to gain distance, he gunned the engine and entered the wash at top speed, pushing into the raging stream. The engine sputtered, then took hold. His speed steadily increasing, the water hit the windshield and spurted through that bullet hole with such force that the water jetted all the way to the back of the bus. All the kids, screaming with delight, were safely delivered home and Pete realized that was an experience he would not repeat.

On the final day of camp that summer after the last of the kids had left, after we had cleaned up the yard, after we had scoured the cafeteria, and after we had packed for our departure the next morning, we sat on the floor of the sister's trailer in front of the open freezer eating Otter Pops. We were hot, exhausted, and over-the-top happy. We had begun something we didn't really understand. We had started to form relationships that have lasted through the years. We thought we were coming to do camp, but what we received from the O'odham was a love and loyalty that is still with us today.

Over the years we have been invited into homes and into lives in a spirit of trust and mutual respect. Some of our campers and counselors are now with God. We have suffered with losses and rejoiced with successes. There is much pain in the lives of our desert friends, but they know how to live and celebrate life and its many joys. Today many former campers are part of tribal organizations. Some have gone to live in cities outside the Nation. Some have gone on to college. Some work in the colleges.

An O'odham elder came to camp one year and she told the children, "You could be the first O'odham lawyer, doctor, or astronaut."

We left PisinMo'o two days after camp ended.

Home for three days, and then we were off to Tijuana with a new group of fourteen teens and adults. Tijuana was a week of fresh experiences. Martin with his friend, Lisa, as well as Greg, our former youth minister, and his wife Kate were living in Colonia Tenochtitlan. They had prepared for our arrival and had met and gotten to know many of the local residents.

The sisters who lived in the house next to the church were now friends. As we got to know them and they saw how we interacted with the kids in the colonia, they slowly began to trust us and accompanied us on many of our excursions.

They even went with us when we went to the main prison, La Mesa, and the parish priest accompanied us to say Mass for the inmates.

We were warned that it would be an ordeal to get into the prison. We would be thoroughly searched before entering to make sure we were not bringing in contraband. This prison was surrounded by high walls with guard towers at intervals. Guards walked the wall patrolling from above.

Upon entering, the doors were locked behind us; that was the first of many times when I was alerted to how different life is inside these walls. It was ominous, entering the enclosure and having the door clang shut behind us; knowing that even if we wanted to leave, we could not do so on our own.

The males and females in our group were separated. We women were ushered into a small room where each of us was searched by a female guard. Arms askew, we were patted down over our whole bodies. Once searches were completed, we were let out into the jail compound where prisoners, spouses, and children were all milling around together. We knew there was a Catholic nun, Mother Antonia, who lived in this prison and had a ministry in the Tijuana jails. Somehow we thought it would be fine to go into La Mesa with a group of teenagers because we had the nuns and a priest on our side.

In order to get to the room where we were allowed to celebrate Mass, we had to walk through the prison all the way to the back of the compound. We stayed close together, each protective male in our group staying adjacent to one of the girls; but there was a constant push by prisoners in the crowded walkways. Several inmates asked to carry the box of song books and crates of oranges we had brought. Fortunately, on this trip, we held on to both.

Mass was miraculous. No matter where we are, when people come together to pray it is a superb experience. After Mass Pete and Greg led a sing-a-long and we passed out the oranges. Everywhere we went in Tijuana people loved the music. I was continually surprised at how much American music the Mexican people knew and having Pete and Greg with their gift of music was a blessing.

We visited La Mesa several times over the years. One time we let one of the prisoners carry the oranges and we never saw them (the prisoner or the oranges) after that.

The walls of the prison were lined with small shacks where inmates and their families had businesses that provided everything a person might need, for a price, of course. There were food stands, places to buy drugs, and shops with cooking utensils plus innumerable other trinkets. It was a small city and everyone knew who had the power.

One memorable day we waited at the gate for the guards to let us out after we'd celebrated Mass and done our usual singing. For some reason the guards on our side of the gate were very slow. Prisoners started to crowd us and push while the sentries on the other side looked on in amusement. Pete was searching for the guard with the key who was nowhere to be found.

Reaching his limit of patience Pete yelled at the guards: "Let us out!"

The one and only time we ever saw Mother Antonia was that afternoon when she came out of her room above the gate and called vehemently in Spanish at the men to let us out. Rapidly the key was found and the gate was opened.

We also went to other Tijuana jails. We became friendly with the sisters who ran Casa de los Pobres, a soup kitchen in the western part of the city. They took food to the downtown jails, Ocho and Judicial. The jails did not provide anything remotely nutritious for the prisoners to eat, so any real food had to be brought in by friends or family. Over the years, as our group presence in Tijuana increased, we took on the feeding of prisoners in these two jails during the month of August when the sisters were gone for retreat and rejuvenation. We made bean tacos and coffee with lots of sugar, cinnamon, and canned milk in it. We walked from cell to cell in

Judicial where the prisoners sat in cramped chambers. A small cell could have twenty-five men and women sitting with their backs against opposite walls and their legs overlapping in the middle. There was little space to move. When we got near the cells the captive's arms reached through the bars in an attempt to grab the tacos or coffee we handed out. As I placed each taco I looked into desperate eyes that spoke to me of a pain I could never understand.

One day, in the process of distributing food, Pete noticed a woman alone in a corner cell. The people in the other cells told him she was loca, or crazy. He took a taco, walked over, and spoke gently to her.

She whispered to him, "I no crazy. I don't want to be in cell with men. They have their way with me."

Everywhere we went we took a first aid kit. We regularly encountered people with badly infected cuts. One day at Judicial, Pete was told there was a man who needed help. He approached the cell and the man showed him a wound in his buttocks. There was a bullet hole that had penetrated the muscle from the front of his hip through his fleshy backside. When Pete put a long handled Q-tip into the wound it went all the way through. It had been festering for days. Pete went back several times that week and each time he cleaned and dressed the man's wound.

The other jail, Ocho, was configured with a central courtyard and multi-storied cells rising around the four sides. As in Judicial, the group took the containers of tacos and coffee from cell to cell. Here Pete brought his guitar and sat on a chair in the middle of the courtyard on top of a fetid drain. With cells all around and above him, he sang. The jail was a cacophony of sounds with doors banging, radios blaring, and people yelling. As Pete started to sing the other noises slowly stopped. Floor by floor, cell by cell, the guards and the prisoners became quiet. At the end of each song they erupted into cheers and requests for more.

Many months after one of these encounters, our friend Greg A. was in one of the colonias talking with a young man who had just gotten out of jail.

Deeply into their conversation this young man mentioned, "When I was in Ocho, this man used to come and sing. It really helped me get through a time that was so hard."

Whether we were in Tijuana or PisinMo'o, we began each day with group prayer and ended each day with prayer and processing. We saw our trips as working retreats. We are Catholic and brought that tradition with us everywhere, even though our group participants came from many backgrounds.

After a very long day of work, it was sometimes difficult to concentrate on reflection. Each night we began with music and that helped set the mood. Again Pete, and sometimes others, played and everyone sang. It was great fun to listen as a group evolved and got more and more into the singing. Some groups were wondrous in their sounds.

Both on the Reservation and in Tijuana we became known as "the group." As the years passed it was apparent that the people in both places trusted us and accepted all the newcomers because they were part of "the group." We used this as part of our pre-trip preparation: the people who had gone before set the tone for the next group and the current group would set the tone for those to come in the future.

The element of trust was always on our minds. We never wanted to do or say anything that would harm the relationships we were building. One time in Tijuana one of the women was talking to me and telling me how she wished that they could cooperate in the colonia the way our groups cooperated. I was surprised at her comment, because I didn't know the politics of what went on when we were not present. Something happened in each place when we brought our groups. For a short time the routine was broken and old habits were loosened. I always prayed that the lessons we all experienced during these trips would be lessons carried into everyday life for all of us.

The adults and teens we brought with us had similar reflections. "It's easier to share deep feelings with people we don't know."

We were privy to many profound realizations that never could have happened in other circumstances. It is a gift we cherish, that we have been able to share in many life changing experiences with so many thoughtful, caring people.

A friend who was our age made one of the trips to Tijuana. When we gathered for a post-trip meeting she told the group she had been talking to her daughter about the daily prayer and processing.

Her daughter listened about the shared prayer and asked her, "Mom, what did you ask for?"

Surprised, the woman responded, "Why, it was always a prayer of thanksgiving."

One of the stories I liked to tell our groups was about Corrie ten Boom. My recollection of the events may be slightly different than they are in Corrie's book, "The Hiding Place", but this is how I remember what I read:

Corrie was a deeply religious Christian woman who lived in Holland. Her father had a watch shop in the city of Haarlem. Corrie, her father, and her sister Betsy lived in the floors above the shop. Corrie and her sister were both middle-aged single women at the onset of WWII. When the Nazis invaded and occupied Holland in 1940, Corrie and her family began to help the Jewish people they knew. They opened their home to some and helped them get out of the country through an underground resistance movement. Eventually the secret work of the ten Boom family was discovered by the Nazis and they were sent to concentration camps just like their Jewish friends and neighbors.

Corrie's father died shortly after being imprisoned and then Corrie and her sister Betsy were sent to Ravensbruck Concentration Camp in September of 1944. On the train ride to Ravensbruck they overheard the prisoners saying that they could not have any kind of religious materials with them. Corrie and Betsy worried about this information because they had been able to keep a Bible with them the whole time they had been confined.

Upon arriving at Ravensbruck they managed to get to the toilets to hide the Bible in a heap of broken benches before being strip searched. Returning to the line they were told to strip off all their clothes and then they were sent back to the same toilet room to shower and put on a new dress from a pile of clothes on the floor. Corrie retrieved the Bible and hung it, in its pouch, from her neck underneath her new thin dress. When the guards patted down each woman who came from the showers they examined the women in front of and in back of Corrie, but they never touched her.

Assigned to a room with several layers of wooden bunks, Corrie and Betsy found their spot, but soon realized the room was infested with fleas. Prodded by the scripture they had recently read that stated they were to give God thanks in all things, they began to pray for the events of their days. Betsy wanted to pray in thanksgiving for the fleas, but Corrie resisted. Finally Corrie succumbed to Betsy's pleas and voiced her prayer thanking God for the fleas.

The days passed and Corrie and Betsy would bring out their Bible and pray together. The women around them began to join in. Being able to share the scriptures was enriching and inspiring to everyone. Each woman was vigilant about making sure there were no guards *around, in fear of being caught and punished. Then one day they had a shared realization: the guards avoided coming into the room because of the fleas.*

Betsy died at Ravensbruck and Corrie lived to be released. She spent the rest of her life traveling the world and spreading the good news of Jesus Christ.

After I read her book, we began a family custom of holding hands at meal times and thanking God for the events of our days. This custom spread to our youth group dinners on Monday nights and then to our *Truck of Love* group trips and meetings.

Our days accelerated as we continued to say yes to requests: for speaking engagements, additional trips to Tijuana, and additional weeks in PisinMo'o for camp. We visited many of the Catholic parishes in the area with our stories and music. People came forward to help us with various tasks. There was a real community growing up around the work of *Truck of Love*.

In the spring of 1989 when we went out to the Arizona villages to talk about camp, we arrived in the village of Charco after dark. We wanted to show Bryan and Gary some pictures, but there was no electricity in the village and so we stood in front of the van lights to look at photos.

At that time, the homes in most of the southern villages were the traditional homes made of adobe walls erected on top of the desert floor with thatched roofs made of cactus ribs. The homes were low to the ground to enable easy repair. The dirt floors were swept to a hard, dust free finish. These structures only allowed for minimal electricity and no refrigeration or plumbing. Outhouses were the norm. The people cooked on outside fires.

During one of our visits we went with the sisters to an outer village to meet a woman for whom they had a great affection. This woman lived in a traditional house. She was unable to come to Mass, even in the village, because she stayed at home to care for her two grown children.

The day we visited was a warm spring day. She welcomed us into her home and as my eyes adjusted to the dark, I saw that the one large room had a long platform off to the left that held the food and cooking utensils. There was a big table in the middle of the room with a single un-lit light bulb hanging on a wire from the ceiling. At the table sat a young woman in a wheelchair. When I shook her hand it was soft, puffy, and unresponsive; she had a severe case of rheumatoid arthritis that caused enormous swelling and stiffness of her joints. There was a double bed in the far right corner and just behind the door to our immediate right was an oversized crib in which the woman's son rested. He was twenty-one years old at that time. His body was about the size of a six year old. He was curled into a fetal position, unable to move or speak. He was clean and diapered in what looked like a piece of a white sheet. Day and night his mother cared for him and his sister. The people of the village helped her as needed. She didn't get out much so the Franciscan sisters came to bring Holy Communion to her.

I've often told the story of this woman. She is a devoted mother who spent her life in this small village caring for her son and daughter. She will never be canonized as a saint by the Catholic Church, but to me she is just that; she spent her life with devotion and honesty, loving God, and doing what had to be done. I'm sure she has had desperate days, but the day I met her she seemed joyful in her life.

Kate, Greg, Martin, and Lisa became a huge part of our organization that year. We found there were not enough hours in each day. They helped coordinate trips, deliver goods, organize volunteers for the clerical necessities, and do anything that needed doing. Their youth and energy kept us going when we were just too tired to think.

That summer we had eight teens from the O'odham Nation come to Hidden Villa. They attended leadership training and stayed on to be camp counselors for Hidden Villa before joining us for the trip to PisinMo'o.

The camp was growing, the Tijuana trips were multiplying, and Pete was making monthly trips to Tijuana with food and clothes. In the midst of all this we were moving from the home we had rented in Los Altos for eighteen years. We had no idea where we were going. The house was being sold and we did not have the money to buy it, but summer was upon us and we had obligations with *Truck of Love*.

The intensity of that time is still palpable. Our hours, days, and weeks were filled with inspiring experiences. One night before going to feed people in the garbage dump in Tijuana we had a group prayer reflecting on the Beatitudes.

In the morning we packed our beans, tortillas, fruit, and water into the vans and took off for the dump. People saw us setting up and came slowly across the compacted trash to where we had parked the vans. We had a towel and soap and some wash water and one person was assigned to help people wash their hands which were black from the burned garbage through which they had been digging. We all liked this particular job because we got to touch people's hands as they used the soap and towel. It was reminiscent of Jesus washing the feet of His disciples. It also helped us to see if a person needed some medical care for the prolific cuts.

During our reflection that night after our trip to the dump we stopped to meditate once again on the Beatitudes. This time we each wrote down a "be-attitude" inspired by the day. The group reflections all began with the words, "Blessed are."

Blessed are:

Those who live from the faith of Christ; they live in a happiness that overcomes poverty and loneliness.

The children of Tijuana; though they suffer deprivation, their faces radiate joy and hope.

The dirty, for they will be cleansed.

Those who search for God's presence in all they do; their search will not be in vain.

Those who learn from their mistakes; they shall know the truth and be set free.

Those who won't be moved from doing right, regardless of danger or reputation. They will reap 10X10X10 in their hearts and in their souls.

The final night of this trip, while we were praying, a knock came at the door. It was tempting to ignore, because we were busy at prayer; but one of the Spanish speakers in the group, Nancy, got up and went to the door. There was some muffled conversation and then Nancy came to whisper in my ear.

She said: "There's a man who says his child is sick and a friend told him we might help."

I got up and went to the door with her (because I didn't and don't speak Spanish). A man stood at the threshold in the dark courtyard and told us about his infant daughter who had been sick for several days. He said he tried taking her to the doctor, but the doctor would not treat her unless he could pay $200.

I asked, "May I see the child?"

The mom came from out of the shadows into the light cast by the open door. She carried a very small bundle in a blanket. I pulled back the cover and saw an incredibly tiny baby that I estimated at about three months. Her skeletal face rested at an odd angle in the mother's arms. Her eyes did not focus, her mouth hung open like a gaping bird; she was not responsive, but she was alive. The mom said she was suffering from diarrhea and vomiting. It was apparent she was badly dehydrated and would die without treatment.

It was our last night with this particular group in Tijuana. I looked into my money pouch to see what was left after the week's activities. I found exactly $200 which I gave Nancy with the instruction that she was to take this family directly to the clinic.

This was one of several times when we were in Tijuana that I had the opportunity to reflect on how cheap life is. For the want of $200 this child was going to die. Now she lives. Her name is Delia.

As we wound down that summer, we went home from Tijuana to a house we had to leave. We'd lived in Los Altos for eighteen years. It was the only home our children knew. We began to look for other rental properties, but every landlord wanted us to earn four times the amount of the rent: if a house rented for $1,000 a month, according to them we needed a monthly income of $4,000. With my salary of about $1,800 and Pete's check of $500 from *Truck of Love*, we had no way of coming close to that amount. We kept assuring landlords that we lived simply and we always paid our bills, but they were business people and wanted to insure they got their money each month.

In the midst of our search for a new home, the earthquake of '89 occurred in October. This one was so big everyone remembers where they were. Pete and I were in J.C. Penney department store and watched as the displays flew in circles and the plate glass windows crashed straight down to the ground. Pete tried to push me under a small chair and I quickly argued that my head would survive, but my body would be dead, so we stood and rode it out.

Walking to the parking lot to retrieve our car, it was eerily quiet. Lights at intersections were out and drivers were extremely aware and accommodating to each other. We slowly made our way home, fearing our 100 year old house would be badly damaged. Driving down our street the roadway was covered with water from what we later discovered were all the backyard pools that had sloshed over their sides. We walked into our home to find almost everything on the floor.

We had a huge bookshelf on which our TV rested. All the books, statues, vases, and the TV were in a pile on the floor.

Then the aftershocks started. We spent a couple of very tense days during which everyone's nerves were on edge. We had an eight foot long dining table with benches and with each aftershock, whoever was in the house would race to get under it, but there were too many of us to fit so there were always a few people left frantically turning in all directions to find an unoccupied doorway.

The day after the earthquake, we got a call from one of the local grocers who offered us all his damaged boxes, cans, and jars of food. In the midst of cleaning up our own home, we picked up hundreds of boxes of cans and jars covered with the remnants of broken containers. Joanne, our homeless friend with the voices in her head, spent many days talking to her ephemeral friend; washing, drying, and sorting the cans and bottles of food for later distribution to the people we served.

In reflecting about the earthquake we realized it affected a broad variety of people. Previously our daily work was mostly working with chronically poor people, but the earthquake changed that. Suddenly we were working with people of means who suffered great loss.

We spent the rest of the fall months recovering from the earthquake and looking for housing. At last we saw a house in Mountain View near St. Francis High School, where I worked and our children attended high school. The house was owned by a minister and his wife. They understood our lifestyle and gave us a chance. We moved from Los Altos to Mountain View at Christmas that year, but before we left we had a funeral for the house with our youth group members.

The teens had spent every Monday night in our home for ten years of dinners. They were attached to this tradition and worried because our new place would not accommodate the custom. We had our final youth group meal and when we were done we took the special pronged instrument that we had used every Monday night to serve spaghetti and buried it in the back yard under the redwood tree.

The move completed, we were back to business.

Each year we carried on the tradition we had started in 1988 of having a springtime *Truck of Love* dinner. The first dinner had been the fundraiser for the O'odham teens to come to Hidden Villa for leadership training. The dinners morphed into occasions to thank all our donors and volunteers.

In 1992, Larry, our cook from summer camp, came to California to cook our dinner. Knowing he could not make the customary tortillas (cemait) in our kitchen; he made 200 of them at home, wrapped them, and brought them in his suitcase. This was no small project: each tortilla is hand shaped and cooked over a mesquite fire and is about eighteen inches in diameter. When he got to California, we showed him to the kitchen at St. Williams where he finished off the O'odham feast with chili chicken, beans, and potato salad.

These dinners were possible with lots of volunteers. The teens from the youth group played a huge role as did the various people who had made trips with us. Our many donors loved to attend the dinners and we always felt uplifted even though we were exhausted by the effort.

The summer of 1992 was another marathon. I was gone from July 5 until August 16. We had ninety-six different adults and teens on seven separate *Truck of Love* trips. There were five O'odham as well as two teens from Tijuana at Hidden Villa for leadership training.

At the end of camp that summer we attended a death anniversary celebration in the village of GuVo for one of our camper counselors. Alton was one of our original Hidden Villa group. He returned for a second year at Hidden Villa and each year thereafter we would wonder, "Is Alton going to come to camp?" He was tall, thin, and wore wire rimmed glasses. He was very quiet and he always wore his earphones through which he constantly listened to music. His loving parents encouraged his gentle spirit and tried to provide the best opportunities for him. By the time he was going into his senior year of high school, he was becoming more and more a part of camp activities. Some of our counselors even remarked how they had seen Alton playing guitar for his whole group of kids.

The previous year, as we were saying goodbye, he had asked, "Pete, will you give me guitar lessons next summer?"

Delightedly Pete replied, "Of course. I'd love to."

Sadly Alton did not live to be at camp in the summer of '92. Alton returned from boarding school during the first week of June. He was due to start summer school in order to complete some requirements for graduation. Camp was only six weeks away. On his third day home he went driving with some young friends. Something happened that resulted in Alton being dragged by the car for several miles over the dirt road back to his home village. He died before they could get him to a hospital.

The night of Alton's death anniversary celebration in his village we were truly honored to be present amid his friends and family. The sacred O'odham tradition of marking anniversaries is a wonderful way to keep the memory of a loved one alive in the present.

By the time Pete and I took the first newcomer group to Tijuana, the veteran's group had already been there for ten days. In Tijuana we intended to have a school in the garbage dump where we would teach English and math. The sisters planned to join us and do some religious activities. There was also a house to rebuild and a church construction project down the hill from Tenochtitlan in Colonia Divina Providencia.

The school in the garbage dump was enormous fun. Each day we brought our tarps, blackboards, books, pencils, chalk, paper, beans, tortillas, oranges, and cookies. We fed the kids before we tried to teach them anything. We attempted to put the tarps up with sticks to provide shade, but they blew away in the wind. We ended up sitting on the ground on top of the tarps: a school with no building.

At the end of one of the school days while we cleaned the area, packed up our stuff, and made several trips to load up the vans, our nominally Jewish friend, Cathy, picked up the large picture of the smiling Jesus the sisters used in their class. As she walked we heard someone say, "Look, Cathy found Jesus in the dump."

Indeed, we all found Jesus in the dump. He was in every face we encountered: Jesus suffering, laughing, eating, hugging, playing, learning, and spending time with us.

There was one young boy who lived in the dump who was noticed by all of us. The children loved to play soccer and there was a large flat area of dirt and rocks where they kicked and ran after an old ball. In the midst of this daily rampage was a little boy who might have been four feet tall. When the ball sped toward him, he balanced on two crutches and swung both his legs straight out from his waist. Most of the time he connected with the ball and raced off on the crutches following it down the field. He was amazing.

His name was Mario and he loved life. We took him to the beach where he rode the merry-go-round that we pushed faster and faster – at his request. One day he went sailing off. Running to pick him up we asked if he was ok. He answered (in Spanish) with an impish grin, "I'm fine, except for the birdies and stars floating around in my head."

He rarely, if ever, accepted help. One day we took all the children from the dump to a large park. There was a zoo with a variety of birds in cages. One of our male volunteers saw that Mario was lagging behind, so he put Mario on his shoulders to help him stay up with the group. Mario kept making

Mario

his helper stop as he marveled at the birds and animals and the huge green lawn.

That night our volunteer reflected, "I have travelled all over the world, but I have never seen birds, animals, trees, flowers, and grass like I did today with Mario on my shoulders."

Many nights, we reflected with the group as well as the adults and kids from the colonia. More and more the local kids and adults accompanied us on our days of discovery and service in and around Tijuana. One particular night we had a discussion about values. We invited our Mexican friends to enter the discussion. Our interpreters made sure everyone knew what was being said. English and Spanish words and phrases peppered the air.

Someone asked, "Who are the poor?"

Of course we knew the answer; they were the people living in poverty in Tijuana. We were sitting in the room with them.

With the help of our interpreter, we all brainstormed ideas. There were no right or wrong answers – we listened to each other and shared our ideas. This is what we heard:

The poor are *economically deprived* (viviendo en pobreza); *from the heart empty* – del corazón vacio; *lonely* – abandonados; *uneducated* – sin educación; *elderly* – ancianos; *without work* – sin trabajo; *without food* – sin comida; *without health* – sin salud; *without self-esteem* – sin auto estima; *homeless* – sin techo; *addicted* – adictos; *without hope* – sin esperanza.

Another warm summer night as the sun went down, we met with the youth group in Colonia Divina Providencia where we did skits together. We met in their little church, a small concrete block building with a concrete floor and rough benches for sitting. Amid lots of laughter we watched. One of the skits was supposed to show a family at home in the evening. Our group did their skit and showed a family silently sitting together watching TV. When it was the turn of the Mexican teens they put a blanket on the ground and they all got on it. They lay down in a row with one person's back to another person's front. There were perhaps a half dozen children on the blanket packed like sardines in a can. They made believe they were sleeping – making snoring sounds. Then at the verbal signal of one of them they all turned over together so as to be on their other side, facing the opposite direction.

I had never thought about sharing a bed with more than one person, but it was common in the small dwellings for everyone to sleep on the same bed (if they had one) or certainly together in whatever small space they had.

During each trip we had time to go to downtown Tijuana to let the group shop for about an hour. As they wandered through the shops; we went along the streets and invited the moms and street kids, who were selling all sorts of things, to meet us at an appointed time at a nearby restaurant where we treated them to dinner. Sometimes we had forty people crammed into the restaurant where the owner would look on in wonder and some skepticism about what these gringos were up to. The waiters and owners got to know us as we paid our dinner bills and left generous tips. It was never more than $200 to feed everyone.

The mothers with their small children were able to leave their hard, hot work on the sidewalk and have a bit of fun. Each time we bought some of their gum, hand-woven bracelets, dolls, or whatever they were selling so they wouldn't miss out on the money they would have earned on the street.

As the years went on the women and their children got to know us. When we appeared they asked if their friends could also come. We had so many people that we started to transport them to a local park where we served them beans we had cooked along with fruit, tortillas, and cookies. Then the kids could be kids and just play as the mothers watched with huge smiles.

We walked along the streets and invited the moms and kids to meet us where our vans were parked in the Woolworth's parking lot. We had some opposition to this plan from the guards in the parking lot who informed us that "these people" were not allowed in the parking lot. We hurried them into the vans as fast as we could to keep them from being harassed.

On one occasion, when we were gathering the street people, an older well-dressed Mexican man was watching us herding kids and Moms into the vehicles. With some visible concern he stopped to ask, "What are you doing with these children?"

Assuring him of our intentions, "We are going to the park to play and eat."

He remarked with a huge smile, "It is so wonderful to see someone treating the children so kindly."

These mothers and their children worked the streets because they were the wage earners in their families. They sat on the street day after day, often subjected to cruel treatment from tourists as well as store keepers.

Another event we had continued from the very first trip was to gather the kids from the garbage dump and take them to the beach. A young man from Tenochtitlan, Emilio, followed us everywhere we went. He was tall, sturdy, and mentally slow. He loved being around the group and would do anything we asked. He was strong and did a lot of lifting and carrying. He spoke rarely, but the first time we took him to the beach he kept repeating: "Mucha agua! Mucha agua!"

When we had school, the beach trip became a reward for attending school. We knew the children a little better and now we wrote down their names as they got into the vans. We really didn't want to lose some three year old in the sand. Of course the kids all knew one another and they looked out for the little ones. The beach was a place of refreshment. The sea breeze was clean, the sand warm and soft under our feet, and the water gave us new energy. A few of the kids would show up with bathing suits, but generally they went into the ocean in their clothes. The children were very adventurous and our teens stayed with them to make sure they didn't get out too deep; but Pete knew that there was always someone who would venture too far, so he often stationed himself a little way off shore.

One of the girls from the colonia, Gloria, told me how Pete had put her on his shoulders and walked into the ocean with her. She was a shy girl who was afraid of the water, but that day she recalls her fear left her and she began to grow in confidence.

After a long fruitful summer full of working and living with groups, sleeping on floors, preparing food for hundreds, and being dirty and tired, we found it was difficult to return to the Bay Area and home. We had post-trip meetings with our volunteers and listened to each person talk about their struggles in returning here to a place where expectations were wildly different from where we had been. Getting the two places to weave into a fabric for our lives was sometimes a challenge.

I was given a book by Meighan, one of our teen volunteers. It was a compilation of poems by a Native American woman, Nancy Wood. In it she had a poem titled *Two Worlds*. It spoke to me and many in our group because she talked of living in one world where we exist, but don't survive, a world where we have power but not strength. She compared this to a world where there is harmony and where we listen to our spirit, a world where we have dreams.

So many of the participants of our trips, young and old, came from high powered families where they had influential jobs, or they attended schools where expectations were for pure excellence in academics and extra-curricular activities. We met many people who were stressed by daily activities and opportunities. They lived for tomorrow, often missing what was in front of them today.

On the first night of most of our trips, we read aloud a book titled, "The Precious Present", by Spencer Johnson. It had been given to us by another of our teen volunteers and we found it very helpful in bringing us to the present moment: where we are now. It is a gentle story that explains what we all know: we can't do anything about the past and the future is yet to come. The present moment is all we have. To live this moment is the best thing we can do for ourselves.

I was certainly a victim of too much future planning. As the message of this engaging book began to take hold in my soul, I found myself not worrying about what was to come or what mistakes I had made: as I lived each moment, life unfolded as it was meant to be. I trusted more in my God and the way He was leading me and us. When I prayed the *Our Father,* I paid special attention to the line "Give us this day our daily bread."

We returned to Tijuana that Christmas and I was reminded of this lesson one more time. We went to La Mesa prison early one evening to celebrate Mass. As we trudged through the mud down a corridor stinking of rotting waste, we came to an enclosure where we were told to wait. It was cold and dark and the smells of food cooking and decaying garbage engulfed us to the point of nausea. While we waited, Pete and one of the boys, Mike, brought out their guitars and began to play amid the chaos of vendors and thousands of voices shouting to each other. As the first familiar Christmas song lifted into the night air, heads began to peak out of barred windows above us and men and women appeared out of the shadows; first to watch, then to smile, and finally to sing, clap, and laugh.

Madre Ancila, who was with us, said, "For a moment these poor people forgot where they were."

On the home front life was still frenetic. Pete had begun to serve a breakfast of beans, tortillas, and coffee to the day workers; who, in anticipation of getting work, gathered on sidewalks by the side of one of the most trafficked areas of El Camino Real in Mountain View. Contractors or individuals who wanted cheap labor came early in the morning to offer the men jobs. Most of the men had come to this country from Mexico and Central America to find work so they could send money home to their struggling families. Often several men lived in one small apartment. They rotated sleeping in whatever makeshift beds they had.

At the end of each day the employer brought them back to the same spot and gave them their day's wages. Unfortunately there were a few unscrupulous bosses who let the men get out of their trucks and then they would speed away without paying them anything. Some gave them less than they had been promised. The men didn't argue or make demands because they were desperately afraid of being deported or physically injured.

Pete had seen that there was no help available for these men and with his attitude of find a need and fill it, he brought his pots in the early mornings. He started with one morning, and then his project grew to three mornings a week. Several of our local volunteers helped him make this happen.

Over the course of a year, word got around that Pete's beans were the best north of the Mexican border, so the numbers of men wanting a little sustenance before they went to work increased.

One beautiful Tuesday morning he pulled up in the *Truck of Love* van and asked some of the guys who were waiting if they would help place the food on the sidewalk (they knew where by now). Set up was swift and the crowd started to grow in anticipation of breakfast. This morning he had five dozen doughnuts along with the bean mixture which had been perfected through months of asking the guys how they liked their food. There were also five dozen tortillas and five gallons of pre-sweetened coffee. The men were making their burritos and happily drinking coffee when Pete noticed the traffic on San Antonio Road had stopped. He didn't pay much attention to this strange anomaly until the men dropped their food and ran in all directions.

Six men wearing black flack vests emblazoned with "Immigration" in white letters came from behind Pete and instructed him to get down on his knees and lock his feet one over the other with his hands behind his head. Just then six more men with crew cuts and dark glasses carrying rifles stood in front of the other agents facing toward the street. One of the men asked Pete if he knew why they were there.

He innocently responded, "Because I'm feeding hungry men before they go to work?"

One of the agents sternly stated, "We're looking for illegals."

Pete's temper flared as he asked the men, "Are any of you or your friends hungry? If so I seem to have plenty of food left now."

Only two or three arrests were made that day and Pete was allowed to leave after they wrote down his name and address.

Pete also developed a relationship with Mama Branch in East Palo Alto. She was an elderly woman who helped the people of her community. Pete took food and clothes to her in order to supplement what she already had. She and Pete became great friends.

For many years before his death her husband had been a minister in East Palo Alto and she was a woman of intense faith. In addition to serving the spiritual needs of his community her husband had also responded to their physical needs. Mama Branch carried on his legacy.

Poverty was endemic among the residents of East Palo Alto. Most people we knew would not venture into the area which had the dubious distinction of having the highest murder rate in the valley.

Pete never departed from Mama Branch without a shared prayer – she was a woman who knew how to pray.

One day after prayer, Pete asked, "How do you stay so positive when you deal with some of these people who always want and are never grateful?"

She told him, "I just love the hell out of them."

Mission San Jose Summer Day Camp in the summer of 1993 was full of emotions that sometimes seemed to be at war with each other. The day we arrived in PisinMo'o, there were kids all around us as we hastened to unpack the van so we could be available to play. We were excited to be there after our two day journey - to feel the scorching heat of the sun on our backs, to see the children so eager for camp, and to introduce the new volunteers to the people.

In the midst of the arrival chaos, Sister Patrice pulled me aside and said, "See those two girls over there? Their mother and father were buried last week. They need to know that you know."

Two nights later we went to the funeral of a young man, just twenty years old, from the village. As usual it was a hot night. We walked in the dark and dust to the small home where his body was laid out in the casket under the ramada. We could barely see all the people as we stood outside in the shadows. Children ran around in the warm night, dogs barked and chased after them. The smell of food for the funeral feast permeated the air. Men and women cried aloud in their grief. Underlying all of this was the drone of voices methodically praying the rosary.

Suddenly I was grabbed and hugged by one of our campers, a boy about seven years old who stood nearly four feet tall and was very round in stature. His shiny face smiled up at me and I could see his bright eyes reflecting what light was coming from the house.

He exclaimed excitedly, "I can't wait for camp to begin!"

We were yanked from one experience to another. Camp began a couple of days later and we were immersed in activities with hundreds of children. As usual we had a variety of counselors - many from St. Francis High School. This particular summer there were two students with us who made a big impression on the O'odham.

When we arrived in the village on the first day, some of the little O'odham girls took me aside and asked, "Who are those girls?"

I knew who they were talking about, but I acted like I had no idea what they were asking and I said, "What girls?"

They pointed to the girls and asked again, "Who are those girls?"

I said, "They're sisters, Miyko and Tempra. They're really nice; you're going to like them."

"But they're black," the girls continued.

"They are my friends and they really want to be here. Please give them a chance," I replied.

That afternoon I could not get the girls to go over to meet Miyko and Tempra; but as the days went by, and camp proceeded, everyone was thrown together in activities. I noticed that pretty soon those same girls were hanging all over Miyko and Tempra. By the end of the week they were exchanging phone numbers and promising to write to each other.

At the end of the camp, several of the adult members of the Nation came to me and asked if we could please continue the week of leadership training and add a second full week of camp, making this a three week experience. They said the children needed us.

I told them, "I'll try."

I could not imagine how we could make this a three week trip, plus travel time, but I was willing to think about it. Meanwhile we had to get to Tijuana.

Miracles were happening all around us. That summer the six little boys who lived near us in Colonia Tenochtitlan, who we affectionately referred to as the "rug rats," appeared again on our doorstep. They stood in a group at the door and looked. They came inside and sat. They got to know the teens in the group and wanted to play ball. They wanted to be with us, but their behavior was problematic; they took food without asking, they wouldn't be quiet when we needed to have meetings and discussions, they wouldn't obey us, and we got irritated.

We met with all our volunteers and we all decided that there had to be a response to the bad behavior, but we weren't sure what that needed to be; they simply wanted to be with us. They were really hungry, they were certainly dirty, and it was obvious no one had taught them manners. As a group we thought we would try the "positive approach." We invited them in before they had a chance to stampede in. We asked them to sit with us as we sat in a circle to sing. We each attached ourselves to one of them for English classes. We made sure to hold their hands when we circled up to pray.

Some days we patted ourselves on the back and thought "Good job, well done." Other days we figuratively "tore our hair out" as they were back to all the bad behaviors.

But we were witnessing some slight, subtle changes. One day seven of us were sick - laid out in our sleeping bags on the floor. They came into the room and silently sat by us. One night, when we told them we needed quiet time; we heard them outside practicing the English words they had learned in our Sunday and Monday night English classes. The final night we were in Tenochtitlan that summer, we gathered them together for our last prayer and each of them offered a prayer of thanksgiving for our group. The big surprise came when we learned that after the group had left the colonia; they stayed and worked all day with the leaders we had left behind to help clean up the area we had called home for five weeks.

When we left Tijuana for the last time each summer we went home to all sorts of activity. One Christmas season a donor sent us a check and enclosed a note saying she wanted the money to help a needy family have Christmas presents and food. This was the beginning of what became a huge part of our winter season each year.

This program eventually grew to serve several hundred families. Pete and his team of volunteers visited the needy families and got names and ages of each person who lived in the household. They got wish lists from the children and clothing sizes from the mothers of the children who would be grateful for a new winter coat or shoes for their kids. Then as individuals or groups called, Pete assigned a family to them.

He emphasized, "You are making a commitment to this family. I am counting on you."

The reply was always, "Oh, yes, don't worry. I want to do this. I am very excited to make this happen."

Once a person had signed up to help a family, Pete moved on to other people, assuming this family would be taken care of.

A couple of times this backfired on us and we had to shift into high gear on Christmas Eve when a mother would call and say, "Mr. Pete, you said they would call me, but it is Christmas and I don't have anything for my kids and I don't have any food."

A few Christmas mornings Pete piled whatever he could gather into the van and took off to make some child's Christmas wish come true.

There was a large parish in the south of San Jose that routinely adopted more than sixty families. They scheduled a day to wrap the collected gifts and send people with maps to personally deliver them to families all around San Jose.

We had many companies, groups, and individuals that collected gifts and we had a day when we met at St. Nicholas School in Los Altos where we wrapped hundreds of gifts and sorted bags of food. Then drivers, also aided with printed directions (this was before GPS), were sent out in all directions around Mountain View, Alviso, and Palo Alto to deliver these gifts of love. We called our program "Adopt-a-Family."

One recipient of this program was a huge family living in Alviso, a little town that rests at the end of the San Francisco Bay.

The household was composed of six families living together in a rickety pink house. When asked if they wanted to receive Christmas gifts from *Truck of Love*, they had a family meeting to determine which families were in most need. One of the family members told the others that he did not think it was right to ask *Truck of Love* to help all 29 of the people living in the house. He suggested the families with new babies, those with illness, or those with no jobs would sign up. They all agreed and after Christmas break the children in this household went back to school in new clothes, able to say, "I got this for Christmas."

Those six families eventually split into several groups: two families returned to Mexico, one family worked for and received a Habitat for Humanity house, one moved to Modesto, and one bought a house. Two of the girls went to Santa Clara University and are now teachers.

Many people told us this experience of adopting families was a way to put the meaning of Christmas back into their lives.

One woman said, "I have everything I need, but I feel like there is something missing from Christmas. There are too many parties, too many gifts, too much food, yet no sense of fulfillment. The act of helping a family that would otherwise have no celebration around this day when Christ was born is a way to understand this wonderful gift we all receive in the Christ child. It is in giving that we receive."

During this time of the year our phone constantly rang. We received countless calls from one person after another who wanted to be put on our Christmas list. I was reminded of the Mexican Posadas when a couple who have been chosen to be Joseph and Mary go from house to house. They are turned away from one house after another until finally some kind person invites them into the warmth of their home. There is such joy in the acceptance of the travelers and so much anxiety and sadness while waiting in the streets.

It seemed like Mary and Joseph had our phone number. "Please, can I get on your Christmas box list? I am alone with my two children and we won't have anything for Christmas."

"My Thanksgiving was alright. I took a can of spam and browned it in the oven and we had some peas and rice."

"I just got out of jail. I lost my job and I don't know what to do."

"Please can't you take just one more on your Christmas list? I have AIDS and no one will help me."

In the summer of 1994 we expanded our Arizona trip to three weeks - three days of leadership training and two full weeks of camp. This gave us the opportunity to become very comfortable with the community in and around PisinMo'o.

The desert spoke to us: getting up early in the cool of the morning as the sun is rising, birds starting their songs as the light peaks over the hills, dogs sleepily wandering around looking for someone to follow, horses and cattle lazily meandering through the village stopping to munch on spindly desert weeds; the hot evenings watching the sun set, sitting in a circle of chairs carried outside to the back of the cafeteria, singing songs as the disappearing light of the sun radiates off the clouds in a multitude of translucent colors. We felt like these reflective times encouraged us to be able to manage the blisteringly hot days chasing kids, playing games, and getting wet with the hose.

We loved our three weeks in PisinMo'o. It was hard to say goodbye, but we had commitments to be in Tijuana.

That summer in Tijuana we met the mother of the "rug rats." We discovered the boys were all from one family. The mom was about 33 years old and she had 12 children. She was, by this time, also a grandmother. She came with the boys to have dinner with us and we learned what a rough time she'd had in life.

She invited us to come to her home. The night we visited the boys were ecstatic to have us in their house, one simple room with a concrete floor, no windows, and one light bulb hanging from the ceiling. One of the boys took me outside where he proudly showed me his pet chickens. Each one had a name.

We spent several weeks that summer down the hill in Colonia Divina Providencia. We taught English and math in the mornings and in the afternoons we helped build a bigger church to accommodate the growing community. The people of Divina were exceedingly gracious to our groups. Several days each summer the ladies brought lunch to us, real Mexican food: homemade tortillas, nopales (cactus) salad, beans, rice, and always some kind of meat. They were amazing cooks.

One broiling afternoon as we dug into the side of the hill to make it flat for the new church walls, we were overcome with thirst. One of the kids went home to tell his mom that we needed something to drink. He returned with the most delicious cold peach Kool-Aid that I ever tasted. I was too thirsty to ask if it had been made with filtered water. I prayed it was safe and opened my mouth wide. It had a magnificent peach taste and cooled my parched throat.

In order to get to Divina we either drove down the hill or walked. Each day there would be a brave group that left our church home on foot to venture through Colonia Tenochtitlan and endeavor to navigate down the hill to Divina. This was remarkable because of the severity of the angle of this slope. I maintain it was an incline of about seventy degrees, Pete assures me that it was only about a forty-five degree rise - or fall - depending on the direction we were going. It felt like we were tumbling rather that walking down the hill. Most steep mountains have roads that are switchbacks: gradually leading the traveler back and forth until one reaches the bottom. This road was a long ribbon of treacherous road going straight down for at least a quarter of a mile. It became a real badge of honor to not only walk down the hill; but also to be able to navigate up the hill after a long day playing with children and digging and pounding the dirt for the new church. Often we walked down, but hitched a ride in the vans going home.

The walkers were fortunate to encounter a woman we lovingly called the "Chicken Lady." She had a small roadside stand that we passed each day. She sold sweets, and soda in a bag. She emptied the cold coke into a plastic bag, tied the top with a string, and put a straw into the hole, saving the soda bottles to return for the deposit. The first day we passed her stand, she motioned us over because she wanted to meet us. We stopped each day and she prayed over us. She loved that we were in her colonia working with the children and helping build the church. One day she told us the story that caused us to dub her the Chicken Lady: Her husband had been sick and near death. She was praying because she knew that if she could make him some chicken soup she would be able to restore him to health. She didn't know how she was going to get the chicken because she had no money. So she kept praying.

She was at her snack stand next to the street and two young men came driving by. She didn't know them, but one of them held a chicken out of the car window and told her it was for her. She gratefully accepted this gift from God, made the soup, and restored her husband to good health.

She adored her God. She used every opportunity to tell us about God's goodness and love. She talked and talked and some days when we were hot and tired, we tried to rush past her stand before she saw us. Rarely could we sneak past her without stopping.

Walking through Divina enabled us to experience some of the life of the small colonia at the bottom of the hill. There was one road in and the

Chicken Lady in snack stand

same road out. It was a dead end. The homes were small, some shored up by used tires, barely clinging to the hillsides. The yards were dirt. Dust covered everything, but every Monday morning as I walked past the houses the women would be boiling water in huge pots to do their laundry. I watched as they scrubbed with their hands until the t-shirts were white as new. I marveled at the expertise they had with a washboard and felt ashamed I had a machine at home that could not come near to accomplishing what they did. They had a pride in their work and the care of their families. These were some of the same women who took the time to feed us on numerous occasions.

One of our constant companions when we were in Tenochtitlan was a very young girl named Maria. She lived behind the church with her grandmother, who often chained Maria's ankle to a post in the yard so she wouldn't go anywhere. She was never schooled - ever - and was completely illiterate. She would show up at our door early in the morning and stay until we asked her to leave at night. She was absolutely content to be with our group doing whatever we were doing. One year when we arrived, her head had been shaved because she had lice. As her hair grew out, her head took on the look of a black tennis ball. She grew up with us and we worried about what would happen to her as she got older. It was with great sadness that we arrived one year and she was very pregnant. This was the first of several children she bore.

We found gifts for our weak spirits in a variety of places and situations. The summer of 1995 in Tijuana several people reflected on the lack of tension in our groups. They talked about how accepted and safe they felt. I kept coming back to those reflections, wondering what made *Truck of Love* trips a time and place of peace, joy, and contentment for our participants. My answer is found in why we kept the name *Truck of Love.*

When we incorporated as a not-for-profit corporation, several people suggested we change the name. We were adamantly against it. This was the name Gordon Stewart's daughter, Leslie, had created and we believed it reflected what we were doing: delivering trucks full of God's love to the poor.

Gradually I began to see the true significance of this name. Jesus had told us that the greatest commandment was to love one another, ourselves, and our God. At face value that seemed to be a simple and easily fulfilled request.

But what if all I really did was love? How would that look? Would my day start any differently? Would I treat my children and husband another way if I got up in the morning and said to myself, "Today is a day to love."

What seemed simple on the surface was a tremendous daily challenge. I saw that each person in our groups was attempting to love. I saw it when one of our teens gently coaxed a little child off the jungle gym, for the 100th time. I saw it when one member of our group had an asthma attack in the middle of the night and several of her friends in the group surrounded her and supported her as she struggled to breathe. I saw it as we walked out of the desert at dusk one night and some in our group were afraid of snakes and their friends coached them calmly back to our vans. I saw it when we painted the kitchen of a friend in Tijuana and one of the girls in our group painted flowers on the cabinets.

At the end of one of our visits to the juvenile jail in Tijuana a young man gave us a poem. One line said "If you want to come to know love, what you must do is open your heart."

I had listened to a talk given by Richard Rohr some years before. He is a Franciscan priest who, at the time, was part of an intentional community trying to live the message of Jesus. The day I heard him talk he reflected on how he learned that a Christian community had to be not only nurturing to those who were part of the group; but in order to stay vibrant and growing, the community needed to reach outside itself in service to others. Those thoughts resonated for me the more we got into the dynamics of what we were doing with *Truck of Love*. It is tempting when we have something so good to shut the door and savor it and not let any potential hazards in to create disruption.

Once more I was reminded how Pete and I complimented one another. I would be content to sit in a room and savor all the good that was happening. He was always out stirring the pot. He plowed the dirt and I sifted out the rocks. His presence in my life caused me to move out of myself into the unknown.

In one of our newsletters around this time we used a familiar quote from Scripture, "This is the message you heard from the beginning: We should love one another.... This is how we know what love is: Jesus Christ laid down His life for us. And we ought to lay down our lives for our brothers [and sisters]. If anyone has material possessions and see others in need but has no pity on them, how can the love of God be in them. Dear children let us not love with words or tongue, but with actions and in truth." (1 John 3:11, 16-18)

We knew God was calling us to this work, but I can't say we always wanted to answer this call. There were many days and nights when I wanted to do nothing more than sit down to watch a TV show or read a book, but we seemed to always have someone living with us. I had a repeating dream of empty rooms. Many a time our kids would walk through the living room and wonder who it was sleeping on the couch that day. Most of the people who shared our home were already friends, but we learned the hard way to think before we invited some people to stay.

Pete took pity on one mother with five small children. He saw them near dusk one evening on a busy street corner in

Los Altos. The mother was trying to keep her older kids from running into the street while balancing a young child on her hip. It was obvious she was in distress. Cars slowed and honked at her, but no one stopped. Pete drove around the corner, parked the van, and got out. He walked to where she was and asked if she needed help. She told Pete she had no place to stay, no money, and her kids were hungry. It was too late to find any agency to help, so Pete brought them home.

I guess that ought to have been the first warning sign. What mother with five small children would get into the van of a complete stranger?

We'd had many people stay with us in our little three bedroom, one bathroom home. By the time this family tumbled through the door, it was almost bedtime.

Our own children were welcoming and gracious to them, but they whispered their discontent into my ear, "What is Dad thinking?"

I gave the family something to eat and showed the mom how to pull out the couch to make a bed. We had sleeping bags for the children. Our own children went to their respective bedrooms, having their evening freedom interrupted by this family that now occupied the only community space in the house: the living room and dining room.

My personal experience of bedtime with my children was usually one of peacefully saying goodnight and sleeping until morning. We closed the two doors that separated the bedrooms from the living room and dining room where this family was located. I expected some noise, but as the minutes went on the racket got louder and louder. From my room in the back of the house, I felt the house move as the children jumped from one piece of furniture to another. The screams and sounds were more reminiscent of playing in the park than my vision of bedtime.

Finally I got out of my bed, opened the door to the dining room, peeked my head in and said to the mom, "Please get your children to lie down and be quiet."

The second time I opened the door I spoke directly and firmly to the children.

Finally on my third trip, I threatened to have Pete take them back to the street where he had found them.

Morning could not come fast enough. As soon as possible, I fed them breakfast and, corralling them with great difficulty, Pete loaded them into the van. As a group, they were like silly putty. We'd get one child by the hand and two others would be back jumping or pushing in any direction but the one we wanted. Pete was determined to find a shelter that would take them.

As they pulled away from the house, I silently vowed that we would never repeat this mistake. Pete took them to every place he could think of and finally found housing for them; but there was one small problem. The space for them was not available until the following day.

He called on the phone and pleaded, "I found them a shelter starting tomorrow, but they have no place to stay tonight. Can I bring them back home?"

I reluctantly agreed. I could not put them back on the street.

By the second morning the five youngsters didn't want to leave our home. I believe it may have been one of the few times in their short lives that they had been welcomed anywhere, where they had been treated with dignity and respect, where they had experienced what a family could be.

Though in my heart I was resentful and even a little bitter at the treatment we had received at their hands, I tried not to show them how I felt inside. I did, however, feel as though we had all laid down our lives for them.

When I confront my own lack of faith in situations like this, I recall Jesus asking that the cup of suffering be taken away from Him. It is human to resist pain. I prayed for myself and our family that we could continue to find compassion in our hearts for people who were put into our path. I also began to research the community resources that were available for a mother with five children.

As we prepared each group for a trip to Tijuana or Arizona, I saw the fear in some of our participants. I recognized that fear of the new and unfamiliar because it was in me. My mantra during those years for myself and for the group was, "With God's help, we can do anything together." And we did.

However, that spring we did something that caused real fear in my heart. We tried a trip with old people - like us - to Tijuana. We were in our early 50's, but thought that was old. These were parents and grandparents. Some of them were encouraged by the teens who had made trips with us. Each of them wanted to have this experience, but not necessarily with a group of teenagers, some of whom were their own.

From the beginning I was apprehensive. What if they did not like "my" Tijuana and "my" Mexican friends? After lots of prayer and reflection, repeating my own advice, "With God's help, we can do anything," we began the preparations for our trip.

From our pre-trip meetings and then the long drive down Highway 5 to the border, it was a joy. Finally there was someone else who uncurled themselves from the ride with similar aches and pains of limbs stiffened from several hours of sitting. Adult reflections were informed by years of experience and lived faith. Prayer times were extraordinary as we shared our thoughts and feelings with others who had some life history.

There was a home for elderly that we regularly visited when we were in Tijuana. We went with our song books and sang with the people. In this particular place I wandered into one of the rooms and encountered a somber lady who was confined to bed. She was a tiny woman with a long thin face and short straight grey hair that was combed behind her ears. She sat under the covers leaning back on her pillows as she sternly stared at me with piercing dark eyes. Both her legs had been amputated near her hips. She refused to be in a wheelchair and I was told she was pretty cranky. I do not speak Spanish, but the first day I was there the aides handed me a bowl of food and told me to feed her. They explained to me that it was very difficult to get her to eat and then they disappeared.

I went over, sat beside her bed, and spoke to her gently in English as I showed her the bowl of mashed up meat and vegetables. I brought the spoon to her tightly closed lips and she pushed my hand away. I kept talking and smiling and gradually she opened wide and received what I had to give. I immediately saw why her food was mashed – she had no teeth.

To the surprise of the nurses, she ate all her food that day. She did not attempt to speak to me at all during the time I was with her, but I saw her eyes follow me as I left.

Each time we returned to that home, I found this little woman and sat with her when everyone was singing in the other room. Slowly she began to know me. She smiled and tried to talk with me, but, of course, I could not understand her. We did, however, seem to have a connection. Over some bowls of mashed-up food we formed a friendship.

By that summer we tackled summer camp without the direct help of the sisters. There was a definite shifting of duties. One of our volunteers, Cathy, became the camp director. Several of the O'odham stepped up to help get vans from the districts and O'odham presenters for sessions with the children. We had Larry, who was our chief cook and supervised a kitchen full of women helpers. Thankfully the camp was becoming more O'odham.

On the weekends we liked to get out of the village and experience O'odham culture. Our cook, Larry, invited us to go to Baboquivari, the sacred mountain where I'itoi's cave is located. O'odham tradition taught that I'itoi, also called Elder Brother, is the spirit of goodness.

Larry explained there was a picnic area below the mountain where those who chose not to climb could relax and wait for the rest of the group. We left early on a Saturday morning when it was still relatively cool. The climb was steep and Larry and I were the last to arrive at the cave. Larry explained to me that the opening into the cave was very narrow and the person entering had to be in a good spiritual place in order to fit through. Sister Carla had accompanied us and she had already entered. I looked at the opening: a tiny slit in the rock; but I could not see inside, it was too dark. Hesitantly, I twisted my body so I could squeeze through the fissure. As I slid head first into the cave I fell inside onto a soft dirt pad in the dim cool space. When my eyes adjusted I saw the others gathered around Sister Carla who was lighting the sage to do a traditional blessing.

It was a very small space where the O'odham had come for centuries to pray and offer gifts to I'itoi. I was emotionally overcome with the significance of this place in the life of the people. It was grander than the greatest cathedral ever made by man. I felt privileged to be invited into this extraordinary experience.

Before leaving the cave, following O'odham tradition, we each left a gift for I'itoi. The climb down the mountain was infinitely easier and sandwiches with lots of water were welcome relief for our hunger and thirst.

In Tijuana that summer our friend, Nancy, led a group of vets before we arrived. We finished out the summer with two ten-day group trips for Tijuana newcomers. This summer we felt closer to the community. The groups were greeted with great anticipation by our Mexican friends. We were part of funerals, birthdays, weddings, and baptisms.

The sisters in Tijuana had prepared two girls from the garbage dump community to receive their First Holy Communion while we were there. We planned and prepared for a celebration after the First Communion Mass. One of our volunteers had a dress made for the girl she was sponsoring, but the second girl told us she had a dress that she had gotten out of the garbage dump that she wanted to wear. We smiled and said out loud, "How wonderful." Privately we were horrified; what kind of dress could this be?

The day arrived and we sent vans to the garbage dump to pick up the girls and their families. They arrived at church in their Sunday best and the girl with the dress that had been retrieved from the garbage was resplendent in a pristine white dress and veil. Apparently someone had thrown away this dress and veil in a plastic garment bag. It was perfect and she was radiant.

By 1996 the grueling schedule of family, trips, speaking engagements, and local work was getting to us and we were exhausted. Thank God our auto pilot was working. We knew what we needed to do and we did it, but the effort was crushing.

Reflecting on Christ's poverty, we discovered a passage from Mother Teresa's Missionaries of Charity. We were blessed to work with them in a colonia outside of Tijuana and had a yearning to understand why they did what they did and how they labored through each day with such joy.

In their rule it is written: "Christ, who being rich became poor and emptied himself to work out our redemption, calls us: to share in His poverty so that we might become rich through His poverty; to bear witness to the true face of Jesus - poor, humble, and friend of sinners, the weak and the despised..."

The redemptive quality of Christ's poverty echoed in my soul. This was the poverty of spirit that recognizes the power of God in every act of life. The poverty that deserves none of what the world has to offer, but recognizes that everything is a gift from God. The poverty that enables us to give when there is no apparent result. The poverty that encourages us to keep going when there is no energy. The poverty that lets us receive without guilt, but with a sense of gratitude to our Creator.

As I look back on this time, it is apparent that we had to hit the downtimes in order to understand our full and total reliance on God for everything we are and have. We can do nothing on our own, but again, with God, all things are possible.

These insights always come to us when we most need them. For some time Pete had been sharing with me a series of recurring dreams he was having. This may have added to my exhaustion as we grappled with what to do in the face of what appeared to be yet another call from God.

Pete felt that he was being called to be homeless. He worked with homeless people in the Bay Area, but he really had no knowledge of their unique journey in life. In our discussions and prayerful discernment, we tried to figure out if this was a real call and what it meant. This process lasted over a period of about two years.

In the meantime we had work to do, trips to complete, camps to run, and a family that needed us. We had to be fully present to all these people and events. There was no time to be distracted.

Our trips to Arizona and Tijuana that year were tremendously life-giving. We left behind the comforts of our home and our cherished family to go find what we sometimes forgot was always with us. We experienced "life in our face" as one of our counselors, Nora, declared. We went from the vast expanses of land where the horses and cattle languidly meander through the village to a city of 3,000,000 in Mexico. We played with children who were not always cooperative, sweated as we dug and pounded dirt, sang and prayed together, and made friends we will never forget. We were continually brought back to an appreciation that God is working in all of our lives. We re-learned that "flexibility" is the word we need to remember as plans changed and we were open to the unexpected. This love that we were trying to live opened us to listen to that inner spirit that leads us to what is truly meaningful in each of our lives: for us that was our family and our work with God's poor.

We left Arizona, drove home, and two days later we were in Tijuana with the first of two groups we shepherded that summer. We arrived in Tijuana already worn out, hoping for a slow start on the weekend. Excited that we could sleep in until time for Sunday church, we were startled awake in the dark at 5 a.m. by the blaring horns of a mariachi band playing Las Mañanitas in the courtyard directly outside our door. We collectively jumped up from the floor while Cathy, who had been with us in PisinMo'o, and who was also overwhelmingly exhausted, uttered an expletive that we laugh about these many years later. Stunned in our fatigue, we deliriously staggered to the door to greet the whole community who were joyfully serenading us and welcoming us back into the colonia for the next few weeks.

We had a new favorite phrase: love evolves. During that winter we made a difficult choice to stop the group trips to Tijuana. It had been thirteen summers since the first trip, but we were stretched beyond our limits.

There was so much more going on at home with the homeless, the people in East Palo Alto, and the plethora of other little projects. We announced the change, but kept a commitment Pete made to take a truckload of food and clothing to Colonia Tenochtitlan each month. Pete still visited with our friends in the garbage dump and the little ladies who sold trinkets on the street. He connected with some students from San Diego State University who went with him across the border where he took them to feed the people in the dump and the street workers.

Our friend, Nancy, who had been with us for several years had formed a tremendous connection with the people in Tenochtitlan, committed herself to assisting Pete with the transition. She continued ministry in Tijuana for another decade and now almost twenty years later, she is working her own ministry in Ensenada, south of Tijuana.

Our resolve was rooted in Scripture: "There is a time for everything, and a season for every activity under the heavens: a time to be born and a time to die, a time to plant and a time to uproot...." (Ecclesiastes 3:1-2)

It was time to concentrate on more local projects. Change was good. It was time for something new. In the spring instead of having our annual *Truck of Love* dinner, we gathered a group together to paint a house and revitalize a yard for a local family in need with an organization called Christmas-in-April.

Welfare laws were changing and we were receiving more calls for local help. Mama Branch's house burned down and she referred her people to us for help with food, clothes, and other necessities.

Pete's dreams continued and began to be more specific. He and I agreed that he would make this journey into homelessness. I asked him not to say anything to anyone. I did not want our children worrying about it, so he waited to talk with them until six months before the proposed date of departure.

He met with them one by one. By this time, they were used to us being a little different in our goals and dreams. They knew there would be no arguments to discourage this trip and so Pete received their blessings - slightly different from each of them.

Our grandson, Gregory, was ten at the time and Pete took him out to breakfast at a restaurant. Pete told him what he was planning to do and Gregory looked at him and the plate of food in front of him and asked, "Is that all you're getting, Grandpa?"

It was life as usual for Gregory.

Pete and I discussed the specifics. He dreamed he was to leave from a state other than California and the date for departure was August 14, 1997. We didn't understand how this could happen, but we trusted that in time it would be revealed. In the meantime we planned for and completed our eleventh summer camp in Arizona.

With the one and only summer trip behind us, Pete and I returned home and began to prepare for his homeless experience. Our oldest son, Tim, was performing at the Ashland Shakespeare Festival in Oregon that summer. He wanted us to see one of his plays, so we scheduled a trip and bought tickets for the night of August 13. It seemed that Pete would be able to leave from a state other than California on the morning of August 14 (which was a specific detail that had been in Pete's dreams).

The few weeks between Arizona and Ashland sped by. Pete had to let local people know he would be gone. I had to be brought up to speed on what I needed to do while he was away. He bought a hiker's backpack and systematically packed it with what he thought he needed. He planned to work, so he took one set of clothes suitable for a job and I made some signs that said "north," "south," "east," and "west" to facilitate his hitchhiking.

We went to the play in Ashland the night of the thirteenth and attempted to sleep on the floor in the living room of our son's small apartment. Our alarm was set, but we were awake much earlier than the 5 a.m. bell. I made coffee and we said a quiet prayer. Pete put on his backpack and kissed me good bye.

He walked out of the door, my eyes riveted to his figure I prayed for him as he strode up the path to the sidewalk and out of sight. I prayed for his safety, his health, and his strength. I had no idea what was in store for him.

It was a Thursday and I had made him promise that he would call me each Sunday. I also insisted he take $100 with him because all the homeless people I knew had some money in their pockets. He spent $20 the night before at the play so he walked out the door with $80 in the bottom of his shoe.

People asked me what I thought of this trip he was taking. I willingly accepted that this was something he had to do. I don't recall feeling at all stressed about his going. I think one reason may have been a dream I'd had about a year before he left. I do not usually recall my dreams, so the fact that I remembered this was significant:

> *I dreamed that Pete and I were lost and I was leading him through a maze of underground spaces. I put him on my back to walk up a very weird set of stairs. I was surprised how easy it was to carry him on my back. Then we were in a strange room and I was looking for a way out. A beautiful blond haired child (who looked amazingly like our two year old granddaughter, Kayleigh) was in this room. She extended her hand toward us to lead us to safety.*

The first phone call came not on Sunday, but the very next day. He was in northern Oregon and he had a job washing dishes in a restaurant, the first of several jobs he was able to get. He kept a detailed journal about his trip and we eventually transcribed it, with the help of some dedicated friends, into a book that we published under the title "Old Men Dream".

He learned a lot. He got all the way to the east coast. He had jobs driving a truck, washing dishes, and working in a laundry. He earned so much money in the first couple of weeks that he finally decided not to look for any more work. He hung out in parks, got lots of rides from strangers, walked hundreds of miles, and met wonderful and interesting people. He got deathly ill after eating with a new friend out of a dumpster behind a Chinese restaurant. That friend cared for him as he lay in agony beneath a bush that was his shelter in

Savannah, Georgia. For a time he couldn't see and when he came home he had to be treated by a specialist lest he permanently loose his sight. He helped people with the extra money he had in his pocket. He learned he could find anything he needed. He was followed by some guys with a gun, let out on a road to nowhere by an elderly couple, and met an old, raggedy man on the steps of a church who told him, "God loves you. He loves the little child in you. He wants you to love Him like a little child."

Being homeless revealed some things that were unexpected. We were so used to giving that we didn't ever think about what it was like to always be receiving. Many times Pete ate in soup kitchens or slept in shelters. When he asked, "Is there something I can do to help clean up?"

The response was usually, "Oh no, we do that."

It was hard for him to be ignored because of who he hung out with or where he ate or slept. He felt like he was judged without being engaged. People treated him in ways that he felt were demeaning. The time came when he was so beaten down by illness and bad attitudes that he felt the despair and depression creeping in. It was apparent that if he was homeless much longer it would be difficult to come back to a regular life. He began to understand why people were chronically adrift.

He returned to me and our family on October 6, 1997, after fifty-two days on the road. There were times when he called me during his trek, when he sounded sick and I thought, "If I ask him to come home, he will."

But I knew he had to complete the journey. He arrived home with $80 in his pocket.

Pete was home, but there were very few moments to reflect on the previous fifty-two days. It was time to start the Christmas Adopt-a-Family program. Pete got to work immediately between trips to the eye specialist for the unknown ailment he had contracted on the road. The phone rang persistently. The previous year we had helped almost 200 families with gifts and food. This year would be no different.

We saw God's hand in our lives. There was no Christmas trip that year to Tijuana and we had made plans for a family celebration with my brother's brood on December 27. He lived over the hill near the beach in a little town called Aptos. We loved the drive and were looking forward to seeing the cousins. He and his wife had four grown sons.

Christmas day was a busy time, so I didn't have a chance to call my brother until the morning of December 26. My nephew answered the phone and in a somewhat frantic tone, told me the paramedics were at the house and he didn't know quite what was happening. He would call me back. I sensed something was terribly wrong and decided that rather than wait for a call, I would start over the hill and go to the hospital near their home. When I walked up to the nurse's station at the hospital and asked for my brother I was gently ushered into a room where the nurse explained to me that he had died.

It was a time of intense family unity. My brother was ill, but we did not expect this. He got up the morning of the twenty-sixth, went outside to sit and look out above the roofs that lay below his deck to gaze at his beloved ocean. This was the place he treasured most, his place of reflection.

I returned to work at the school after Christmas vacation, but I realized afterwards that I was not functioning at full speed. I wanted to be alone. Pete took me away for a weekend. I needed to have some space from the constant needs of others. I needed time to myself. For many weeks, I came home from work at night and headed to our bedroom where I quietly read.

Pete's stepdad died a few months before my brother, and much to our surprise he left us some money. We had approached our children and told them that we wanted to give the inheritance to them. They were adamant that we use it for a down payment on a house of our own.

We had rented all the homes where we raised our family. We never thought we could own a home because we didn't have enough money for a down payment. We'd never been able to save because we spent our earnings on everyday life. We asked around, found a real estate agent and started looking at houses. In the midst of dealing with my brother's death, we got ready to move into a place of our own.

God's hand was writing with crooked lines. Our third grandchild, Timothy, was born in February. I ended up in the emergency room suffering from what turned out to be a case of shingles, precisely on the evening we signed the papers that gave us the keys to our new home. I was sidelined for the two weeks when I needed to pack up the old place and paint the new space. Friends and family came forward to help, while I lay on the floor of the new house and watched them paint, clean, and put paper on kitchen shelves. This was a huge exercise for me in letting go of expectations. I loved to control my situation and this time, when we were experiencing this great change in our lives, I had to lie there and let others take care of me. One of the hardest parts turned out to be that I had to stay away from my newest grandson lest I give him chicken pox.

We moved into our 80 year old house in downtown San Jose in March. We lived in San Jose just a few days and then Pete loaded the van for another two day delivery trip to Tijuana.

In July we were off to Arizona. Summer camp leadership training that first week drew teens and adults from all over the reservation. One girl was a new mother at the age of sixteen and another young man was struggling with his sobriety. We spent the three days of leadership training talking about racism, stereotypes, and conflict resolution. It was a time of powerful community building when the O'odham and the teens we brought with us began the relationship that helped them through the upcoming days of camp.

Early one morning we loaded everything into vans and took off across the desert in the dark to pick bahidaj (cactus fruit). The saguaro cactus is protected from outsiders by the federal government, but the O'odham pick the fruit each summer as they have for thousands of years. We learned how to bless ourselves with the juice of the first fruit and to offer it back to the earth by placing it at the base of the cactus. The fruit we collected was boiled into cactus syrup.

Walking out into the desert could be treacherous. There was another cactus called a cholla: also known as the jumping cactus. It was not necessary to touch it to be caught by its hooks. Near proximity caused the curved spines to jump to a person's skin. Each summer at least one of our counselors got a cholla barb stuck in them – a hand, an arm, or an ankle. The cholla could not be removed by grabbing with the fingers or it became lodged under the skin of the helper. Whoever was nearby got two sticks and attempted to pull it from the skin. The ends of the needles were hooked and it took a lot of strength to pull it free. Sometimes it felt like we were ripping a huge piece out of the poor victim. Afterwards the wound ached for hours, a vivid reminder to look before moving in the desert.

Getting up early to experience these wonderful traditions and staying up late meant that by the end of that first full five days of camp with the children, we were ready for a break.

There is a place called Topawa, about an hour from PisinMo'o, where the Franciscans have a retreat center. It is not far from there to the Mexican border. From the retreat house we had a clear view of the sacred mountain, Baboquivari, where we had climbed to I'itoi's cave a few years before.

It was necessary to get out of PisinMo'o if we wanted any kind of peace, so on Friday night we packed up and drove to Topawa. Sister Carla was with our group and she encouraged us to make a hiking trip to a place called Window Rock. She would lead us there the next morning. We made sandwiches, filled water bottles, and set our alarms.

We left before dawn so we could be there near sunrise before the heat of the day. We planned to be back in Topawa by noon and have a good rest before finishing up our second camp week with the more than 100 children who each clamored for our attention.

To get to Window Rock we drove south from Topawa and turned off onto a lonely dirt road that led us twelve miles to where we parked and prepared for our hike. It was an impressively beautiful sunrise and the desert beckoned us. We hiked up the mountain of reddish brown dirt and rock to where we saw an opening that looked like a gigantic window carved into the formation. From there we had a panoramic view of the desert with Mexico directly south of where we stood. There were puffy white clouds off in the distant sky and the desert floor several hundred feet below. We each found a place of solitude to ponder where we were and what we were doing. The silence was all-encompassing; the only sounds were the wind and the birds.

I settled into a warm rock and I saw Pete traverse the side of the hill to sit cross legged in a carved out niche in the rock face across from me. We sat there for some time, writing in our journals, gazing at the expanse of desert; and then as it began to warm up one of the group announced it was time to go down to the cars for sandwiches.

As I began to move, I glanced at Pete who looked like he was jumping down from the rock. I thought it was strange; maybe he had found a new way to get down.

Then I heard the crunch and heard his cry, "Get some help! I'm broken."

I looked over the edge of the cliff and saw him lying face down about thirty feet below. His right leg was pointing at an odd angle. He had been traversing the rock and his hand with the short fingers had missed their hold. Down he had gone. The whole group quickly climbed to where he was lying.

I repeated over and over, "Oh, God. Oh, God. Oh, God," as I navigated the steep terrain.

I called to the group not to move him. I didn't know if he had broken his back. There were fourteen teenage girls, one teenage boy and three adult women. Cathy and one of the girls went for help. Cathy had to drive twelve miles back out the dirt road and find a place with a telephone. That could take some time. The rest of us tried to make Pete as comfortable as possible.

His leg was bleeding profusely where his foot had been almost severed. The teens removed their shirts and wrapped his leg. One girl sat at his foot and applied pressure in an attempt to slow the bleeding. Another scraped the dirt away from his mouth and cradled his head to keep him from having to eat the soil. The others took off their shirts and tied them together to fashion a shade screen to prevent him from burning to a crisp under the glare of what was now the very hot sun. Pete was sweating and the girls poured water into their hands so he could slurp it from his face down position.

It was four hours before the first paramedic arrived. He came with a body bag and no painkilling drugs. In their experience the people who fell off Window Rock didn't live to talk about it. He radioed for more help. It was another hour before a few more paramedics arrived with the needed painkillers. During this time the teens sang camp songs and Pete told jokes and sang with them. He was in extreme pain, and later likened it to feeling like the pain that Christ must have felt as he hung on the cross.

The paramedics initially thought they could carry him down the mountain, but they abandoned that idea. The terrain was very steep and Pete is not a small person. They radioed for a helicopter. The first helicopter attempted to balance on a ledge across from where we were, but the ledge wasn't wide enough. They were called away. A short time later another helicopter arrived that lowered a basket. The paramedics lifted him into the basket as the helicopter hovered over us, kicking up the dust. The noise, the dust, and the heat were intense. They finally got him situated and lifted him straight up off the mountain and aimed toward where a third helicopter was positioned on the desert floor that was ready to take him into Tucson.

Once he was gone from the ledge, the paramedics emphatically told us to get down the mountain as fast as we could. They had just received a radio message saying a class five monsoon was fast approaching. As I gingerly descended the mountain, trying to avoid being another casualty, I looked up and saw a wall of black clouds racing across the desert aimed directly at us. I knew we had to drive out that dirt road before it became impassable. There was no time to eat. We had to move.

We piled into the cars as the helicopter, with Pete securely in place, lifted up and flew north. I could see it flying into and around the clouds and worried they would not get to the hospital. We took off down the dirt road, dodging holes and bouncing hard over high spots, praying the whole time for the rain to stay away.

It got darker and darker and the wind picked up. We arrived at the main paved road just as the first drops of rain began to fall. By the time we got to the first wash it was a raging river. We had to stop. We got out in the pelting rain, found the food, and finally took the time to eat. It was almost 5 p.m!

Pete had been laying face down waiting for that ride for over seven hours. We sat at the wash for an interminable two hours. Friends from other villages, having heard about the accident, came to wait on the other side of the wash. The 9-1-1 phone call had been made from the district office and word travels fast on the reservation. Some of us stood in the rain and tried to yell information to each other across the furious water. I needed to get to Tucson, but there was no way I could get past the wash and this was the only road to Topawa and then on to Tucson. By the time I arrived at the hospital they had already taken Pete into surgery.

I was in denial about the seriousness of the injury. As I'd left the group in Topawa, I told them that Pete and I would be back at camp before the end of the second week. While he was in surgery I called each of our children. They were ready to come to Arizona immediately, but I asked them to wait until we knew more. I sat in the waiting room and prayed, asking God to help us all. There were so many people who depended on Pete. The children at camp had another week they were eagerly anticipating. Pete was a huge part of the spirit of the camp. What was going to happen?

Late that night, after several hours of surgery, I was brought to him. His ankle had been shattered and the doctors had put it together with a series of metal rods and wires they called an external fixator. I couldn't really see much of it because they had the whole thing wrapped with a mountain of gauze. It was clear he would not make it back to camp that week. I sat and dozed in a small hard chair by the side of his bed that night and the next several days while he was in and out of consciousness.

The phone started to ring. Friends from years gone by were calling to give us their support and encouragement. Friends from the tribe came to see us. One by one our children began to arrive. Their presence meant the world to us.

Tim and Ian listened to my dilemma about camp and the group: Pete and I were the drivers of the two vans that transported the group to and from California. I had no way to get the group home to California. Tim and Ian offered to be the chauffeurs.

That weekend, our daughter Julie and her family arrived to see us. On their way out of PisinMo'o the group stopped to say a brief goodbye. They looked tired, but very happy. They had finished camp in grand style. They brought Pete cards from the campers and lots of good energy for healing.

Then our son Peter and his pregnant wife Kerri arrived. By that time Pete and I knew it was going to be a few weeks before we could leave Tucson. Pete's leg was badly infected. Every couple of days, in an attempt to save the ankle and foot, the doctors took him back to surgery to clean out the wound. I had been dozing by the side of his bed for more than a week.

Peter found an extended stay type of motel down the street from the hospital where he and Kerri stayed. He conveniently rented it for a week and gave me the key when he left Tucson to return to California. He saved my sanity and my life. That began my routine of staying at the hospital all day and then walking to the motel before dark each night.

Pete was a favorite of the nurses. They loved him because he was good natured and fun to be around. One of them made sure he always had grape juice. He was in so much pain that he had no appetite for food and the grape juice was a real highlight in his days. He was completely confined to bed because the external fixator made it nearly impossible to move. We had no idea how we were going to get him home.

Our longtime friend Michael called from California and said he would cover the cost of our trip home. We looked into some kind of special flight, but there was nothing available to us. We settled on an airline that had seats in the front that faced each other. We thought we could stretch out his bad leg and get him home with less discomfort. The day approached, arrangements were made; but the doctor would not release him until he was out of bed and sitting up in a chair. The morning of our flight they took him to physical therapy for the first time. He was in such agony that I didn't know how he could survive this.

The ride home was indescribable torture. It began in a transport van from the Tucson hospital to the airport during the afternoon rush hour traffic. The half hour ride took the better part of an hour while the stopping and starting of the lurching van put intense pressure on Pete's leg. In addition, the van's air conditioner had failed so we sweltered in the more than 100 degree heat inside the swaying metal box. At the airport we transferred Pete to a primitive airport wheelchair, then the long ride, with no leg support, to the gate where we waited for our flight to be announced. Getting on the plane, we put some pillows on the floor for his bad leg to rest on. When the stewardess informed us that we could not have anything on the floor for takeoff, we respectfully ignored her and thankfully, she chose not to insist.

All our children met us at the San Jose airport in California and helped us get Pete into the waiting ambulance for the trip to a convalescent hospital that our insurance required before they would release him to go home. Our children escorted me home to San Jose, to the house we had just bought that had not even begun to be familiar.

Our boys had gotten together during the weeks we were in Arizona and constructed a ramp into the back door of the house. They knew that we would be using a wheelchair for the foreseeable future. We got a hospital bed delivered the next day and I set up the living room as the place for Pete because we couldn't get a wheelchair through the bedroom door. I couldn't wait to get him home.

Two nights in the convalescent hospital and I finally had him all to myself. We had been in the hospital in Arizona almost a month. I had one week before I was due to return to school – I stretched it into two. We were so happy to be home together. We couldn't wait for him to be back on his feet and back to his normal activities.

On the first visit to the doctor in California he laid out the reality of our situation. The foot was still badly infected. The ankle would probably never heal properly. The bottom of the foot would have no feeling. Amputation was a solution that we ought to think about. Amputation would eventually mean no more visits to the doctor. We talked and decided we would do it. The surgery was scheduled for September 9th.

Recovery took time. People stepped up and took over many of the *Truck of Love* tasks that needed to happen. They delivered vans and truckloads of food and clothing, took care of Thanksgiving food baskets, did the Christmas Adopt-a-Family program, wrote thank you notes to donors, and they came and visited with Pete while I was away for long days at school.

When we were at home alone we talked about all that had happened. We recalled the hours on the mountainside and how the young people had been so wonderful. We called that day both the worst and the best day of our lives; it had been a genuinely joyful day. We were filled with gratitude for those young people who were so brave, generous, compassionate, and caring. They took care of us that day. They lifted us up and we felt the presence of God. Pete felt there were angels who guided him down that mountain side. He fell onto a ledge that was just about eight feet wide. Had he rolled anymore, he would have fallen off a 100 foot cliff.

The days alone at home were long for him. I came home each night after an 8-10 hour day and he greeted me at the front door in his wheelchair.

"Where are we going?" he'd ask as I wheeled him out the back door and down the ramp.

After he transferred himself to the front seat, I would fold the wheelchair and struggle to get it into the back end of the car.

Off we went for a ride or a meal. There was a drive-thru Burger King where we sometimes ordered our food and ate in the parking lot so I didn't have to maneuver the wheelchair in and out of the car and the restaurant.

By November of that year he was the proud recipient of a prosthetic foot and was finally able to get out of the house on his own with crutches. He had his independence back when we fitted our van with hand controls so he could drive.

PART

III

"Forget the former things; do not dwell on the past. See, I am doing a new thing! Now it springs up; do you not perceive it? I am making a way in the wilderness and streams in the wasteland."
Isaiah 43: 18-19

1999 - 2009

We went back to camp the following summer. It was hot and difficult; Pete's leg swelled up and he had a hard time walking with his two crutches. By the time camp was over, we made the decision that we could not spend more than a few days in the desert. We could no longer do camp.

We had private conversations with some of our long-time volunteers and they assured us they would keep camp going. We made our announcement at the final dinner with all the volunteers.

One young man came crying, "Pete, you have been like a father to me. You taught me how to be a father to my children. I will miss you so much."

We were touched beyond measure at the outpouring of love and affection from the O'odham. We knew we would return – we just could not spend three weeks in the desert heat any more.

Life did not stop for *Truck of Love*. Life was changed, but was full of possibilities. Pete had been a powerhouse of moving furniture and clothing and he could no longer do that. We found other outlets for the donations people wanted to offer.

Pete had more time to spend with individuals. He helped one man get his driver's license. He provided bus passes to many people on the streets of San Jose. Our home was downtown and soon people knocked on our door day and night for assistance with food or housing. He got acquainted with the local shelters and made sure people were connected with available resources. He kept on doing what he was so good at doing: building trusting, loving relationships with people.

In the summer Pete and I helped the Campus Ministry at St. Francis High School create and implement a program of immersion in downtown San Jose for students in the Holy Cross High Schools of the Southwest Province. It was a pilot program that brought together students and teachers from New Orleans, Los Angeles, Hayward, and Mountain View Holy Cross schools to experience inner city poverty. We had great fun and learned a lot about the services available in our own back yard. The week-long experience was so good that St. Francis decided to do it every year with their own students.

One day when I was at the local Jesuit retreat house for a retreat with senior students, one of the priests I knew approached me and asked if Pete and I would consider facilitating a married couples retreat. I was hesitant because we do not have degrees in theology or spirituality, but he assured me that our many years of marriage qualified us quite well. This began several years of happy collaboration with El Retiro where we assisted with retreats for married couples. It was a joyous time of reflection for us as well as the couples involved. It amazed me that we could do simple exercises on communication and a couple who had been married 60 years would approach us and say they had never talked about the basic subjects of communication, faith, or forgiveness we had introduced. Pete played his guitar and sang with our participants, which was an added attraction for many.

A happy offshoot of this was an invitation for our daughter Julie and me to lead a mother-daughter retreat. Julie was living in Kirkland, Washington, and she traveled to join us for the weekend of the retreat. She and Pete incorporated some songs into the reflections and activities. The mothers and daughters had a grace-filled weekend which we repeated the following year.

We found there were multitudes of ways to serve. Literally when one door closed, another opened.

Pete continued to make his once a month trips with food and clothing to Tijuana. We still had the Thanksgiving food program and the Christmas Adopt-a-Family program that Pete coordinated.

In the summer we tried to get to Arizona for a couple of days. We wanted to keep connected with the camp. The California group of volunteers coordinating camp had met with the O'odham leaders and the name had changed to TOTOL (Tohono O'odham Truck of Love). It was a superb collaboration of two cultures for a common purpose.

It was difficult for Pete to be in Arizona - he felt useless. He had been the one who played with kids, who loaded and unloaded vans and trailers. Physically, he could no longer do those things. He had been a dynamo of a human doing. We reflected on Mother Teresa who said that we needed to be human beings, not human doings.

It was time for us to live life differently. More opportunities were coming our way to be present to others through retreats, talks, and prayer. We had to learn to appreciate this transformation through the seasons of our lives.

Pete was also experiencing a lot of physical pain which changed his disposition and challenged him in fundamental ways that were foreign to him. On the outside people still saw the cheerful Pete who was and is an inspiration. But privately we had some very difficult times. He was taking so much Vicodin that it affected his behavior. We talked about it, but he was in pain.

Finally he went into a program provided by our insurance company. It was thirty days of daytime meetings and intense group therapy. Gradually, he began to come back to us as the

Pete we knew and loved, although we still dealt with his feelings of inadequacy and uselessness. It didn't seem to help that I could see the positive effect he had on people with his music and his presence. He had to understand that for himself. It was a long journey, but progressively he has come to accept and savor his new place in life.

Through it all, we have never wavered in our knowledge that God is with us. We feel God's presence more at some times than others. Watching a sunset in Arizona or witnessing the first steps of a grandchild have become conversations with our God. We find that God surprises us in most unexpected ways. Each smile, handshake, or hug opens a dialogue with God.

Two of our long-time volunteers, Scott and Mandy, formed their own not-for-profit organization and called it Truck of Love South. As Pete stepped back from deliveries of food and clothing to Tijuana and Arizona, they stepped in to supply these communities. They, along with another wonderful friend, Cathy, kept camp going those first years of our absence. Subsequently others, Chrissy, Meighan, Amanda, Theresa, and Eli, took on leadership roles. We found that we did not need to be concerned because there were many other people willing to step up and fill in the gaps we had left.

Cathy had been coming to camp continually since the fifth year. She arrived a few weeks early to help line up speakers and special tribal groups for camp. Chrissy worked with Native Americans in the Dakotas and brought a wealth of experiences to camp. Meighan was a teacher at St. Francis and helped create the leadership training. Amanda had great knowledge of child development and communication and was a tremendous support to counselors. The others, Theresa, Eli, Tim, and Mike, all had great relationships with the O'odham. It was apparent that camp flourished under the new leadership.

Our work in San Jose expanded. Pete met social workers, shelter managers, and soup kitchen volunteers and they knew they could call him with requests that other agencies were unable to fulfill. One day he received a call from a local social worker who had an older couple who were about to be evicted if they did not clean up their apartment. Pete went to visit with them and when he knocked on the door the woman who answered could pull the door back only about two feet. He gingerly squeezed inside only to see that, floor to ceiling, every space was filled with boxes and piles of newspapers. There was a narrow aisle through the detritus that led from one room to another.

He asked, "Where is your husband?"

She indicated he was in the bathroom.

Pete talked to her about the necessity of cleaning out their apartment. As he walked through the tight corridor between the piles, the floor creaked and groaned and he worried about his own safety. The social worker had told him that the tenants under this apartment had departed because they were worried about the integrity of the structure.

Pete left that day saying "I'll be back in two days with workers and a dumpster."

As he drove away, his mind raced with all he needed to do: order a dumpster, find workers, and figure out where he could take the couple while the clean-up was happening so they would not hinder the workers.

The following day as he listened to the local news on the radio in the van, he heard the reporter talking about an elderly couple who had been killed that morning. They had been found crushed at the bottom of a pile of newspapers and rubble after their concrete floor fell through to the apartment below them. Information was being withheld pending notification of next of kin.

These years were a continual revelation of God's goodness when we were placed in situations that became moments of grace. One day Pete was on his way back from a brief delivery trip to Tijuana when he stopped in a parking lot near where he had lived as a child in Southern California. He was taking a break from the drive, sitting in the van, tuning his guitar; when there was a knock on his window. He looked up to see a very drunk woman leaning toward him. He rolled the window down and she started to babble something he could not understand. Picking on his guitar, he began to sing and the tears rolled down her cheeks smearing her mascara. He invited her to get into the van and asked her where he could take her. She gave him the name of a nearby motel and then passed out.

He arrived at the motel and jostled her awake enough to ask her what she would like to eat. She sloppily said she would ask Carl. Pete helped her get to her room and knocked on the door. Carl, a boy of about fourteen, opened the door. He was there taking care of his six younger brothers and sisters. His mom hurried to the bathroom. Pete asked Carl what they wanted to eat and he yelled through the bathroom door to his mom.

She said, "Get as much from him as you can."

Carl and Pete went off to the store. Carl talked about their life and how they had previously lived in Las Vegas, but they moved from place to place. Carl thought Pete was just another of his mom's "johns." Pete made it clear that the only thing he wanted was to help them with some food. Carl made it clear to Pete that his mom was doing everything she could to keep them all together.

Many people asked us how we could do this work. They worried that there were too many people in need for us to be of any real help. Our instinct was to help the person who was in front of us. When I would be overwhelmed, I remembered that Jesus did just that. He walked from town to town, he stopped and ate with people, he went fishing, and he was present to the person he was with. When we talk about following Jesus, it isn't just looking and recognizing the events in Jesus earthly life; it is about being Jesus to each person we meet. In acting like Jesus we give Him our very being.

We didn't always want to do what we thought Jesus would do. Sometimes it was inconvenient. There were plenty of times when Pete would leave me in the evening when a knock on the door or a phone call caused him to go out to rescue some unfortunate person. I was not always gracious when our plans got changed.

In the summer our long-time homeless friend, Art, died. He had slept on our couch and in our vans. He spent one Christmas morning with our family and was very moved when our children gave him a Christmas present. He abandoned his own children and intentionally became homeless when his wife attached his paycheck after a nasty divorce. He was independent, stubborn, and self-centered.

He was a veteran, and as the years went by we received calls from the veteran's hospital when they were dismissing him back to the street after being treated for a bike accident or some other problem. He lived eighty-three years, most of them on the streets, sleeping in dumpsters, and eating in soup kitchens.

He asked the nurses to call Pete when he was hospitalized for the last time. He wanted Pete to sign him out of the hospital. Art was too sick, and Pete refused his request.

The nurses called us late one night. Art had died. Pete asked if they had notified his daughter, but they were unaware that he had any family. Pete called his daughter who was more upset about the lateness of the call than about her father's death.

We were grateful that we had been able to be present to Art and that he had died with dignity in a hospital instead of in a gutter on the street.

Our relationship with Art was not perfect. We were not always glad to see him come up the path to our house. When we moved to San Jose, we hoped he would not find us, but one day, there he was at our front door. For better or worse he was part of our lives and we were part of his. We had to repeatedly remind ourselves that he too was a beloved child of God. Could we have done more? I don't know. We tried our best. Will we be nicer to the next irritating person we encounter? I hope so. That is the beauty of this life. We have so many chances to get it right.

Increasingly *Truck of Love* became the "go to" place for people who fall through the cracks. There are so many agencies that help the poor, the sick, the elderly, and the indigent, but many of them close on Friday afternoon and do not answer their phones until Monday morning. Others have such corporate restrictions that their ability to help is hampered by rules and regulations. *Truck of Love* is a small organization. Our only mandate is to serve the poor. We can do this anytime and anywhere.

We lived in downtown San Jose, the center of Silicon Valley, one of the richest areas of our country; whereas the wealth of the area increased, the poverty and homelessness increased as well. Rents were too high for a person earning minimum wage. We were quickly becoming the homeless capital of Northern California.

One night a woman knocked and when I opened the door, she asked, "Is this Kindness House?"

The people on the street had named our house. We made a sign - "Kindness House" - and put it above the front door to remind us of our obligation.

We had now been doing this work for many years. People's stories seemed to be very similar; only the faces changed. It was easy to look and see if a person was in distress. If only each of us would have the courage to open our eyes and hearts to acknowledge the people who are put into our path. If each person in this world did one good thing for another human being, we would not have the poverty that exists.

We prayed for people to let go of fear. It was apparent to me that the opposite of love was not hate, but it was fear. It is fear that keeps me from looking at the homeless person on the street; I am afraid of what he or she might do or say. I am afraid that I will be hurt. I am afraid of the dirt and smell and anything else that is not part of my daily life. I am afraid that I don't know what to do or how to help.

One day I was in San Francisco with a group of sophomore students from the high school. We were working with the St. Anthony Foundation doing a day of service in their soup kitchen and in the very poor neighborhood around their offices. My job was to help prepare lunch in the kitchen. We had a great morning full of laughter and comradeship as all the volunteers worked together to get the food ready for the several hundred people who were lining up outside the doors to eat. We were told that we would not be serving the food, but we would eat with the hungry clients.

At the appointed time, I went outside to line up with the homeless people so I could reenter the building to eat lunch. I nervously walked to the end of the line that snaked past the doors of the church that was just next door. The men in line were jockeying for position, but a couple of the men became very concerned for me and made sure the others didn't jostle me too much. They were very kind to me and I began to relax.

As we stood there, waiting for the soup kitchen doors to welcome us, the doors to the church flew open and the congregation came pouring out from the daily noontime Mass. The church people had to walk through the soup kitchen line to get to the sidewalk and they came straight towards us, heads down, barreling through with no acknowledgement of our presence. I was stunned. These people had just been to Mass, the most sacred of our prayers as Catholics, but it didn't feel like they had understood the message of Jesus in the scriptures.

When the crowd from the Mass had dissipated, our line began to move. The kitchen was ready for us. I followed the person in front of me. The men showed me what to do when we got close to the counter. I picked up my tray and walked along the line as one volunteer after another spooned food onto my plate.

None of the volunteers looked up at me. Just twenty minutes before we had been laughing and having fun chopping, cutting, and preparing this very food, yet at this moment, I felt like I was invisible. I felt like I didn't matter.

When we created the program for the summertime San Jose Immersions, I always tried to challenge our groups in new and interesting ways. I heard that one of the nearby schools had a similar immersion program and they spent the night in one of the homeless shelters. I wanted to try that too. I went to the shelter and we made the arrangements.

The day this was to happen, we ate in a downtown San Jose soup kitchen and then we were off to wait at the shelter with the other people who hoped for a night of respite from the elements.

In order to get into any shelter the people had to be there by a certain time of day. No late arrivals were allowed. There could be no drugs or alcohol (not a problem for my closely supervised group of teenagers). We arrived with just the clothes on our backs because we didn't want to take anything valuable with us that might be a temptation to others.

We toured the sprawling one-story facility. They had a huge room filled with several hundred bunk beds that were platforms with no mattresses. There was a corridor off which there were some individual family rooms for mothers with children. The staff met with our group and explained the rules of the shelter and gave us a short educational program about homelessness and hunger in the Bay Area. They told us that bedtime would be 10 p.m.

Outside it was a pleasant evening and so we hung out in the courtyard with the other people who would be sleeping there that night. We met several of the homeless men and women who were open about sharing their stories with us. As each person revealed their personal story they universally ended what they had to say by telling the teens, "Make sure you stay in school and get a good education."

Shortly before 10 p.m. we went inside to get ready for sleep. Along with the hundreds of other guests, we were issued a plastic mattress and a thin blanket. There were no pillows. Our group was assigned to the floor in a vacant meeting room; thankfully we would not be in the room that held almost 300 people. The lights went off at 10 p.m. The teens were nervous and there were lots of giggles and whispers. I encouraged them to quiet down and we tried to sleep. One of the girls in the group was sitting up. I asked her to lie down, but she kept her upright position all night, afraid of falling asleep in this place.

We heard grunts and snoring from the hundreds of people in the next room and all night doors creaked opened and slammed shut. Every fifteen minutes a staff member walked through our room. As I lay awake, I could hear the even breathing of most of the teens and I was thankful that some of them were getting a little rest.

Promptly at 5 a.m. harsh bright lights flashed on. It was time to get up. Exhausted, we folded our plastic mattresses in half, gathered our blankets, and walked through the large sleeping room as people began to roll out of the bunks. Some were making their way to the bathroom, while others were already in line for breakfast. By the time our group had stashed our mattresses and washed our faces, the line for breakfast had about 100 people in it. We found the end of the line and waited.

At 6 a.m. the dining room opened for business and we filed in to pick up our plate of food. I was so tired my stomach was in knots. I didn't know if I could eat anything. The shelter served a hefty breakfast, enough to last a person the better part of the day. It was especially good because many of the people didn't know when or where they were going to get their next meal. Others needed to fuel up for a long day of work.

I came away from that night knowing I never again wanted to sleep in a homeless shelter. It was awful. I realized how hard it would be for a person to have a job and live in a homeless shelter, though a few did just that. How could a person ever be able to make any progress in their lives? I met many people that night who had potential and desire, but their living circumstances made it almost impossible to do anything but spend their days finding food and shelter. Their lives were a merry-go-round: eat, sleep, and look for food and shelter again and again and again.

The twentieth summer of the camp in Arizona, I made the commitment to go and be the coordinator for the kitchen. Pete planned to be there for a couple of days at the end for the anniversary celebration.

That year I brought five students from St. Francis High School who had never been to the reservation. We slept and prepared our meals in the house Father Elias had once occupied, which was now empty because there was no priest living in the village. Cathy and Chrissy arrived a week before us and set off bug bombs in this notoriously insect-infested dwelling. They swept out buckets of dead cockroaches and crickets before our arrival.

There was a room at the back of the house that we used for storing our personal items and where we all slept packed together in our sleeping bags head to toe and side to side, much like sardines in a sweaty warm can. The second night my air mattress started to lose air and for the next three

In the company of dogs

weeks I slept without any cushion on the very hard concrete floor.

I crunched my aging bones off of my hard mat each morning at about 5 a.m. and staggered into the shower before I strolled over at sunrise to start my day of cooking in the feast house. The first morning I realized I would have the daily company of a pack of straggly village dogs that followed anything that moved in hopes of some reward. I shooed them away from the front of the feast house as I unlocked the door.

This summer the camp was conducted in and around the feast house, a long adobe building with outdoor cooking pits surrounded by a fence of ocotillo cactus branches. It is an old style community building that is used for a variety of social events. Inside it is one very long room illumined by a couple of light bulbs hanging by wire from the ceiling. There are several long tables that are lined up down the middle. A sink with running water sits at one side and on the same side there is a small four burner stove with an oven that has one rack. Across the room are two freezers and a refrigerator.

The tables lined up in the center of the room became our preparation area. We served two meals each day, breakfast and lunch, to the hungry campers and staff. We didn't use any mixes or pre-made food and we spent the better part of each day creating the meals for the 180 ravenous mouths.

Coordinating the kitchen was great fun, but the long hot hours were brutal. There were fifteen O'odham who came each day to help cut, chop, carry water, take out trash, and build mesquite wood cooking fires in the outdoor adobe pits. They also created the traditional foods on the menu. Each of the ladies was an experienced cook, and they sat at the table methodically chopping, sorting beans, wrapping plastic forks in napkins, or any other necessary chore. Slowly each meal took form and was served. The cleanup was done in the same wonderfully systematic way. They were used to working together in a kitchen and each person did what was necessary to serve the camp.

The first early morning that I entered the dimness of the feast house, I went to the sink to wash my hands. Suddenly there was a crashing and a loud yelp and something jumped at me straight out of the cupboard under the sink and disappeared into the dark corners! Heart racing, I jumped back in terror and saw that it was a cat that I had disturbed.

I opened some of the drawers at the sink and saw lots of evidence of mice, so my first job before the group arrived for the early breakfast was to clean out the cupboards. I quickly learned to cover all the defrosting meat at night lest the hungry cat take hunks out of the hamburger packages or whatever meat we might be thawing. I graduated to weighting the covers because the desperate cat learned how to move the plastic buckets I was using. Some mornings I arrived to find huge holes in the plastic encircling the meat or whole tomatoes reduced to tiny red blobs.

We had a full week of leadership training that year. By the time we all sat down for the first session I counted sixty-two participants, forty-seven of them were O'odham. I was stunned, tears of joy poured down my face. This was more people in leadership than we'd had that first day of camp twenty years before!

Original outhouses behind cafeteria

We saw lots of progress on the reservation. The young people now took an active interest in the traditions, culture, ceremonies, and language of their people. The tribe was providing more services to meet the needs of the elderly and the youth. There was diabetes awareness, healthy eating programs (we had training with the O'odham kitchen helpers about healthier ways to cook traditional foods), programs about culture and language, and more drug counseling available. More of the youth were attending college and graduating. Youth recreation services were improving in the districts. One of the youth directors from the northern part of the reservation brought some of his kids to camp each day.

We spent time savoring the sunrises, sunsets, the monsoon rain, the ragged dogs, but most specially the people.

Because of the casinos that the O'odham had built, there was money coming to the Nation. Youth Recreation Centers were built in each district. PisinMo'o was the sight of one of the new centers and the PisinMo'o youth director invited us to use the new center for camp the following summer. In discussions we learned that many of our former campers were being hired by youth services to work in these centers.

The following summer the youth director in PisinMo'o opened the new recreation center to our staff and campers for the whole two weeks. We were in the lap of luxury. There were separate rooms for the various speakers and activities. There was air conditioning. There was a covered court for basketball, volleyball, and outdoor games. There was an industrial kitchen for food preparation. It was an impressive place and we were honored to be able to use it for camp that year and in subsequent years.

During the construction of the Recreation Center, camp had been on the move. We commuted to San Simon School for a few years and then used the feast house and other spaces in the village. The year we came home to the new Recreation center was a time of rejoicing. The relationship among the O'odham and *Truck of Love* is one that has grown and developed over the three decades of camp.

Two room school where camp began (storage room on far right)

Chrissy says, "Community dinners, baseball games, playing with kids - all these things strengthened our relationship with the community and helped to make camp part of the community instead of just an activity that happens for a couple of weeks each year."

The years passed swiftly. Pete and I began to talk about life after St. Francis High School. I turned sixty-four in the spring of 2008 and I was ready to end the 5:30 a.m. alarms waking me up. When we talked about our summer plans, we knew we had the San Jose summer immersion with St. Francis students. We also knew we wanted to make an appearance at camp in Arizona. We had no other summer plans and thought we might do an exploratory trip to other parts of the U.S. to see if there was any place we might want to live other than California.

For several months we had been driving up and down our state looking at home prices and we came to realize that we probably couldn't afford to stay in California. If I retired from St. Francis, we would have just our social security, Pete's $500 each month from Truck of Love, and a small amount in a retirement account that I would receive through the school.

In late June, we started east. First on the itinerary was a stop at camp. Once again we were able to connect with old friends and enjoy the chaos that 180 children bring to any event. The O'odham participated with all their energy and we saw many great things happening for the community.

We went on further east to Savannah, Georgia, where Pete had spent many nights when he was homeless just ten years before. He took me on a tour of the square where he slept in the bushes when he was so sick. From there we went to Peachtree City, Georgia, where we had a speaking engagement. Our last stop before turning back west was to visit with our son Peter and his family, who lived in Charlotte, North Carolina.

Everywhere we stopped we asked ourselves, "Could we live here?"

We called our daughter from San Angelo, Texas and said, "We love it here. There is a wonderful river that runs through town. The people are so friendly. We think we might like to move here."

Her reply stopped us. "Who's going to visit you in Texas?"

Coming home we were completely undecided, though we knew one thing. There were a lot of beautiful places in this great country and we could probably find a place other than California to settle in our final years.

We didn't have much time to savor our trip or what we had seen. Back in California, we threw ourselves into our local work. I was still employed at St. Francis High School in Campus Ministry where I coordinated the Holy Cross Service program for the 1400 students. I also went on most of the retreats our office conducted with staff and students. My days were full and my work weeks could keep me away from home for sixty to seventy hours. Pete joined me at school for many retreats and service projects. In addition to his work with the poor in and around San Jose, he managed to coordinate volunteers to make sure more than 150 local families had food and presents for the Thanksgiving and Christmas seasons.

In our spare time we began to have conversations with each other and with our children about the future. St. Francis offered a one-time retirement package to longtime employees. They were trying to gently ease out the old timer high-priced personnel by offering a percentage of annual earnings over a period of three years, including a health care allowance. I began to make calculations based on social security, costs of health care for Pete, the cost of our mortgage in San Jose, and other factors.

Our son Peter called one day and pleaded with me to take the retirement package. He assured me, "If you ever need anything, there are enough of us to help."

I kept calculating.

Then I started to look at houses online. I compared prices and taxes from state to state. We looked at our life together, the changes that had been forced on us, and the decisions we had come to after much prayer and discernment. We knew that it was time to move on and we knew God would be with us on our journey.

I had several friends who cared for elderly parents long-distance and I saw they worried a lot because they didn't live near them. Pete and I began considering only places that would be near at least one of our children. By this time our kids were grown and were living all over the world: Norway, New York, Washington, California, and North Carolina. We decided I would take the retirement package and June 17, 2009 would be my last day of work.

There was a lot to do. We'd lived in this, the first home we'd bought, just ten years, but it was almost ninety years old and needed some sprucing up. A couple of years before we had hired a man to remodel the bathroom and convert the attic into two small rooms where we could spread out sleeping bags. Pete is very talented, but being a carpenter, electrician, painter, and general handyman are not among his gifts.

The people we helped had many gifts and it was about this time Ben came on the scene. Pete had met him when Ben lived on the streets of San Jose. He was known and feared by those who were acquainted with him because he had a wicked temper and could be violent. He also had a very soft side. Pete got to like him; Ben was a simple man with few needs. He started coming to our house. He stood next to his bike on the sidewalk in front of our door and talked about life and people. He had prison tattoos from head to toe and, as he rode his bike around downtown San Jose, he was often targeted by the police. We didn't see him for a while and discovered he was in jail. If someone pushed him, he always pushed back.

When he got out of jail, we found things for him to do. He accompanied Pete on his rounds and helped him with the physical activities that needed strength. Ben got to be a regular and some nights we invited him to stay for dinner.

Pete learned that Ben was good at fixing things and asked him to permanently adjust the seats in his truck so it would be easier for him to drive with his prosthetic foot. Ben was eager to work and completed the task quickly. Then Ben was absent again. We went to visit him in jail where he talked about wanting to make some changes in his life. We liked him a lot. We knew when he got out of jail this time he would need help staying out. He had already spent the majority of his life behind bars.

Pete and I talked and decided we would invite him to live with us for the few months before we put our home up for sale. We asked Ben if he wanted to stay in our basement room for a little while. He was eager to do this, but he insisted he pay us in some way. We agreed he could make some of the little adjustments to the house in order for it to be ready for sale. Our hope was to give him some breathing space between jail and the streets to help him start some new patterns in his life.

We began our new routine. Ben moved into our basement room. I would give him his work list before I left in the morning. When I came home in the evening he proudly showed me what he had accomplished. I praised his work, which was fantastic, and he then stood in the kitchen door while I prepared dinner. He talked to me and I listened. He watched what I cooked and asked me how I did things.

He wanted to learn how to cook so "I can do that when I get my own place."

I learned about his life. "I never knew my mother. My Dad used to beat us pretty bad. He always had some woman staying with us. When me and my brother were young, our Dad sent us to buy and sell drugs."

Ben had spent twenty-nine of his forty-three years in jail. He really didn't know how to live in the outside world. He told me that when he was in federal prison they loaded him and other prisoners into buses and transported them to other states. He spent weeks and months going from one federal prison to another because he was one of the prisoners who was unwelcome in the system.

Ben loved being in our home and being included as family. We marveled at God's providence. He was with us for three months, and in that time he made our old house look like new, rebuilding windows, scraping and painting all the inside doors, stripping the hardware of paint, and repainting the outside of the house.

In February when the "For Sale" sign went up in front of our house, we had already decided that we were moving near Peter, probably to South Carolina.

Each day before I left for school I dusted the floors and made sure all the clutter was put away. We were told it might take a couple of months to sell our home, but we really didn't need to be out until June when I finished the school year. We prayed it would sell, but not too soon.

Nine days after the sign went up we had an offer that we accepted. We tried to delay escrow, but we had to be out by the end of March. A priest friend who lived in a huge rectory in downtown San Jose offered us a small apartment in his building. We moved in with the priests so I could finish out the school year.

Our real estate agent in San Jose got us in touch with an agent in Charlotte, North Carolina who agreed to help us find a new home. I made arrangements to be in Charlotte over Easter break from school. Pete was going north to deliver some of our family treasures to Kirkland, Washington where our daughter resided with her family.

My visit to Charlotte at Easter resulted in our purchasing a home in the country outside of a town called Rock Hill. Because we were selling a home in California where prices were inflated and buying a home in a place where housing was cheap, we were able to pay cash for the new home that sits on more than an acre of woods. We had a few tense days during escrow when our San Jose house was devalued by the bank because we were in the midst of the economic downturn. Our check for the sale arrived two days before the deadline to pay for our new home.

We couldn't believe it was all happening. Though everything had gone relatively smoothly, the next months were far from easy. Pete was personally visiting with each of the hundreds of people he had helped over the years of ministry in the Bay Area. Many people were worried about what would happen to them, but he connected each person with some services that would assist them. I spent the last few months at St. Francis High School doing what I had done for the previous twenty plus years in Campus Ministry: we had retreats, service projects, immersion programs, liturgies, Confirmation, and Baccalaureate Mass to complete before I would be free.

Our Board of Directors also decided that we needed to do a *Truck of Love* dinner just as in the old days. They would not let us sneak out of town. We sent out the invitation to the people on our mailing list and on May 2, we celebrated Mass with Saint William's Parish and had one of our simple feasts of beans and tortillas with ice cream for dessert. Almost four hundred people came from all over the country. It was a phenomenal celebration of our shared ministry with many of the people who had gone on trips with us and who had supported us with their prayers and other donations.

We could see that God was at work in all of this. Just a few short years before we had wondered what we would do when we got old. We had never been able to save. We had always rented our homes. We had even started looking at very small apartments that we might rent for less money. Then Pete's dad died and suddenly we were homeowners in one of the most expensive areas of the country. We lived on my salary, with Pete's supplemental $500 a month from *Truck of Love*. We always paid our bills and homeownership actually helped us financially because of the tax breaks. Now we sold this house which had appreciated quite a bit and so we had enough to settle in a place where we would have no monthly mortgage payment and where the homeowner taxes were one-tenth what they had been in California.

People kept saying, "You deserve it."

We know deserve has nothing to do with it. We did not earn it. From the beginning it was a gift and it continues to be a gift.

I finished school at noon on June 17. My boss, Sal, walked me to my car; we shared a long hug and reluctantly said our goodbyes. I drove to San Jose where Pete and I put the last few items in my car and in his truck and we left town. I wanted to be gone. We were exhausted and got about two hours down the road before we stopped for the night, but we were on our way to our new life.

PART

IV

"Do not be anxious about anything, but in everything, by prayer and petition, with thanksgiving, present your requests to God. And the peace of God which transcends all understanding, will guard your hearts and your minds in Christ Jesus."
Philippians 4: 6-7

2009 - 2016

Once again, we had no idea what to expect. The only thing certain for me was the desire to find a church community that would nurture us in the next stage of this journey of life. I looked online at Rock Hill and saw there were two Catholic Churches in the city, plus something called the Oratory. Because of my research, I decided we would try a parish called St. Mary's, described online as hosting the Dorothy Day Soup Kitchen. They also had a gospel choir. At this phase in our lives we were looking for a church home where the people lived the gospel. We hoped and prayed this would be it.

First we had to get there. The initial stop on our cross country journey was PisinMo'o where the twenty-third camp was in preparation with leadership training. That year they had a total of 230 children and adults who came to camp. We spent two wonderful days enjoying the heat, the sunsets, the people, and the atmosphere of inclusion and acceptance that had become a trademark of the camp experience. We left PisinMo'o and continued east. Our PODS containing all our worldly goods were not scheduled to arrive until the end of June and so we had a little time to see some of this beautiful country.

We were a caravan of two: Pete's Toyota truck and my Toyota Camry. We communicated by cell phone, a luxury we had never had on our group trips because they occurred before the common use of cell phones. If one of us saw a sign that inspired us to stop we called the other and soon we would be in some little museum, restaurant, or roadside attraction. We were free! We had no place we had to be and had nothing that we had to do. It was a strange feeling to be responsible for just ourselves. We were driving into an unknown life. It was exhilarating.

We got to North Carolina a couple of days before the PODS and so we stopped to stay with our son, Peter, and his family. It was summer. They had a swimming pool and Pete is half fish so he and the kids swam and played and had a great time.

The second day we decided we wanted to be in our new home. Pete had not been there, he had only seen the pictures I shared. We had our Map Quest directions and took off for parts south: Rock Hill. Our new home was in the country and there was no straight route to get there. Pete followed me as I read the maps and navigated the wooded rural roads to our new residence. We pulled up to the little house, opened the front door, walked into the empty space, and breathed a sigh of relief. We were home.

We had borrowed a small coffee pot from Peter's house. We had mats, sheets, and blankets to put on the floor of what was to be our bedroom. We had pirated two folding chairs, also from Peter, and we went outside to sit on our back deck. We marveled at all the green. We were Californians who were used to brown grass on the hillsides in the heat of summer.

The San Jose home had been in the middle of downtown. Our backyard there had been about twelve feet deep and extended the width of our small home. In the few years we were there, I had planted every plant that could possibly fit into my small space – I loved to work in the garden.

Now we looked out at our new backyard with the sizeable lawn that led down the woods. I felt a twinge of apprehension as I viewed this huge expanse of grass I was now responsible for cutting. It took many days and a few trips around the yard to lose that feeling of intimidation at what we had so casually acquired.

The silence of the country was a blessing. Those first days we ate most of our meals outside on the deck, the only sounds being the songs of the birds. Our PODS arrived and soon we were settled and ready for our new life. I spent some time making our nest. I did not plan to do much of anything those first few months other than make sure we had a comfortable, livable home.

The second Sunday that we were in Rock Hill, we went to church at St. Mary's. We arrived at the church, which is in a traditionally black neighborhood, and parked our car. Walking into the gathering space we were warmly greeted by a smiling woman who welcomed us with huge hugs. We were immediately certain that this was the place for us. The priest was a gifted homilist and the people were actively engaged in this most sacred prayer. We were energized by the Mass and the knowledge that this would be our church home.

Gradually a few of our neighbors stopped by to welcome us. The initial question was always, "Do you have a church?"

When we proudly explained we were Catholic and we were going to be members of St. Mary's Parish, we got a variety of reactions. Some would step back like we had a contagious disease and say, "Oh...." Others would say, "Catholic?"

Usually the conversation would end. We quickly felt that we were in the midst of a place where being Catholic was to be in the minority. People were polite and friendly, but we knew it would take a while before they realized we did not have cooties.

Pete didn't wait too long before he was out on the streets looking for something to do. He frequented the soup kitchen at St. Mary's. Named for Dorothy Day, one of our heroes, the kitchen had served the neighborhood near the church for over twenty years. Up to 100 people ate there six days a week. Pete sat in the dining room and struck up conversations with the patrons. He soon learned that people in this area were very poor. He discovered there was no bus system in Rock Hill even though it was, at the time, the third largest city in South Carolina. People walked, rode bikes, or drove mopeds.

Pete started to give rides to a few people. He also began to take excursions into the country and around the city to get to know our new hometown.

We discovered there were many organizations that were serving the poor, but they were all locations that were difficult to get to. Pete had always roamed the streets to find people in need and he continued this habit in Rock Hill. As he drove, he kept his eyes alert for anything or anybody that seemed out of place.

One Friday in August, six weeks after moving in, Pete was happily driving toward Main Street in Rock Hill listening to an oldies station when he saw a group of children walking along a set of the many strands of rail road tracks lining and defining the boundaries of our little burg. He could see they were not children out to play. They were walking with a purpose. He turned his truck around to meet them as they crossed the trestle going over the main highway and then he stopped, got out of the truck, and stood watching them.

As they approached they looked at him apprehensively, but they could see he was old and had a prosthetic leg, so their alarm bells stopped long enough for him to get a good look. They were six young-looking boys wearing ragged clothes with black garbage bags slung over their shoulders. They continued to walk toward him and eventually came right up to him.

The largest boy, looking directly at him, said, "Hey."

They were extremely dirty and their clothing was completely tattered. One had a pair of shoes held together by duct tape. Pete introduced himself and without another word the biggest boy said, "We don't need no evangelizing!"

Boys on the tracks

Pete acted as though he didn't hear this comment, though he rarely began his interactions with religious talk. Instead, he took the offensive, "Are you hungry, or thirsty?"

Each of them chimed in with, "Yeah," "Yes," "Sure am!"

Pete said, "Wait here. I'll go into town and get you something. Free of charge."

He found a Subway Sandwich shop where he purchased their lunch. Returning to the railroad tracks, there they were sitting on the ground, hitting blades of grass with their hands waiting for his reappearance.

He smiled, held up the bag of food, and greeted them with, "I'm back!"

They all jumped up as he handed the bag to the biggest boy who seemed to be the leader. He doled out one sandwich and one drink to each of his friends. Pete sat on a rock near them as they eagerly dug into the food, each one saving a portion of their sandwich, wrapping it up, and putting it in their bag for later.

Pete asked, "Where're you from?"

The leader replied, "Up north."

"How old are you?"

The leader said he was fourteen and the youngest said he was twelve, but he looked to be about ten.

"Can I help get you into a shelter for the night?"

The spokesman said, "No, thanks. We're on our way."

Individually they politely said, "Thank you, mister."

They each got up and resumed walking along the railroad tracks, continuing their journey south.

We had arrived in Rock Hill in the midst of the great recession. The unemployment rate in the area was between twelve and twenty-four percent, depending on who we talked with. The first two weeks we were in our new home, we contracted some young men to build a screened in porch and a sidewalk to go from the new porch around the house to the front yard. Two very old black men came to make the sidewalk. One of them could hardly walk. He wore knee pads and it was his job to lean over the wet concrete to smooth it into a sidewalk. After kneeling and bending for some time, he needed the assistance of his partner because he had tremendous trouble getting back to a standing position. All the time the two men were working, they repeated over and over how blessed they felt to have work. They hadn't worked in some time and they had bills to pay. I was torn. It was apparent that they were hurting physically, but they needed the money. This was the first encounter I had with the working poor of South Carolina.

Pete made the rounds of various agencies that helped the poor. He discovered a women's shelter that needed their washing machine repaired, and *Truck of Love* paid to fix it. He bought soap for another shelter. He met an eighty-three year old man who was a bricklayer all his life and was subsisting on $127 a week. Pete bought him shoes and socks.

By the end of that summer, I was ready to get more involved with our parish. I read an announcement in the Sunday bulletin that said there was a Bible study class each Wednesday night. I thought I'd give it a try and so one Wednesday evening in September I arrived at the church and tentatively opened the door to the Martin de Porres Hall and walked in.

I was warmly welcomed by a little woman with a big smile and a lazy southern drawl. The man who was the coordinator for the class was a gentle man who was very involved in parish life. He and I had a brief conversation one night about what the parish called the Social Concerns Committee. I mentioned Pete and I had worked with the poor in California and he said we ought to come to the next meeting of the committee.

The Social Concerns Committee had been meeting at the parish for many years. This was a group of concerned parishioners who were anxious about the patrons of the Dorothy Day Soup Kitchen. Their discussions were focused on how to provide help for the clients of the kitchen who had needs that went beyond the one hot meal each day. Pete and I went to their monthly meetings and listened. Here we were in 2009 in the heart of where many of the battles surrounding integration had taken place. We discovered that St. Mary's had a long history of serving the expressed needs of the community. We were very interested in helping.

In the summer of 2010, the committee found a volunteer interested in creating an office at the parish to serve the extended needs of the diners at the soup kitchen. She was given a small space next to the church office where she set up a computer and waited two mornings each week. Each day a few people came by to ask questions. She was excellent at researching solutions and soon she had more work than she could do. She reported to the committee about a need for drivers.

I volunteered to drive on the Tuesdays and Thursdays that the office was open. Pete was at the kitchen many days, so when she wasn't in the office, he provided transportation for people. I thoroughly enjoyed driving people to doctor's appointments, to the DMV to get an ID, to the unemployment department, or to the pharmacy. Spending time with people as we went to and from appointments gave me an opportunity to learn about their lives.

I learned things that turned around some of my opinions and solidified others. One man told me he left school in the eleventh grade because the schools had been integrated and he didn't want to be bused to a school where he wasn't wanted. He spent his life doing low wage jobs because he didn't have a high school diploma. Subsequently I met many individuals who reiterated these sentiments and life story. I learned about unintended consequences.

As I got more involved in the Social Concerns Outreach Office at the parish, Pete cruised the back roads helping people he encountered. In the autumn of that year he stopped to help a couple whose moped had broken down on the side of the road. Once they realized he was genuinely trying to help and not harm, they led him deep into the woods south of Rock Hill to meet the Foleys.

When Pete was introduced to Mrs. Foley, he couldn't see her husband who was standing behind a tree. The young man who introduced her to him was reverent in his approach to her. She appeared to be in her mid-sixties and was toothless. Her gaunt face showed many years of hardship and neglect.

"Who are you?" she asked Pete.

He said hello and introduced himself. He went on, "I try to help people who need help."

She gave him a slow shallow grunt then stuffed her mouth with an enormous amount of white bread and walked behind a large tree. An older man came into the open from behind that tree and faced Pete as Mrs. Foley disappeared.

The young man introduced Mr. Foley, who wasn't able to talk very well.

The young man took up the conversation."Mr. Foley's been sick and can't talk too good, mister. What'cha think's wrong with him?"

The entire right side of Mr. Foley's face was swollen and his eye was almost shut. He held his jaw as though he was in pain. It looked like he had an infected tooth.

"Can you talk?" Pete asked Mr. Foley.

He nodded his head and said, "I got a tooth ache."

Pete offered to take him to a dentist to have the tooth looked at, but Mr. Foley declined, saying he was a Seventh Day Adventist and that he did not believe in doctors or medicine.

"Well then, what if I go to the health food store and see what I can get to help you?" Pete asked.

Mr. Foley mumbled, "That's ok, but NO doctors!"

Mrs. Foley came from her hiding place behind the tree. Her cheeks bulged with the bread she had been chewing. She quietly removed the mass of soft dough from her mouth and fed it gently to her husband who could barely swallow it. She fully intended he not die of starvation.

Pete left them to eat and drove off to the store.

Mrs. Foley, cheeks bulging

After getting advice from a helpful pharmacist, he returned armed with three-bee pollen (which acts as a natural antibiotic) and clove oil (to reduce the pain). He gave them the pharmacist's instructions.

Three days later Pete went back into the forest with high hopes and was not disappointed. Mr. Foley had undergone a remarkable healing. His demeanor was jubilant, and he was dancing around like a little boy.

Pete was now accepted as a member of this small community living on their own, off the grid, in the woods.

A few days after meeting the Foleys, Pete sat with them on a log near their fire. He watched as they lifted rocks from the fire pit with sticks and placed them in a large pot of water. Soon the water was boiling. Silent couples came through the surrounding trees to sit and wait. They each carried small bundles. One couple brought an onion. Another pair brought celery. Several more added carrots, potatoes, and anything else they had retrieved from various dumpsters located behind local grocery stores. Finally after several more rounds of hot rocks, the soup was steaming and the vegetables were cooked and all began to eat.

At Christmas that year. Pete managed to get donations of food and clothing for the Foleys' small band of followers who numbered about 28. He pulled his truck up to where they were and one of the men named Scout helped Pete unload. As they worked, Scout told Pete that his wife had recently gotten sick and died. They had buried her there in the woods.

Scout lamented, "I just wish I coulda given her her dream."

Pete asked, "What was her dream?"

He was surprised when Scout replied, "She always wanted a pair of pink satin high-heeled shoes."

They continued to unload the truck and had gotten down to the last bag of food, when Pete saw one previously unnoticed plastic bag on the floor behind the driver's seat. He picked it up and looked inside, then handed it to Scout saying, "Here they are."

Inside the bag was a pair of pink satin high heeled shoes. With tears in his eyes, Scout took the bag and walked into the woods.

Just after the New Year, the Foleys and most of their followers left our area. They were told that the land where they were residing was going to be clear cut. Big machinery was about to come in and wipe out the woods that kept them secret and safe. They had to move.

After they left, Pete kept driving the deserted rural roads and stopped when he saw people living in a situation that looked like they could use some help. There were lots of people squatting in abandoned houses or mobile homes. He was able to help many with food and tarps and other necessities.

One morning he drove into a yard to check on a couple he'd met a few days before. As he pulled into his destination he saw two county sheriffs' cars. The officers were out of their cars, writing in their journals. Pete turned off his engine and waited to see what was going on. The man and woman he had intended to visit had just been handcuffed and were being led to the back seat of one sheriff's car. They looked pretty forlorn. As the sheriff closed the back door to the patrol car the couple noticed Pete, and said something to the officer.

The officer walked slowly to Pete's truck and asked, "What's your business with these two?"

He said, "I'm here to bring them some food and other things they need."

The officer countered, "They're not supposed to be here. You just get outta here and don't interfere with what we're doing."

The officer walked back to his car and got in. The sheriffs' cars pulled out and Pete began to drive behind them. He wanted to see where they were taking the couple so he could follow up and find out if there was some way to help them.

One sheriff's car pulled into the left lane and the other managed to get behind Pete's truck with his lights flashing, directing Pete to pull off to the side of the road. Pete drew to a stop and rolled down his window. One officer exited his vehicle and approached Pete.

The officer demanded, "Let me see your license and registration."

Taking both back to his car he took his time researching Pete's origins while the other car carrying the couple took off and disappeared down the road.

Returning to Pete with his documents, the officer warned, "Either go home or go to jail."

Pete questioned, "Where are they being taken?"

"To county jail." was the reply.

Pete checked at the county jail and was told they probably meant the city jail, but he would need a booking number, which would not be available for about a week. Predictably, when he checked a week later, the authorities could give him no information.

This incident had severe repercussions with other people he was helping in the area. In the next place he visited, the people didn't want his help. They thought he was the one who had caused the couple to be arrested. They thought he was a snitch. Building trust among people who had been hurt so much was a slow arduous task that had many pitfalls.

In the spring Pete was driving down one of the endless heavily wooded back roads when he was flagged down by a ragged man, with long scraggly brown hair, who was missing most of his side teeth. His remaining teeth pushed out in front, giving him a strange beaver-like appearance.

When Pete stopped and got out of his truck, the man introduced himself. "My name is Lester. The Foleys and Scout told me to look out for you. Maybe you could help us."

Pete asked, "What do you need?"

Lester said, "If you can, me and my friends need some tarps, water, and food."

"Sure. I'll go see what I can find." Pete joyfully drove off to the store.

Excited to be asked for help, Pete returned from the store to find Lester sitting near the spot where he had originally flagged him down. Lester got into the truck and they drove the short distance to his encampment. He had a blanket spread under some trees with a fire pit a short distance away in a clearing. Pete dropped off the water, some tarps and the little bit of food.

Getting back into his truck Pete told Lester, "I'll be back in a few days to see if you need anything else."

Pete visited each week and brought Lester a few essentials for survival. He noticed Lester's tattoos: big spider webs on both elbows indicating a long time in prison, and two teardrops under his left eye. He was a kind and gentle man who seemed to be the leader among this group of people living near him in the woods.

Shortly after meeting Lester, Pete was introduced to Lilly. She sat under a tree wearing the same dirty faded blue checkered dress he'd seen her wearing each time he visited. Over the dress she wore an apron that must have been white some time long ago. It had a border of Easter lilies outlined with red piping.

Pete had not paid much attention to Lilly. She was watching Lester unload the truck and it occurred to Pete that he'd never really talked with her. In her apparent state of innocence he wondered how she managed living in the woods.

Pete asked Lester, "Is it ok for me to go over and talk with your girlfriend?"

"Yea, guess so."

Lilly volunteered, "C'mon over."

Pete walked to her and sat down on the ground by her side.

Before he could say hello she said, "I could hear you talking to Lester from over here. You smell nice."

A little flustered and somewhat confused by her comment, he changed the subject. "How are you?"

She launched into her story. "I've been blind since birth, and Lester ain't my boyfriend, he's my partner. We been together since I was young. Lester's a lot older than me and some peoples they think I'm his daughter, but I'm not. You must be something to have Lester let you come in and out of here so freely. He never lets anyone know what we need or where we are. How'd you find us anyhow?"

About that time, Lester came over to tell Pete that he had finished unloading the truck. He asked when Pete would return and eased Pete away from Lilly. He was very protective of her. Pete assured Lester that he would return in a few days and headed off to his next destination.

During this time I was having more experiences in the Outreach Office at the parish. In the spring, the woman who started the Outreach Office began to need some extra help. Instead of driving, I sat at the desk one day each week and interviewed the people coming in who needed help. It was enormously different to be the one responsible for the referrals rather than simply driving a person to an appointment. Suddenly I needed to know about the available resources. The learning curve was steep. There were huge disparities between California resources and those in South Carolina.

There were many people in the parish neighborhood who lived in rundown family homes. Because they could not afford to pay the monthly utility bills, some had no electricity, heat, or water. Their houses provided only shelter with a door to close out the weather or anything undesirable from the outside. The inhabitants attempted to do enough odd jobs (mowing lawns, raking leaves, cleaning gutters, etc.) to pay the taxes. Some of our clients lived in sheds or rooms that had no electricity and no heat in the winter. We started giving $10 money orders for kerosene because people heated their small spaces with portable kerosene heaters. That gave a person enough heat for one or two nights.

These individuals had no medical insurance. We discovered that our parish and Outreach Office was located in one of the most medically underserved areas of our state. There was a local clinic that saw people on a sliding fee schedule, but their lowest rate was $25 per visit. The people we saw could in no way afford to pay this amount.

The Dorothy Day soup kitchen had volunteer nurses that ran a blood pressure clinic on the second Tuesday each month. The patrons of the soup kitchen went into the room to have their blood pressure taken, lured in with the offer of free toiletries. When a person had dangerously high blood pressure the nurses brought them down the hall to the Outreach Office and it became our responsibility to find a doctor who would see them and write a prescription. With the local clinic charging $25 for each visit, we had a hard time paying for these individuals to see the doctor each month because the doctors would write a prescription for only one month's medication at a time.

We saw a lot of people with severe dental pain. There was nowhere for them to get help. The least expensive dentist asked at least $200 for an extraction. Many a client left our office saying they were going to pull out their own teeth. The Outreach Office coordinator sent a letter to local dentists asking them to help our clients. Several responded that they would do emergency extractions for free. This began a program that has grown exponentially.

Pete and I came home some nights exhausted by our adventures. Retirement was quickly becoming a full time job. We contemplated people's responses to the work we were doing. When Pete told new friends that he was working with people who lived in the woods he got a couple of reactions.

One was incredulity that anyone actually lived in the woods, and the other was a question: "Aren't you afraid?"

I always went back to scripture and remembered that one of Jesus' most frequent phrases when he appeared was "Fear not."

Do not be afraid. Jesus knew that this was a common human emotion. He also knew that fear holds us back from life: Fear prevents us from experiencing this amazing world in all its grandeur. Fear causes a part of us to prematurely die. Fear is the opposite of love. Love casts out fear. If fear begins to creep into my heart, I bombard myself with prayer knowing that God always takes care of me.

Pete and I meet people each day who live in horrendous of situations, but when we build a relationship, we discover that person is no different from us. They care about family and friends. They want and need our respect. They have a deep need to belong. They laugh and cry just like everyone else. They have lost jobs, spouses, children, cars, homes, healthcare, and friends. They get up each morning and face each day. They find others who live in similar circumstances and they work together to survive. We find close communities in the most unlikely places, people who are brought together by mutual need. They are not so different from me. They may be dirty. They may eat scraps that others have thrown out. They may collect cans and recyclables to earn a little money, but they get up each day in the hope that today will be ok; that maybe today they will find that job, or get that place to live, or be reunited with their family.

That spring Pete regularly visited Lester in the woods, as well as stopping to see others who lived nearby. One night there was a particularly violent storm that swept through the area and Pete was apprehensive about a mother and four year old daughter he had met who had set up their home under a tarp strung between two old houses in the thick woods.

Pete headed in their direction after the storm and was greeted with this story: The night of the storm, the mom, Renee, had a hard time getting Jasmine, her daughter, to sleep because of all the lightning and thunder. Finally they both slept, only to be interrupted abruptly in the middle of the night when Renee heard a loud crack and became pinned to the ground under the tarp by a huge hickory tree. Renee could hear Jasmine screaming above the thunder and rain, but was unable to get up to go to her. Jasmine was also pinned under the tarp, but on the other side of the fallen tree. All Renee could do was pray. Her eyes were wide open looking into the tarp, listening to Jasmine scream, when the outline of a man appeared.

She screamed "Get me outta' here!"

The lightning flashed, the thunder struck, and the man put his finger to his mouth and he said, "Don't be afraid."

At just that instant Jasmine stopped crying. Renee felt an unexplained calm, like everything was going to be ok. A few minutes later Renee's neighbor, Fredric, rescued her and Jasmine from under the tarp.

Renee asked Fredric, "Did you see the fella standing over me, or was that you?"

"Wasn't me. I heard Jasmine scream, so I come a' running."

Renee asked Jasmine how she remembered the situation. She said, "I was scared until the man standing over me told me not to be scared."

"What'd the man look like?" Renee asked Jasmine.

"He looked like blue light, and he had a smile, and I wasn't scared anymore."

Pete went out to the woods most days and I was in the Outreach Office a couple of days each week. The months passed quickly.

One day in the fall when Pete arrived in the woods there was a new person. There had been a cold snap and the trees were losing their leaves. The ground was a red, yellow, and golden brown mat. Pete parked his truck off the road where it was hidden from view.

Lester and Lilly approached him. They knew that on this day he was bringing some clothes. He greeted them and Lester began to unload the goodies Pete had brought for the community. There were bags of underwear, socks, shirts, and pants, along with some shoes and coats.

Pete noticed a small man sitting with his back to them a few hundred feet away. His legs were draped over a log and his bare feet were dangling near a small fire.

Pete asked, "Lester, who's that?"

He said, "Don't know. He showed up late last night."

Lester left to get the people from the other small camps to tell them Pete was there with some stuff. Lilly and Pete stayed behind to organize the storage boxes he had brought at an earlier time.

Lilly asked, "What's he wearing?"

She was referring to the man across the meadow.

"Looks like he has a ripped t-shirt and short pants. I don't see any shoes. He's gotta be cold. Let me go talk with him."

Pete walked across the meadow and into the trees where the mysterious man was huddled. Getting close, he saw he was young, probably in his teens. His face was swollen and his eyes were black and blue.

"Where's your coat, young man?" Pete asked.

He said nothing.

Pete went on. "You ought to go over there and share some food and warmth with your neighbors. They're very friendly. I'll introduce you, if you don't mind."

The new arrival began to shiver uncontrollably and then gave Pete what we call in our family "the naughty look," the look that our three year old granddaughter mastered. It's the look that says "You are very bad and I don't want anything to do with you."

"Can't you see, mister? I wanna be alone! Now, go away!"

Pete returned to his work with Lilly who declared, "Take me over there, Reverend Pete."

Pete guided her to the log near the intruder and then excused himself because he needed to leave to buy the rest of the food. He returned to see the young man was sitting eating soup with some of the other people.

A few days after their first meeting Pete got more of Edgar's story. "My Ma and Dad and me was living in Tennessee. My Dad was always a drunk and he beat on my Ma. One day she just left. My Dad drove our truck to a rest stop on the highway and left it there.

"We hitchhiked to this area of South Carolina where Dad had some friends. They let us live in a broken down trailer. My Dad drank all the time and used up all his money on liquor.

"I got tired of getting beaten up when my Dad's drunk. I just left and started walking. I's sixteen. I never been to school. Don't know how to read or write."

Each day Pete could see Edgar's mood change. He began to smile. He made friends in the group among the other children.

He told Pete, "I never been happier then now that I got here."

As the weeks and months went by, Pete began to be in the woods more frequently. Just before Christmas he was sitting with a group of kids, the children of the adults who called this place home. Many of the children went to school, but this day several were sitting and talking with Pete. One of the older boys, River, about seventeen, was a simple child. He probably had the mental age of five or six.

This day he asked Pete, "Can you get me a Nativity set for Christmas?"

One of the little boys asked, "What's Nativity?"

River sweetly replied, "It's when Jesus is born and everyone cares about each other."

We wrote about River's comment in our newsletter and one of the girls, who many years before had gone with us to Tijuana, read this story. Subsequently we received a package in the mail from her. In it was a small Nativity set with a note saying that she had read our newsletter to her own children and they wanted the children in the woods to have this gift.

Pete and I agreed that this was the best time of our life. We loved our routine. Each day Pete went off to meet with the people who lived in the woods. His people were the ones who are "off the grid."

My days were a little different. I took care of the home front and some days I'd go off to the church Outreach Office where I met with a variety of people who had an assortment of needs. Other days I worked at a shelter with an agency that helped men, women, and children who are victims of domestic violence. I loved that we had the freedom to choose what we wanted to do and how we got to spend our days.

Because we lived in a small town, sometimes my work at the Outreach overlapped my work with the shelter. One afternoon I walked into a tutoring session with a woman at the shelter, only to have her tell me that I looked familiar. She was ready to change her life and get out of the downward spiral that had held her captive. It turned out that I had helped her get her South Carolina ID card when she had come to the Outreach Office. Now I was helping her learn math so she could get her GED at the age of thirty.

One weekend during this time I was talking with my grandson, Ethan, then seven years old, about my tutoring experience and this woman's desire to get her high school diploma.

He asked, "Grandma, why has she been going to school for thirty years?"

I explained, "She hasn't been going to school all these years. She left school before she was finished and now she

196

wants to get a good job and she needs to learn the things she missed."

It never occurred to him that anyone would not go straight through school and also graduate from college.

I loved that my sweet grandson enjoyed school and learning. He has great gifts of curiosity and intelligence, plus a family that will always love and support him. The choices he has in life will be unlimited.

The people I work with do not have that support network. When they lose a job, or have to leave their home because it is not a safe place, or get sick and have to go to the emergency room because they have no insurance, often there is no one who will take them home and help them overcome their difficulty. They have no options. They don't know what choices are available to them. Their lives have been so limited by their life experience that they do not have the tools necessary to move out of their situation.

It was now my job to help people find options. One of the things I found myself frequently saying was, "Everyone needs help at some time in their life."

Once a person relaxed and trusted us, we could begin the process of looking at their individual circumstances to see how they could help themselves move into a better place in their lives and their community. It's all about opening lives to the possibilities that are out there, the choices that I hope they can make for themselves.

In the early days of working in the Outreach, I met a woman who has since become a friend. A tall woman with beautiful silky brown skin and slightly graying black hair, Theresa limped into the Outreach Office, cane in hand. As she tottered to the chair, she leaned so far to the right that it seemed with each step she would fall over. She collapsed into the chair and breathlessly began to tell her story.

She had been working nearby at a senior day care center. One day, four months before, in the midst of an ice storm she ventured out the back door of her duplex on her way to work when she slipped on the frozen steps and broke her hip. While she was in the hospital the social worker had wisely filed for disability. Thankfully the hospital had repaired her hip with new parts, but upon discharge they told her to get physical therapy. When she went to the first therapy session she was informed that they could not work with her because she had no insurance, thus the debilitating gait.

She came to us because she needed help.

Terrified she said, "Miss Sue, I don't wanna be on the street. I used what I had in the bank. I know my disability check comes next month, but I can't pay the rent this month."

I took her to the Salvation Army and after we met with the representative and completed the necessary paperwork, her rent was paid. When her disability was approved, we helped her apply for Medicaid. Soon I was driving her twice a week to therapy where she painfully learned how to improve her walk. Within a few months she was walking without a cane.

I picked her up a couple of days each week at her dilapidated residence. As I got to know her, she shared with me the difficulties she was having with her humble abode.

"I got a leak in my roof. I called my landlord, but he don't come to fix it. What you think I oughta do? I'm afraid he's gonna put me out."

Her rent was only $185 a month and she knew she could not find another place as affordable. Gradually she came to the realization that she ought to go to the Rock Hill Housing Authority to apply for low cost subsidized housing.

Getting to know her, I understood one of the major reasons she hesitated in so many new situations was that she did not read very well. She lived in fear that she would have to read and fill out paperwork. Once I assured her that I was there to help, we made the appointment with the Housing Authority. Much to our pleasant surprise, we discovered that because she was over the age of fifty-five and disabled, she went to the top of the list. The normal wait time of six months to two years could be greatly reduced. Within the year she was proudly ensconced in a sweet one bedroom cottage that was priced in proportion to her income.

The new neighborhood was long curving blocks of little brick houses. Windows were boarded up on most of them. Weeds grew in the yards, trees were grey and dying. There were junk-filled yards surrounded by chain link fences. At first I was horrified by house after empty house. I wondered if they could all be foreclosures. I was repulsed by the horrendous desolation. Every so often there was a house that looked like someone might live there - a house with signs of life, a car or an open door.

This was the new and better neighborhood. She had found a place where her roof didn't leak, where the cockroaches did not inhabit the underside of her refrigerator, where the rats did not keep her company as she watched TV, where drug deals did not take place in her front yard, and where the nights were quiet and not broken up with gunshots. She had a fresh life in this quiet neighborhood.

As I drove through this area several times each week, I came to see it with new eyes. I still saw the boarded up windows, the graffiti on the walls, the crumbling doorposts, broken screens, and trash everywhere. But I also saw the house with a row of pansies lining the front walkway, the yard lovingly cared for with chairs on the front porch. I saw children playing in the dirt, like children in back yards everywhere, making mud pies. I saw the corner house with the basketball net where all the teens played ball. I saw people in their front yards talking with each other, smiling and laughing with each other. I saw the rusted barbeque, belching smoke, inviting the neighbors over for a shared meal. I saw a neighborhood I'd be proud to be a part of, where people cared about each other and noticed when a person comes and goes with a wave of the hand or a shouted greeting.

I knew my friend was happy here. She had decorated her house with curtains and little trinkets from the Dollar Store. She got her disability check each month and could pay her rent. She registered to vote for the first time in her life. I picked her up each Tuesday morning to take her down the street to the soup kitchen where she spent the morning socializing while I drove people to various appointments. She waited for me to get her after lunch and we did her small errands. We'd go to the Dollar Store where she purchased a few necessities, go to a doctor appointment, or sometimes get an ice tea at Mc Donald's. She never got out of the neighborhood unless someone took her. She had no car.

One day I had an appointment in York, South Carolina, about twenty miles west of Rock Hill. She went with me because she hadn't been to York in at least ten years. She marveled at all the changes in the countryside.

As we drove in the afternoons, afraid she needed too much from me, she'd repeat, "I hope I'm not worrying you too much."

As time went by I learned her real story. She had been born and raised near Baltimore, Maryland. "When I was sixteen I found out that the woman who raised me wasn't my mother, she was my aunt. My sisters weren't my sisters, they were my cousins. I found out when I was in high school, when my aunt died, but I found out my aunt was really my mother. Miss Sue, they lied to me all those years."

The information sent her into a downward spiral. She left school. "They always told me I was stupid. I never did get to reading very well. It was too hard."

She worked at various low wage jobs, married, divorced after six months, and got into drugs. A boyfriend drove a big rig truck and she traveled the country with him for a few years.

By the time I met her she'd been in Rock Hill some twenty years. She described, "I always had a job, usually cleaning in motels or local schools. I spent all my extra money on drugs."

She also opened her home to dealers who would use it as a place to sell in return for supplying her with the crack that became her habit. In her last two years of drug use she lived off the income of a friend who shared her apartment. She no longer had the desire or energy to do more than find her next high.

One day she woke up and realized she didn't want to live like this anymore. She now says, "I know someone was praying for me."

She found a church, started to go to Bible study, and told the friend he had to move out because he was still using and she didn't want the temptation around. Faith became her guidepost and Jesus walked with her each step of each day. She felt the pull of the drugs, but her God kept her from caving in to temptation.

I reflect a lot on her journey. I have discovered she is a very smart woman. She may not read well, but she knows just how much money she has in the bank and how much she can spend. She remembers experiences, appointments, people, and stories she is told. What she lacks is information. She has heard lots of old wives' tales and superstitions about health and wellness. She has no concept of what constitutes good nutrition. She is a meat and potatoes person with an occasional frozen pizza in the mix. She suffers from high blood pressure, kidney disease, and high cholesterol. We began to talk about how to cut out salt, saturated fat, and sugar from her diet.

She never learned about the importance of voting or thought about the fact that people died for her right to vote. It was one of the most joyful days of my relationship with her, when in 2012 I took her to the polls and she cast her first ever vote for her choice for President of the United States.

Each day she grows in confidence. Her once ghastly temper is being moderated by her desire to be a better person.

She has gone through training and become a volunteer in our outreach office; she keeps the clients organized and occupied while they wait.

Recently she decided she wanted to get her drivers' license. I kept asking, "Why do you want to do that? You can't afford a car."

She repeatedly told me, "I just want to get it. God will take care of the rest."

Each week we met and she took the online tests for the DMV. I read the questions and she gave me the answers. We scheduled an oral test with the DMV and she passed the second time she took the exam.

During this period, a woman approached me at church. "We have a car we'd like to donate. Do you have anyone who can use it?"

Theresa took the driving test and is now the proud owner of a 2003 Camry. She paid for the first month's insurance, the registration, and license fees out of the money she had been saving. Now she is able to get herself to the store and to doctor appointments and maybe even have a part time job.

Theresa is willing to share her journey with others in the hope that they will realize they too can kick the old ways and find new hope in life. She has worked hard to change her former bad habits.

She tells me, "Maybe someone can learn from my experience. I couldn't do it without God and your help."

Pete was asking people in the woods about their journeys that led them to the woods. River approached him and asked if he could tell Pete his story. He told him about his mom and dad's "bad luck." How two years before, their car had broken down and they couldn't afford to repair it. The dad worked in a car wash and the mom had a job in a grocery store. They both lost their jobs because they couldn't get to work. Then they lost their apartment because they couldn't pay the rent. So they started to walk down one of the local highways when they came upon some people in the woods who invited them to share their fire.

He said, "It took awhile to get used to living in these woods. We was so hungry and cold. The only way we got through winter was because these people shared with us. The first Thanksgiving and Christmas we spent here were like any other day. We picked up stuff on the highway to sell for recycling. That's how we made money."

Lester, who was emerging as the leader of this community, approached Pete in March to ask if Pete would lead a prayer service using the Word of God. He also wanted him to use one of the stories that Lester knew Pete was writing about the people who called the woods their home. The day for the prayer service arrived and most of the group gathered in a loose circle, sitting on logs or the ground. Pete decided to use John 3:13-16, that ends with "Yes, God so loved the world that he gave his only Son, so that everyone who believes in him may not be lost but may have eternal life."

He led them in singing *Amazing Grace* which they belted out with great enthusiasm. The prayer service was so well received that the people requested that Pete lead them every Friday.

We had no idea what a significant impact this would have on the group. It was the beginning of a treasured tradition for people who felt rejected and abandoned by family, friends, and society. They were calling Pete "Reverend" because he referred to his job as being a ministry. He told them he was not an ordained minister, but this was a term of respect that they preferred to use.

Pete was approached one day by Liz who came to the forest to die. She was in the last stages of leukemia and had an urgency about telling her story. She was born in 1945. Her mother died in childbirth and her dad never let her forget that she had killed her mom. He became a mean drunk and when he remarried, she grew tired of caring for all the children so she ran away. After many years and many adventures, she was diagnosed with cancer. Deciding she did not want treatment, she found this community in the woods that gave her life a renewed spirit.

When Liz got sicker, the people in the woods panicked and convinced her to go to the hospital. Lester and others from the community rode bikes the seven miles to the hospital to visit with her each day, then one morning Lester went to see her and her room was empty. He inquired about her at the nurse's station and was told she had died in the night.

Because she did not list any next of kin, her body was sent for cremation and would be buried in an unmarked location. The community was devastated. The prayer service that Friday was very difficult. Each person was grieving in their own way and the unspoken question was, "Is this going to happen to us?"

By Monday two couples who had called this place home were gone. They just disappeared. They left without even saying goodbye.

Life had to go on. Liz was mourned, but bottles and cans had to be collected, kids had to get to school, people had to be fed, water had to be transported, and the camp area had to be kept clean. Pete was coming home with stories every day. He tried not to have favorites, but sometimes it was just not possible. When the combination of innocence and attitude, youth and humor, love and enthusiasm are on display nearly all of the time by a single person; he couldn't seem to help himself.

He told me about Picket, a nine year old boy who was just about the mental speed of River, who was eight years older. River followed Picket all over the forest when Picket wasn't at school. Picket and River were two who had been at the Friday morning prayer services from the beginning. They loved the stories from the bible and they loved how Jesus was poor like them.

They sat together and after the scripture readings asked questions such as "Did Jesus live in the forest like us?" or "Jesus was poor like us, huh?" or "Can Jesus cure me?"

Picket was born with no leg below one knee. His daddy carved him a "Captain Hook" style wooden peg leg which seemed to suit Picket just fine, along with a "Tiny Tim" kind of crutch.

River liked taking care of Picket, but sometimes got in his way more than he helped. One day he reached for Picket's hand to help him over a large decaying log and fell backwards, pulling Picket along with him. Their laughter caused everyone who was within hearing to smile.

Picket loved music - any kind of music. He had a pair of earphones which were in his ears all of the time. The earphones had wires hanging down, but no CD player.

Pete asked, "Picket, do you hear music playing with your ear phones?"

"Heck no! Not with the earphones. I hear birds sing and people laugh and that's kinda music to me."

Pete got Picket a used CD player and Samantha, our granddaughter, gave Pete some CD's she thought Picket would like. He loved them and immediately used up two sets of batteries. Pete watched as he and River shared the ear pieces, one ear each, and walked together arm in arm off into the forest by themselves.

River and Picket declared, "We wanna live together in a house someday."

Another day they asked, "Reverend Pete, do you sleep in a bed?"

Pete's stories made me stop and think about my anxieties.

A scripture I love to repeat is: "Therefore I tell you, do not worry about your life, what you will eat or drink; or about your body, what you will wear. Is not life more than food and the body more than clothes? Look at the birds of the air; they do not sow or reap or store away in barns, and yet your heavenly Father feeds them. Are you not much more valuable than they? Can any one of you by worrying add a single hour to your life?" (Matthew 6: 25-27)

I have a motto that I use as a mantra when necessary: "Worry doesn't accomplish anything."

I learned to take care of what is possible and to trust the rest to God. We have never gone hungry. We have always had clothing and shelter. We have everything we need and we even have the luxury of some of what we want.

This trust in God was deeply challenged that summer, when Pete arrived in the woods in the early hours of the morning to find people sitting and waiting with their belongings all packed up. They had been asleep when, in the middle of the night, some of them sleeping near the fire were cruelly awakened by baseball bat wielding men who threatened to do them great harm if they didn't get out of their woods.

By the time Pete appeared, word of the event had spread throughout the group. They were all terrified, but especially the people with children. Some had decided that the solution was to move deeper into the woods. Others wanted to leave and return home.

Several families came to South Carolina with the promise of work. When jobs did not materialize they ended up in the woods. They were doing all they could to work and save money to return to their roots, but work was scarce and living among the trees was the only solution.

This invasion by violent strangers became a catalyst for change for five of the families who had young children. They borrowed the group's cell phone and began a series of calls to home. Each family that had the promise of work and a place to stay made plans to leave South Carolina and return to their homes. Some were able to provide a few dollars for their trip. The community contributed some money from the shared money that each working person made and put in the group kitty - the money they were saving for emergencies or special occasions. *Truck of Love* made up the final $900 and Pete purchased bus tickets for all.

The rest of the community moved deeper into the trees hoping they would be safe. Unfortunately this was not to be so. Again one night, bat wielding men came through. They got close enough to Lester that he could smell the liquor on their breath. Even though the woodland residents outnumbered these senselessly violent beings, they did not confront them. They tried to become small and let the men go by. They really embraced Christ's message of turning the other cheek. Their strategy was to spread out among the trees in the hope that no one would notice them.

Their peace had been offensively and violently disturbed and their fear was palpable for some time. The Friday morning prayer services were a source of tremendous comfort. The scripture readings touched each person in ways that sometimes caused great changes. This was definitely the case with a man named Arthur.

Pete says people have often accused him of being "colorblind." He had never told me that all the people in the woods were white. There had been one or two black people who wandered through, but they never stayed, until Arthur.

Pete was returning to the woods after a week's absence. Lester greeted him and then introduced him to a new member of the group. Arthur was short and skinny, with a milk chocolate complexion. He would not stand out in a crowd except that he had a patch where his left eye used to be and a conspicuous inch-wide white scar that started under that patch and carved a swath across his forehead into the bush of curly black hair that covered his head and ended up near his shoulder blades on the right side of his back. Arthur didn't have much to say to Pete, he just looked scared.

Lester and Pete went off to the store to get some food and do laundry for the group. It was then Lester told him the little he knew. "I seen him standing near a big hardwood tree when we was picking up trash along the road. He looked hungry, so I took my lunch over to him. We started talking."

Lester discovered Arthur was a Christian. He invited Arthur to join their group and stay as long as he needed.

On their way back to the encampment, Lester told Pete he had already talked with Arthur about him.

He told Arthur, "Reverend Pete won't hurt you. He's good to talk to."

As they unloaded the truck, Arthur appeared from the woods and Lester again encouraged him to talk with Pete. Arthur motioned for Pete to come into the woods with him. They found a place away from the others and Arthur began with a question, "Do you suppose God would forgive you for the bad you done in this life if you was truly repentant?"

Pete told him, "I believe God forgives all our sins; scripture tells us that. As long as we are trying to be better and we are sorry for what we have done; God will always forgive us."

Arthur's shoulders began to heave and he bent his head down. Stifled sobs shook his body. Pete backed away to where the others were busy with their day's work. Arthur joined them a little while later, looking very much relieved.

Later Pete learned why Arthur had asked about God's forgiveness: Arthur confessed, "I was a punk kid. I drank and did lots of bad stuff. My grandmama raised me up. She loved me more then I deserved. I just got tired of my life and I took her money and I left."

One Friday morning after Pete read the story of the Prodigal Son during the prayer service, Arthur approached him to say, "I gotta go home and find my grandmama."

Pete drove him to the bus station and Arthur used his own money, saved from many days of working collecting recyclables, to buy his bus ticket. We prayed that he got where he needed to be.

A few weeks later the Friday morning reading was again about forgiveness. This time it was River who approached

Pete. Pete told me so many stories about River that I felt I knew him. He obviously had a deep effect on Pete, who described River as touching his soul. As with all the people in the woods, the first story Pete heard was often just a part of the person's life. Usually there was much more.

Pete figured River was about eighteen years old, but he seemed more like an eight year old. He was small in stature, with a sweet face and an ugly ragged scar on the side of his head. He was one of the most trusting, loving people Pete had ever met. He was a true innocent. Pete had known him for about two years, since he'd started working with the community in the woods.

River lived with the community and with his adoptive parents. Pete had known for some time that he was not their biological child. He also knew that they loved him and protected him with a fierceness that Pete didn't really understand.

One day, after the regular Friday morning prayer service, the group was talking about forgiveness, again, because once more the community had been rousted by unknown men who had threatened them.

The people were dispersing after prayer when River came up to Pete and asked, "Reverend Pete, can I go with you to get the groceries this morning?"

"Sure," Pete said, "Hop in."

As soon as River sat down in the passenger seat of the truck he began to talk. "You know how you was talking about forgiving to everyone? And how I could talk to you about anything, anything at all?"

Pete responded, "You can trust me with anything you want to say. I won't tell anyone."

"Remember how I told you I don't know nothing about my real parents? Well, you can't say nothing to nobody here on who told you what I got to tell you, ok?"

Pete reaffirmed he wouldn't tell anyone unless what River told him was a danger to him or someone else. And so River told Pete a tale of horrendous abuse by a father who beat him and his sister. He recalled one day when his father repeatedly threw his sister against a wall until she was silent.

He ended his tale by affirming the morning's reading about forgiveness.

Hearing River's story made us wonder if he too had been struck in the head. He had the scar and he was slow to learn; maybe he had been brain damaged. We were so grateful that his adoptive parents were loving and kind people. The community had embraced River as if he was their mascot.

River had a habit of greeting Pete each morning as he arrived in the truck. He always seemed to have something urgent that had to be said, so when he ran toward the truck one fine winter morning, Pete was not too surprised.

Excitedly River exclaimed, "Reverend Pete! There's a man named Michael here. He says he knows you!"

Pete looked at the young man who was following River toward him. He was medium height with wavy shoulder length auburn hair. His tan face was covered with a short beard and his intense eyes met Pete's. He was wearing familiar clothing: a loose fitting shirt and khaki pants with sandals on his feet. Slowly, recognition came to Pete of the young man he had met so many years before on the streets of Mountain View in California.

Pete said, "Yes, Michael. How good it is to see you!" and gave him a big hug.

Michael said, "Pete, it's good to see you here."

Pete asked him if he would stay for the prayer service they were about to have. He wanted to introduce him to the group.

Michael said, "I'd love to meet everyone, but I have to be going." He walked away into the woods in the direction of the road.

After he had gone, River looked at Pete and innocently asked, "Is he really an angel?"

As spring arrived more of the people were going to work or wanting to work. The group that Pete saw each day in the woods was a fine example of the desire we human beings have for work. It is a part of who we are. Work helps us define ourselves. Jesus was a carpenter, and his followers were fishermen, tax collectors, shepherds, farmers, merchants, and laborers. Jesus belonged to the working world and valued that part of a person's life.

The community in the woods had evolved from a bunch of individuals taking what they could to survive to a real community of people who prayed together and worked together for the improvement of the community and the betterment of its members.

The first person to get work was a woman named Cinamin. She approached Pete and told him she wanted to wash windows. She asked him if he would buy her a bucket and a squeegee. Once she had these, she hopped on the bike Pete got for her and she rode into the nearest town and began to

Cinamin

knock on doors. Looking for work every day, she soon had enough window washing work to employ two more residents of the community.

Then one day Pete was driving the back roads and went past a brick yard that had a dangerously overloaded truck full of old bricks parked in the front. Pete stopped and went into the office where he asked the man if there were any jobs available. The man was excited, saying he could use anyone who wanted to work hard. They just needed to show up and he would pay ten cents for each used brick that they cleaned: chopping off the old mortar and stacking them on pallets. That turned into six regular jobs. Each person cleaned enough bricks to bring home about $35 a day.

A young man came into the community with just the shirt on his back and the pants on his legs. He was about seventeen and was very smart at fixing things. He began the job of maintaining the bikes and he set up an underground storage area where he collected parts of small appliances and bikes. Jack fixed or put together anything that crossed his path. He even sold some of his projects at the local flea market.

Another woman, a mother, had a job cleaning rooms at a motel. She was saving for her daughter's education.

Those who could not go out to work stayed in the woods and had jobs to maintain the encampment, such as cooking, sweeping, and washing clothes. Once those jobs were completed they went out to the nearby roadway and picked up bottles and cans for recycling and loaded up the garbage in plastic bags. Lester, who was elected the leader, made sure that order was kept and jobs got done.

Jack could fix anything

At that point there were thirty-nine people living in this woodland community. Thirteen went out each day to work. Everyone who worked put a percentage of their income into the group kitty that was kept for emergencies. The recycling money and the money Pete paid for garbage collection was also put into the kitty with a small amount going to the laborers. Even with their income, it was still necessary for Pete to supplement them with food, medical supplies, tarps, water jugs, laundry money, and other essentials that kept them safe. That added up to about $3,500.00 each month.

Pete loved the way the people in the woods were coming together to help each other. One of the women was a gifted teacher and took Edgar under her wing. She spent part of each day in their makeshift classroom, a tree stump where he could lay out his paper for writing. His reading and math skills grew exponentially. She worried he was getting too advanced for her. Pete kept her supplied with books and materials that helped her challenge her avid student.

One of the women who wandered into the encampment became the cook.

She told Pete, "I was five when my momma and daddy sold me to 'Uncle Jim.'"

This began Pete's journey into Bernice's story that left him disgusted and dumbfounded, but with a whole new insight and respect for this diminutive woodland lady. She told him how she was one of ten kids and was hungry all the time. One day her Momma told her she was going to go live with her Uncle Jim who would teach her a trade. Uncle Jim lived in his motel where several young children also lived. She became one of these children who went into the rooms of the motel guests at night. After several years she escaped the motel and wandered the streets and woods meeting men who taught her how to survive.

She had arrived in the community in the woods a couple of years before. She was a very quiet, private person who took on the chore of cooking for the whole group of forty. She made the traps to catch the squirrels for her famous, fabulous squirrel stew. As she told her story, she rolled six small blue pop beads with the fingers of one hand. The pop beads were the only remnant of her birth family. She said these beads kept her calm.

There was an air of contentment about her. At the age of about twenty-four she had found a safe place to call home.

Each person had some gift they could offer to the group. There was Scout who was the lookout. Lester was the leader. Lily was the confidant of all. Bernice cooked. River kept everyone laughing. Jack fixed bikes. Cinnamon went into town to wash windows

Unfortunately the feelings of love and peace and the triumphs of so many were once again sorely interrupted by disturbing events.

One Monday morning Pete arrived at the encampment in the woods to an appalling sight. The adults and kids in the group were gathered around Edgar and River. On Sunday afternoon the boys had gone off together to collect cans along the highway near the camp. Lester, who was continually concerned about safety, reminded them they could not be gone more than an hour.

Dinner time came but there was no sign of the teens. Lester and Scout went out looking for them. As dark descended, the rest of the community fanned out along the highway calling for the boys.

It was close to midnight before Scout heard crying and called for the search party to follow the sounds. They found Edgar and River huddled together in terror under a tree not too far off the highway. They were covered with blood from open wounds all over their faces and arms. River seemed to be beaten the worst, unable to stand because of pain in his side. Both boys' eyes were swollen shut. Unable to see much, they had stayed close to each other as darkness engulfed them.

As the group cared for the boys, the story of their ordeal came out: They went off to collect cans along the highway for recycling. While they worked, a big black truck pulled over and stopped.

Edgar said, "Six white guys jumped out and they jumped us. We tried running in two different directions, but that just made them mad. They caught us and they wanted to know where we was staying an' told us if we didn't tell 'em, they'd beat us to death. They started on River because they thought he was a sissy because he started crying. They knocked him down and started kicking him till he was quiet. Then they started on me. They just kept hitting us and hurting us all over and over again. They told us if we moved from where we was, they'd come to our camp and burn it out and kill us. They said if they ever saw us again, they'd kill us."

They were bruised and sore all over. As Pete listened to their story and saw these two precious boys suffering, he felt his anger rising. Who could do this to another human being? Why?

He went to the police department, but of course they could not file any complaint without the people who have been beaten coming forward. He asked them to be on the lookout for six men who fit the description the boys had given.

We had no idea that calling on the sheriff's office was the worst thing Pete could have done. It was shortly after this that he was stopped by two sheriffs' cars and driven aimlessly around the countryside in the back of one car until they decided to let him go.

Pete became a target. Some people who did not want "vagrants" in their neighborhood began to follow him. His truck was known. When he thought he was being followed he drove away from where the community lived. One day he and Lester were going to a store when a shiny black SUV seemed to be shadowing them. Pete kept driving and drove the twenty five miles through the twists and turns of the solitary timbered roads back to Rock Hill. The whole time, the black SUV stayed close.

Finally Pete arrived at the mall in Rock Hill and pulled into the very public parking lot of the Target store. He parked the truck and waited. The SUV pulled up a couple of spaces away. Pete saw two men in dark suits, each wearing sunglasses, sitting in the front seats. Lester fearing for his life got out and rushed into the Target store. Pete got out of his truck and approached the SUV. He waited at the driver's side for the man to lower the window. The men just sat and looked at him through the window.

Pete called to them through the closed glass, "Can I help you?"

They sat and stared. Then they started their car and drove away.

Lester was spooked. Pete was unsettled. He tried to assure Lester that no one knew where they lived.

It was just a short time later when their tenuous existence was again threatened.

"We been found out again, Reverend Pete. Four men and their dogs come through our camp last night a'yelling to wake everyone up. They told us to get up and to get out of here right now, or they'd sic their hounds on us."

These were Lester's words after the reading with which they opened their Friday morning prayer service.

Pete had been thinking what a beautiful morning it was in the woodland paradise. They'd opened the service with a reading from the Gospel of Mark: "The Son of man is to be handed over and they will kill him..." (Mark 9:31)

Lester went on to tell the group that he had been calm when he told the men, "We's gonna go, but in the morning, and not till after we's prayed up."

Everyone sat stunned as Lester went on to explain, "They got real ugly and they got their dogs to barking. I promised them we'd leave in the morning' after we said our prayers and they was ok with that."

After Lester opened the reflection everyone wanted to speak. Mostly they wanted to talk about being kicked out of their homes. They each had made their tarps into personalized dwellings. One lady had a two room tarp home.

The comments all came down to the same concerns. "Where's this all gonna stop? Where we gonna go?"

Scout shot his hand into the air to say his piece. He said, "I been looking all along for someplace to move if we get throwed outta here. I had my eye on a place just across the river. It's got a real nice clearing and a spot where Jack can dig a pit and store his bike stuff."

After the group prayer and sharing everyone got to work. Both Lester and Pete stared as they watched each person pack up their personal items and start to load the truck for the first of many trips to their new home. As the morning went on, Sukey, one of the mothers, used the groups shared cell phone to call the school district to make sure the kids could get picked up on the new road. She was assured that there were several other children picked up near the new area and the kids would still be able to get to school.

Pete noticed there was no fear coming from the group. They quickly and quietly worked together to get the job done. They had come a long way in the three years Pete had worked with them. They now trusted each other and depended upon each other and loved each other. They had become a true Christian community.

As they worked, Lester reflected, "I know the Lord will provide us with what we need. There's no reason to worry."

Pete thought how interesting it was that Scout had been looking "just in case" something like this happened in the future. He happily took the first load of shovels and people to the new site. As they stood looking at the beauty of the new home site, Lester asked Pete to bless the new land with a prayer. The Twenty-third Psalm immediately came to mind and Pete quoted, "The Lord is my Shepherd, I shall not want..."

Then they all got to work.

During this time I was in the midst of big transitions in the Outreach Office. We had been serving hundreds of people out of a space about eight feet by eight feet. One day our Pastor asked us if we'd like to have a larger space. He ushered us down the hallway to one of the classrooms and asked if we thought it could make an acceptable office, his caveat being that the children's religion program would use the space on Sundays and the Narcotics Anonymous would be using it on Tuesday, Thursday, and Saturday nights. The parish brother would use it for the archives on Thursday and Friday in the mornings.

We were so excited to have the hope of increased space that we enthusiastically agreed we could live in the same room as all these others. We took possession of some donated cubicles and set up our new office: three cubicles each having as much room as the original office, two file cabinets, a table, some chairs, and space left over!

When it was time for prayer on the first morning in our new office, we went out into the hallway and explained to the people who were waiting for us that it was our custom to begin our day with prayer. We invited anyone who would like to pray with us to come into our office and join in our circle. Slowly, hesitantly, one by one people got up from the benches and came through our door. They kept coming until our space was filled.

As we prayed, I heard the "Amen's" and "Yes, Lord's" and more "Amen's." Then everyone went back out in the hallway to wait their turn. We did this every day in the new workspace. About a week into our new tradition the group was smaller, but each person offered their own special individual prayer. They were prayers of thanksgiving: for another day, for God's continued grace, for the outreach office, for getting off drugs and staying clean, for finding a place to live, for God's love. One blind man led off - he could have been a preacher - his voice declaring the goodness and generosity of God in his life and the lives of all of us. At the end the group gave out a resounding "Amen!" and left smiling to wait their turn.

There seemed to be a lot more laughter in our hallways. People understood we were trying to be as efficient as possible, but it was sometimes necessary to wait two hours before they could be seen. They knew that when it was their turn we would take the time with them that they needed. Each of them knew we would listen to them. Each of them knew we cared. And each of them knew we were in God's hands.

When the woodland community had been in their new area for a couple of months, it began to get very cold. The group did not have tents. They had tarps and blankets. They had already dug two pits into the earth, one for bike parts and one for cooking. Each one was eight feet deep, eight feet wide and twenty feet long. A few people were sleeping in these underground pits. The temperature below ground was not nearly as cold as it was among the trees.

Pete asked Lester if they wanted to dig another pit so everyone could sleep underground. Lester jumped at the idea and they shopped for wood to shore up the sides and make the top. They needed another pick ax and a couple more shovels and by the time Pete left them they were hard at work excavating.

River was really good with a pick ax and he sang as he broke the dirt. Edgar shoveled, as he was the best at that. Many of the other folks dug, picked, and carried dirt away from the camp so there wouldn't be a new mountain in the underbrush. They expected it would take two days. They were determined to have a new underground room by the time temperatures dropped into the predicted teens. By this time there were forty-two people in the community and with the additional pit anyone who wanted an underground space would have one.

That winter was brutally cold and the pits kept people almost warm. They used heaters fashioned from candles and clay pots to heat the space when it got too frigid.

It was not too long after we had the digging project that it snowed so much that Pete could not get to the woods for three full days. We live in the country and our road does not get plowed. When it's icy we cannot get out of our driveway.

By the time he did make it back to the woods, they were completely out of food and had been melting snow for water. Lester got into Pete's truck and immediately they went off to the grocery store. As Pete drove toward town, he noticed a sheriff's car following them. He didn't say anything to Lester, but thought to himself, "Not again."

Pete pulled into the parking lot of the grocery store and Lester hopped out of the truck and took the only shopping cart into the store. As he wheeled the cart away he saw the police car park near Pete. With a look of terror he went into the building at lightning speed and disappeared into the crowd of shoppers.

Pete ran interference by getting out, going around the truck, locking the rider's side door, and then walking back around the truck to lock the door on the driver's side. He was watching the sheriff's car out of the corner of his eye.

The officer got out of his car and stood about thirty yards away when four pickup trucks with oversized tires surrounded them. The officer leaned against one of the trucks and motioned for Pete to approach him.

He heard one of the truck drivers call out, "Officer, you need any help?"

The officer shook his head. He was a young balding man in uniform. As Pete got close to him, he could see that the officer was not wearing a badge or name tag.

He did not introduce himself, but instead stated, "We know who you are. If you keep on doing what you are doing with this rabble living out of doors, I'm going to make sure you get in real trouble, and these people are going to get themselves arrested for being vagrants."

Pete looked around at the five fellows in the trucks, and was relieved to see that they looked young enough to be in high school.

He asked the officer, "If you're speaking officially, why aren't you wearing a badge or name tag?"

He did not reply. He simply got back in his patrol car and he and the four trucks left Pete there alone in the parking lot. Lester and Pete finished the shopping and watchfully took a detour as they returned with food for their hungry friends.

The people who were living in the woods were hard working, loving individuals who were there for a variety of reasons. They were not hurting anyone. In fact they were helping keep the roadways clean and free of the garbage that was continually thrown out of the cars speeding past. They got jobs wherever they could. They tried to take care of their families and each other. Every day was filled with the unending work associated with trying to survive outside in the extremely harsh weather conditions.

Each time Pete got stopped by the police, we renewed our commitment to the people we served. We were not breaking any laws. We joked about what we would do if Pete got arrested. We began to formulate a plan, just in case.

In March 2014, I celebrated my seventieth birthday. In April, over Easter vacation, our son Ian and his family planned to visit us from Norway. Whenever they came from Norway our other children liked to gather, so we expected our son Tim from Pittsburgh, our son Andy from New York, and of course our son Peter who lived just half an hour from us. We were very excited to see them all with their families. Unfortunately our daughter Julie and her family were not going to be able to be with us. On Good Friday, Pete came home from the woods early because he wanted to spend time with the family. We loved it when our kids were all in one place. They treasured being together and we had such fun watching the interaction among the cousins.

On Saturday the boys went shopping for dinner. They told me they were going to cook for me that day. They came in with bags of groceries and following them was our daughter, Julie, who had flown in the previous night from Washington and had stayed with her brother, Peter. What a wonderful surprise! I was dumbfounded and all I remember is lots of loud voices and cameras flashing as Julie and I shared a long joyful hug.

When some of the noise subsided I learned that they had been planning this surprise for a very long time. Peter's kids who live nearby us had known and had kept the secret. They were so pleased with themselves. Alissa who lived with her parents in Norway had also been fully aware, but never let on in all the times we talked on Skype. Anthony who lived in California, but who had already been with us for a couple of days, smiled slyly in full recognition that he too had been part of this conspiracy.

With Julie as the spokesperson, they proceeded to tell me that we were going to celebrate my birthday. They sat me down as the five of them got out a bass, a guitar, and a drum. Then they explained to me that when they tried to think of what they could give me they realized that what I really wanted was to hear them sing. I always asked, but they rarely granted my request. Each of them inherited Pete's musical abilities and they were excellent singers and musicians. I was in heaven!

As they sang, I looked around the living room at their children, our grandchildren, and felt overwhelmingly grateful for all of them. The looks on their children's faces were a mirror of my own thorough enjoyment of the moment.

It could not have been a more joyous Easter. Christ was risen! We were filled with Easter jubilation.

In the midst of this hullabaloo of family, Pete mentioned to me that River had been acting strangely on Friday. Listening to what Pete described, I said he needed to take him to the doctor on Monday when he returned to the woods.

River was not well when Pete saw him. He had a terrible headache and had not slept much over the weekend. By Wednesday Pete made arrangements to get River to the hospital in Charlotte. When the doctor examined him he said he thought River was suffering from a glioblastoma brain tumor. River spent a few hours in the hospital before he pleaded to go home. With the permission of the nurses they got him to the truck. Once he was strapped in and on the road, he slumped over and died.

He was delivered back into the arms of his community where they wrapped him in the best quilt and put his ragged stuffed animal in his arms. He was laid to rest in his favorite place.

We were devastated, but as sad as we were about River's death, there was a part of us that rejoiced that he was removed from the brutal uncertainty of his life here on this earth. Aside from the beatings and privation, about a year before, his adoptive parents had disappeared. River woke up one morning and they were gone. They didn't tell anyone, not even Lester, that they had plans to leave. They simply vanished. At that time Lester and the rest of the group decided they would adopt River and make sure he was cared for. Everyone was upset by River's death, but it was apparent that nothing could have been done to save his life. We were grateful he had been on his way home to the people he loved. They never told Pete where they buried him, just that it was one of his beloved spots in the woods.

This passage said it best for me. "If we have died with Him we shall also live with Him. If we persevere we shall also reign with Him."(2 Timothy 2:11-12) River learned about Jesus and walked with Him through his days in the woods. He often asked Pete questions or made comments about his sweet faith life. Jesus was his friend and confidant.

Soon it was summer – time to think about camp. This was the twenty-eighth summer of camp on the Tohono O'odham Nation. Samantha, our granddaughter, was scheduled to go with me for almost the full two weeks – whatever we could squeeze out as soon as her school year finished.

When we started camp we never imagined what it would be like twenty-eight years later. We had no idea what we were doing, but over the years with the help of hundreds of people some miraculous things took place. The summer of 2014 was the third year that camp was under all O'odham leadership. The day Samantha and I drove in to PisinMo'o was the third day of leadership training. We pulled into the parking lot of the new recreation center and stepped out into the scorching heat of mid-day. There were no people in sight. Upon entering the recreation center we could hear the commotion from the main room where the leaders were engaged in activities. We snuck into the room in the middle of a game. A few people acknowledged our presence as we quickly found a seat in the circle of chairs. I immediately saw that the leadership training was in good hands.

Samantha was in heaven. She loved the desert. She was at home with the O'odham. I loved being back. As each activity unfolded, I admired the skills and creativity of the O'odham leaders. They were making the camp their own. I felt pure joy watching them teach each other games, lead activities, or create craft projects.

I couldn't help but think back to all the preceding years. How difficult it had been when we were the drivers, cooks, and camp counselors. Memories flooded my mind. I thought of Mike who had told me, "The year Tim and I ran sports, we'd play steal the bacon, and we decided to make a gigantic bacon worth tons of points and we called it 'the Canadian bacon'... the kids went nuts for it."

As I sat through that week and watched the O'odham guiding each other skillfully through the days of leadership training and then the brutal hours of camp with 250 children, I thanked God for the gift this camp had been and continues to be in the lives of all those who pass through. We are exceedingly grateful to Stanley who, as District Chairman, supports camp, and for the staff of the Recreation Center who graciously invite the camp to use the facility.

That summer as I put out chairs, washed dishes, took pictures, or just hung out, people approached me and thanked me - us - for starting camp. The first generation of campers are now part of tribal police, first responders, teachers, counselors, and employees of districts and recreation centers throughout the Nation. Camp is now serving their children and soon their grandchildren.

Not all our campers went on to live successful lives. Several have died from violence, drug overdoses, accidents, or illness. Some have been in and out of jail on a continuing loop. Others have spent years being slaves to drugs and alcohol. Some came to camp in the daytime to laugh and play with everyone only to return to their problems at home after dark. We knew that camp was a very small part of each life, but it was a time of real joy.

TOTOL Camp in PisinMo'o is a time each summer that the children and adults look forward to. Something happens at camp time. The tradition of "the group" that started many years ago is present each time camp takes place. It is that spirit of respect, love, and inclusiveness. It is a place where each person is accepted as they are, not as someone perceives they should be. It is a place of cooperation, learning, and sharing. Our hope is that these moments live on in each person.

While I was enjoying the ambiance of the desert, Pete was helping the woodland community navigate many changes.

Pete and I talked a lot about this community in the woods. We never experienced homeless people helping each other to this extent.

They started as a few people who lived throughout an area of woods several miles south of the nearest city. They knew of each other, but they lived independently. The first day when Lester flagged down Pete to ask for tarps was the beginning of what became a true Christian community: they now worked, prayed, ate, and played together. If there was a conflict they worked with each other to resolve it. They made their own rules and elected Lester as their leader. They did not allow smoking, swearing, or drinking. They were in good shape; but by the end of that summer *Truck of Love* had hit a low spot in our bank account.

Summer was always a slow donation time because, by my theory, people were on vacation and not thinking about charitable giving. For several months, I had advised Pete he needed to slow his spending. I saw we had way more money going out than we had coming in, but Pete believed that the money would come when we needed it.

Money was probably the biggest source of disagreement between us. Pete was the spender and I was the book keeper. I began to donate his paycheck of $500 each month back to *Truck of Love*. After four months of no paycheck he finally got the message that there was no more money. He was ready to go into our small savings to shore up the group. I agreed, but only if he stopped funding all the extras. Pete went to the community and explained that we could no longer help with the extras: fruits and vegetables, clothes washing, bike parts, payment for picking up garbage, etc. All we could do was help with the beans and the rice.

Pete came home each day and rushed to the empty mailbox. He anguished as he saw the increased difficulties encountered because of the lack of such simple things as clean clothes, fruit, meat, or working bicycles.

His heart was heavy, but he and the community in the woods did their best to make it work. One of the tragic side effects of the new austerity program directly affected an innocent little six year old boy named Jasper. He and his eighteen year old mother, Laura, had arrived in the community about a year and a half before. She'd been a prostitute and was brutalized by men since she was 11 years old. When Lester heard her story, he knew that the community would be a good, loving, and healing place for her to be. When she witnessed the regular Friday prayer services she knew she could trust the people. She began her new life and through the "profit-sharing" set-up the group had formed; she was able to receive $18 a week to keep her off the streets and able to care for Jasper. In return for the $18 she and Jasper picked up trash along the road.

Jasper was a simple child, a handsome boy with beautiful flowing blond hair; he stood about three feet tall. At six years old he was not potty trained. He was mostly wandering the encampment in a shirt and no pants. Mentally he was a little slow. He had followed River and Edgar everywhere before River died.

It was Jasper's birthday one Friday and Pete got a donated cake and gave it to him. Jasper asked what it was; he'd never had a birthday cake. He asked if it was all for him and Pete explained that it was his, but he could share it with everyone.

He said, "That's good, because it's too big for me."

The following Monday, when Pete saw Jasper he was looking more forlorn than usual. It seems that because *Truck of Love* could not buy the plastic bags and pay the people for picking up the garbage, Laura went back to the streets to earn some money. She left the encampment on Saturday and told one of the ladies to make sure they looked after Jasper. They hadn't seen her since.

Pete went to the sheriff's office to file a missing person's report and the officer told him there wasn't much chance they would find her. He got the underlying message that they wouldn't even try to look.

The ripple effects of such a simple thing as $18 a week changed the course of life for Jasper and the whole community. Because we could not buy $60 worth of bags and could not pay them $150 for the 150 bags of trash they collected each week, Jasper became a motherless child.

By Tuesday of that week, when Laura had still not returned, Pete and Lester and the community members who were caring for Jasper met to discuss his future. Because Jasper was slow he needed lots of attention. Each person in the group had their jobs that had to be done and no one felt they could spend their full time keeping Jasper safe. It was decided that Pete would take him to the local police who had a system set up for just such children.

Jasper was packed into the truck and off he went kicking and screaming to his new life. We were grateful that he was so young and innocent and his memory of living in the woods would fade. We prayed he would have a better life.

Pete and Lester had a lingering dread of Laura returning to camp and discovering what they had done with Jasper; he was her whole life.

A couple of weeks later Pete, once again, went to the police in search of Laura. This time he was told that a body had been found on the side of the freeway about fifty miles south. Unfortunately the body had been burned beyond recognition. The police asked if she had any distinguishing marks on her body. Pete mentioned a tattoo between her toes. It was Laura.

Life got a lot harder. The group prayed together each week. They looked for work in the local town, but when they did not have clean clothes and they could be smelled coming from down the street, it was impossible to get hired. There was one ray of hope: the brickyard, which had been temporarily closed, was about to open again. That would provide jobs for about seven people who would receive nine and a half cents for each brick that they scraped clean of mortar. Previously they had gotten ten cents per brick, but the owner felt he wasn't making enough profit.

The community talked each week and agreed to keep struggling together. There was a universal feeling that this community was the best thing any of them had encountered in their lives. They were a group of people who accepted and appreciated each other for who they are as children of God. These were some of the most courageous, hardworking people Pete had ever met. They found joy in the smallest things like the pan of macaroni and cheese that was given to us by a lovely woman who lived in a local retirement community. This pan meant for eight people was cut into one inch cubes and passed around to the forty three people who enjoyed it with gusto. This was a community that embraced the Word in both body and spirit.

We were at a real crisis point in our ministry because we needed to spread the word that we were desperate for donations, but we could not afford to put out a newsletter. We used our Facebook page and announced our dilemma. Almost instantly our faithful donors began to respond. By the time we did write the newsletter, we had received over $50,000 in donations.

This woodland group was an inspiration to us. They were people who had so little, but they celebrated each day. They became a community that experienced the healing presence of God in their lives and as this became a reality in each person fundamental changes were slowly taking place.

Pete talked to me about Verna. She had taken Edgar under her wing and had begun his education. During the previous year and a half she taught Edgar how to read and write to about sixth grade level. She nursed River in the days before he died of the brain tumor. She was a rock in the community – someone they all counted on.

Pete didn't know much about Verna. She kept a pretty low profile. Her talents were revealed very gradually as she helped each person. She and Scout became a couple and seemed to enjoy being together. One day during this time she and Pete were talking and she commented to him that she would never want anyone from outside the community to see the way they all lived.

A few days later she approached him and asked Pete to take her to the bus station. She said, "I've saved some money and I want to visit my parents in Iowa."

Pete drove her to Charlotte and dropped her off at the bus station and told her, "Let me know when you're coming back."

At the next Friday prayer service after Pete read from Corinthians about us being many parts, but all one body, Lester stood up and said, "Wait, I have a note from Verna that she wanted me to read to everyone. Reverend Pete, will you read it? Verna's not coming back."

There was an audible gasp from the whole group. Pete immediately looked for Scout, who had disappeared. Silence settled in as he read the note that explained that she had been in touch with her parents who wanted her to return home. The situation that had caused her to leave them was resolved. She was thankful for all that the community had done for her in restoring her faith in people and helping her move on.

Clearly, we were very sad to see Verna leave, but once again we were so very thankful for the healing presence of this group. Verna was given the support and space to forgive herself and those who had hurt her. She was ready to resume her life.

Scout was alone again. He was still the lookout for the group and the keeper of the group phone, but Pete noticed he went off by himself a lot more. He was at the Friday morning prayer services and helped out wherever extra hands were needed, but he didn't walk with the same spring in his step. He thought he had found a partner for life. He was instrumental in Verna's transformation, but he was left behind.

Edgar was shattered. Verna was his lifeline into learning, but he would not be stopped. He continued to read everything that came into his line of sight.

Change was in the wind. It was also a leaving time for Jack. Pete had met him a couple of years before on the side of the road. Pete took him to meet Lester, the community leader, and Jack became part of the group. As time went by Jack's gifts emerged. He could fix anything. He became the bike fixer and would also collect small appliances and fix them to resell at flea markets.

He never talked about his previous life until about a month before when Pete approached him and engaged him in a discussion.

Jack told Pete that he was the youngest of eight children and was always forgotten. He didn't think his family would miss him and so one day he had simply walked away.

Jack walked until he ended up on the side of the road where Pete found him.

Pete encouraged him to write a postcard to his family to see if he could make some contact. The postcard was returned to the address that we had written on it, stamped "Address Unknown." Jack withdrew into his hole where he continued to work on the bikes and small appliances.

A couple of weeks passed and then one week in the fall, Jack approached Pete and said, "You know what I'd like for Christmas?"

Pete asked, "What?"

Jack said, "I'd really like to take a ride to North Carolina to see if my family is really gone from our farm."

Pete gave Ogi, a friend of the group who had an old truck, the money for gas and he and Jack left early on a Monday morning. Late that same morning Pete got a phone call from

Ogi, "Jack's family was home. They can't stop hugging and kissing him."

Jack got on the phone to say he would not be returning with Ogi; he was back home. Pete asked him what ought to be done with all his tools and parts. He replied, "I don't care. I've got everything I need."

During those few years we saw many people who lived with the woodland community for a short time. They were embraced by the group, prayed with the group, worked with the group, and learned new survival skills. They contemplated old resentments and learned to forgive others and themselves. They often experienced the family they never had, or thought they never had. They used the time to heal old wounds and build new trust in themselves and people around them. When they did all the growing they could with this community, they spread their wings and flew. Many flew out on their own and some, like Jack and Verna, returned to their homes and waiting families.

That spring the families were told they were going to have trouble getting their children registered for school, because eight children from different families could not use the same address. They had all been using Ogi's address where he lived in his dilapidated trailer. During the summer months discussions began to happen. Pete met with one family after another to clarify their situations: where they had come from, what kind of work they had done, and what the prospects

One by one families went home

might be if they could return to their homes. Each month one family would call someone from their old home area, either family or friends. One by one connections were made, old resentments were forgiven and the families were sent back to the promise of jobs and places to live. The community was down to about twenty individual adults and Edgar.

Pete and I were very concerned about what was going to happen to Edgar. He was too happy living with this community in the woods. He was still a child. He had a whole life ahead of him. He was smart and learned quickly.

We asked everyone we knew about the possibilities for a young boy who had no knowledge of his family name or place of birth, who had no documentation. No one had any suggestions. We did not want to see him live his whole life stealing out of dumpsters and living in the shadows of society.

We asked everyone we knew to pray.

Finally, about a year after Verna had left, the community phone rang. Scout answered and with a blank expression said, "Edgar, it's Verna, she wants talk to you."

Verna asked Edgar if he wanted to come live with her in Iowa. Her parents had an empty bedroom in their house. She was studying for the state exam to renew her status as a teacher's aide. Edgar could go to school and live with her parents who were ready to welcome him.

Pete and Lester began to prepare for Edgar's trip. He needed new (used) clothes, new underwear and socks, a first-ever new pair of shoes, some snack foods, a backpack to carry everything, and a cell phone so he could communicate with Verna while he was traveling.

Pete talked to him, "I'm going to give you some travel money. You have to keep it in different places: your shoe, your backpack, or your pocket. You never take out all the money in front of people. Just keep enough in your pocket to spend on food and go into the bathroom when you need to transfer more into your pocket. Don't talk to strangers. If you have questions go to the Greyhound employees and ask them for help."

On a Monday morning Pete put Edgar on the bus in Charlotte, North Carolina.

Each day I asked Pete if he or the group had heard anything. We estimated Edgar would arrive by Thursday morning. Thursday came and went with no word. Lester dialed Verna's number with no response. We started to get worried. Finally on Friday the call came through. He had arrived on Wednesday night, and they were so happy and excited they had not thought to call.

The community in the woods became quieter without children. The remaining nineteen adults went about their daily chores. Pete still met with each person to see what the possibilities were for them to find some new start in life.

Two of the women, the cook and a woman who had been working in a motel, found better employment in the motel that included a room. They moved out.

We prayed for each person to find some way out of the woods. One by one we bought bus tickets, clean clothes, and travel food.

By July of 2016 there were only four people left in the woodland community. They kept up their routine of collecting recyclables and trash and redeeming these for cash. Then one day, Cinnamon was in town and encountered her brother. Previously we'd thought she had no family.

This brother was very happy to see her and told her that her parents had been trying to find her for several years. They were ready to welcome her back. It no longer mattered to them that she was gay. The next day she was gone, returning to her family.

Lester, Lilly, and Scout were the last three left. The Friday after Cinnamon's departure, they had the regular prayer service and Lester talked about how hard it is to say goodbye to friends. Pete left for home telling them he would see them on Monday with the money he owed them for the week's work.

When Pete pulled up to the spot in the woods on Monday, there was a note that simply said "We moved."

Pete attempted to call the community phone. There was no answer. He went by Ogi's trailer, but Ogi was not home nor did he answer his phone.

Pete finally received a call on Tuesday. Scout wanted to meet at Ogi's to get the money. Wednesday morning Pete went off to the meeting. After handing over the $200 he owed them, Lester said, "We'll be on our way."

Pete hugged Lilly, shook hands with Lester and Ogi, and watched Scout walk off into the woods. With a heavy heart he got into his truck and drove away.

Pete wandered around for a few days, trying to connect with other local people he had been helping, but he had time on his hands. He was no longer commuting 45 minutes each way to visit the community in the woods.

Then phone calls began to come to *Truck of Love* from people who needed food, shelter, clothing, car repairs, and any number of necessities. The work of *Truck of Love* continues.

Epilogue

Pete and I spend a lot of time these days talking about the evolution of *Truck of Love*. I recently read a wonderful article by Joan Chittister from the "Huffington Post". I copied this quote and include it here with her permission: "Clearly, the purpose of wealth is not security. The purpose of wealth is reckless generosity, the kind that sings of the lavish love of God, the kind that rekindles hope on dark days, the kind that reminds us that God is with us always."

I do not claim to have continually believed this to be true, but today I can say that I do understand this wisdom.

When I was a very young woman I spent extensive time dreaming about my future life. It was what gave me hope. My childhood was not very happy and my imagination, along with lots of prayer, helped me survive some of the dark days.

I dreamed of a wonderful husband who would love me and provide me with a modest house that had flowers all around it and a white picket fence separating the yard from anyone who might spoil my idyllic scene. This husband was going to be happy and kind. I would cook his meals, wash his clothes, and bear his children. He would come home from work each night and I would give him his slippers and pipe and make sure he rested before I set his dinner on the table.

Then I met Pete who challenged me from the beginning of our relationship to make decisions and speak my mind, who rarely waited for me to do anything for him and was always thinking of my best interests.

Looking back I can see that God has an intense sense of humor. When we talk about our relationship and where it has led us we marvel at the directions our lives have traveled together. It has been a grace-filled spirit-driven life that we could never have imagined let alone dreamed. A wonderful friend once told us that together we made one whole person: our gifts complimented each other so beautifully.

We were two young inexperienced kids who fell in love. In spite of friends and family who objected to our relationship, we somehow knew this was where we were supposed to be. Pete's Baptist grandmother called me the "older woman" because I am a full two years older than he is. To make matters worse, I was Catholic. The Catholic part of my family didn't approve of his Baptist background. When it was time for us to get married, my Methodist father gave me $500 and left the country to visit my brother who had moved to England. He was not going to give his precious daughter away to any other man, especially a musician.

Somehow we knew that we were meant to be together. We both had a heart for the downtrodden in our society. We also shared a vision of our own upward mobility and a place that would be a safe and peaceful home. That, after all, was the American dream.

But then our lives took that terrible turn when our friend Julie was killed. We looked with new eyes. Suddenly what had been important didn't matter anymore.

The early dissention we felt from family continued. His grandmothers disapproved when I was pregnant with our third child in the first three years of our marriage. Some family members thought we were crazy when we started loading trucks full of food and other peoples' used clothing and driving these trucks to Arizona, though they would come to help us load the trucks. Some didn't believe anyone should be helping the poor who were obviously lazy and got too much from the government.

As our lives became more involved with *Truck of Love* we talked a lot about voluntary poverty. Saint Francis of Assisi became our hero and our theme song was *Lady Poverty,* the first lines of which are "Lady Poverty, love me tonight. Dress me in sackcloth, where once I wore white."

I stopped wearing the rings Pete had chosen for our engagement and wedding and we replaced them with simple silver bands made by Mexican and Native American artists. To us the significance was one of solidarity with the work we were doing and the people we were serving.

We could never have dreamed of the joy and contentment that would come from letting go of the expectations of our generation. We have witnessed peers who have worked all their lives for bigger houses and faster cars only to find they bring no lasting joy. Our security is in God who has provided everything we need.

It has been a wonderful life in which we have met and gotten to know some amazing, wonderful, generous, and talented people who come from varied backgrounds and live in all sorts of places. We look forward to many more years of "...reckless generosity, the kind that sings of the lavish love of God."

Reflections from Friends of Truck of Love

I asked for and received many reflections from participants of *Truck of Love* trips, some who drove to places with us and others who lived in those places. I include them here as a tribute to the wonderful relationships we have built. I tried, as much as possible, to copy them verbatim from what was sent to me. Pete and I are blessed by each of you who have participated in this work we call *Truck of Love.*

Rob was a participant on the first Tijuana trip and many subsequent Tijuana and Arizona trips. He has since married our only daughter and become our favorite son-in-law.

I have lots of memories...: Coming across the border back into the US and pushing the van to save gas [because it could take an hour or more sitting in the hot afternoon traffic to go a few hundred feet]

Tom and Keith had left me in charge of music for the first trip as I had a boom box we were going to bring. In the weeks leading up to the trip, I put together mixed tapes of alternate eighties music, stuff we listened to at youth group, and Bob Marley. I still think of that trip when I hear "People Get Ready."

The shock of seeing people living in the dump for the first time, and my asthma acting up from the awful air after just a couple of hours of standing around handing out food

That first trip was life changing in a number of ways.

Laura was a teenager living with her family in Tenoch-titlan when we met. She is now a legal resident of the United States and lives with her husband and three sons in South Carolina. She is learning how to speak and write English.

In the beginning I felt weird, because I was with someone completely different from us, but time passed by and you were in our community and we were coexisting with you all. I guess my mind started to change, because you taught us that in this world [there are] people really really in need of a lot of things. You taught us that we are blessed a lot, because however we were living our parents did the best they could to protect us from cold and rain. We were warm and we had a lot of food for ourselves.

You taught us that it is good to share with homeless people. To help when we can do it. I do remember one time that we went to the jail, I was really really scared by entering there, thinking OH MY GOD, what if these people kill us here, what if the police don't let me go out. I was really scared, but I learned that there are people in jail who have committed no crime at all, but I learned too, that we have to behave because I don't want to be there at all. I saw how the police fed them. I didn't like it at all, but also I saw that the prisoners had the opportunity to start all over again, they were working inside of the jail, they were learning a lot of stuff.

I really had a good and extraordinary experience with you all. I always have a good memory of you. When we were singing with you with Pete playing the guitar. DE COLORES song was my favorite. And YESTERDAY Song, I'm not sure if that is the name of the song or not, but the song talks about yesterday.

It was funny trying to communicate with you, because we did not know much English and you didn't know much Spanish. I do remember one time that my mother told me that she was really embarrassed because you started talking with my mom in English about what happened to you. You were saying something about a tire blowing out, and my mom thought that you were asking about what she had to eat so she was telling you that she was cooking pozole for you all to eat when you arrive home and both of you were talking for long time. Both of you thought that each other understood what were you talking about.

I do remember in the beginning of your visits to la colonia. There were some volunteer dentists that you brought - or I do not know how they got there, but they were Americans they did not speak Spanish, so my mom sent me over there for something. I do not remember why I was there - not sure if she sent me so they could check my teeth or sent me with water and food for them. But they did check my teeth and I had some cavities, a big one on my front tooth. So they fixed almost all my teeth. But they broke the front one when they were fixing it so I had a window in the front of my teeth. Then they fixed that and put something on it so my teeth looked normal like nothing happened. [Truck of Love never did bring dentists to the colonia, but Pete had transported some donated dental chairs and equipment to a friend setting up a clinic in the colonia. There were several American groups that would come to the area to do needed dental work.]

Paul is a coach in Southern California. He is the science teacher who assisted Pete with the "bus from Hell."

I remember my first trip at Christmas as a 27 year old teacher. The warning that this could be a life-changing experience did gratefully come true. When I returned back to St. Francis, I remember taking Sue aside to let her know of my return shock into the Precious Present/God Consciousness/Awareness.

Mike is now a high school history teacher in Los Altos, California

The first trip to Tijuana with Truck of Love was amazing for a number of reasons. I had wanted to go with Pete and Sue in that great big Ford Econoline van ever since I'd met Pete at a confirmation retreat in 1986 – he was an enormous ball of charisma, music, and warmth, and she was a quiet, smiling listening heart and soul – they both were a tonic for a skinny, shy, overly spiritual kid like I was at the time. My parents had been writing checks to Truck of Love for as long as I could remember – they believed in the work Pete and Sue were doing – but I came home from that retreat having put the cause and the people responsible for it together. I was hooked on the idea of going to Mexico, working with the people in the dump, and discovering what it meant to be truly poor in the Western Hemisphere.

Unfortunately for me, my parents, rightly or wrongly, sensed that I wasn't ready. For one thing, I was only 14 in 1986, and I had never been exposed to the kind of poverty that TOL was immersing itself in; they feared that I'd be overwhelmed and not a little disturbed by the situation in Mexico. For another, there was always that extra summer school class to take (my father was very concerned about me getting accepted to a quality college), and I clearly couldn't take a 6-week class and to go Mexico for a week at the same time. And of course, I didn't speak a word of Spanish yet.

It took three years of prayers, frustration, and failed math classes to get to the point where my parents decided they couldn't keep the experience from me anymore. By that time, I had taken three years of Spanish at school, and I had a better idea of what the Tijuana experience would be about after several long conversations with friends who had made the trip. It was going to be a lot of hard manual labor, sleeping on a hard concrete floor, and exposure to the life of the poorest of the poor – not a time of idealistic contemplation or abstract thinking about poverty. I still wasn't 100% clear what life would be like on the ground in Tijuana, but I was still sold on the idea of going. So, off I went on an early morning in the summer of 1989, with Martin, his girlfriend (and later wife) Lisa, Kris, and several other friends and acquaintances.

The first mind-blowing experience I remember in Tijuana on that first trip was visiting Casa de Cuna with Martin, Greg, Kate, and the rest of the group. Once we set foot inside this orphanage, which was loaded with very small children, none of whom spoke English or Spanish, I was totally overcome by shyness. I had no way to prepare for the total inability to communicate, and had no concept of how to minister to kids that age. So as the others swept up these little kids to play with them or carry them around the room, I sat on the floor staring at the entire scene, feeling scared and completely useless, and wondering what I was doing in that place at that time.

Kate, whom I had only known for a few days, sensed my unease and approached me, leading a boy who couldn't have been *more than 2 years old. He had the biggest brown eyes I had ever seen and was looking at me in curiosity and wariness.*

I locked eyes with Kate. "I can't do this —"

"You can do it," she said gently.

The boy sat in front of me. I looked at him, wondering what to do, what to say, how to pass the time. I smiled at him as best I could. He smiled back. Then, after an interminable moment, he took me by the hand and led me to a pile of blocks in the corner. He started stacking them up. I began helping him and also began building my own clumsy structure next to his.

I think I must have stayed next to that boy for the better part of 2 hours, building little houses and laughing with him when our structures fell down. We ended up making little sound effects when the towers would crash to the floor and laughing until we had tears in our eyes.

I left that day both proud of having overcome a completely unexpected piece of culture shock and humbled by what was, as Pete calls it, a "kingdom moment." It wouldn't be the last.

"...and a little child shall lead them..." (Isaiah 11:6)

Maybe the most long-lasting aspect of that first trip to Mexico was a discovery I made about myself and a skill I had that would last a lifetime. Before that trip, I had taken Spanish classes in high school, and had done well in them, so I had a good theoretical knowledge of the language. But in Los Altos in the late 1980s, there weren't that many Spanish speakers who would be forgiving enough of your pidgin language skills to converse with you without giving up.

From almost the first moment we were there, though, I found that I was not only able to understand what the people we worked and lived with were saying, but that I could actually speak to them and be mostly understood. I can remember having several long conversations with people who apparently spoke no English whatsoever, and feeling as if I had known them for several years. By the end of that first week, the people in Tenochtitlan had begun calling me the name some TOL veterans still know me as — Miguelito. I even became something of an interpreter for the rest of the group, too, even though there were a lot of bilingual people with us already.

When I got home, I looked my mother in the eye and told her I had discovered something very important in my trip to Tijuana.

My mom looked at me apprehensively, as if I were about to tell her that I had changed my religion, wanted to move to Mexico permanently, or gotten married to one of the girls I had met on the trip. Instead, I smiled and said proudly, "I can really speak Spanish!"

That trip gave me a confidence with Spanish that I had never had in any other academic subject, not even history. I ended up taking advanced placement Spanish and choosing it as my minor in college, and even taught it early on in my professional career. I've walked a lot of miles since that trip, but that is one skill that Truck of Love opened the door for that has changed and enriched my life immensely. What a blessing!

Cathy met us through a mutual friend and went with us to both Tijuana and PisinMo'o for many years. She has been the one constant at camp since 1990. When she is not at camp she is a swallowing therapist and lives in Berkeley, California.

Just now as I was typing the memory came into my head about our first outdoor shower [in PisinMo'o] (when the district chair failed to unlock the bathrooms!). You may recall it was a hose thrown across the roof of the cafeteria! Fun times! I think that's when I started taking p.m. showers (no choice under the circumstances, right?) and to this day I still do (here at home, too).

I have a vivid memory of the year that Billy Antone came to camp. Up until then all our "guests" at camp were from Nation programs (e.g., dental, diabetes, all things the kids got in school during the year). We used to gather everyone under the wa:to [ramada] in the mornings. I remember standing in the center [of all the kids] jumping up and down, yelling, ringing the bell, whatever I could do to try to get some quiet, order, and attention, mostly to no avail. The first day that Billy was there he just stood in the center of the large circle of children and started to speak so very quietly in O'odham. BAM! You could hear a pin drop! Total silence and rapt attention. That was a pivotal moment in my experience and showed me that the most important thing to think about was promoting the language and culture (O'odham him-

*dag). That's what the children needed most and, even if they did-
n't realize it, wanted.*

*I recall in the early days having to drive the vans ourselves
and getting stopped at the washes. :(It was lovely, though, having a "guide" with me, being able to have a real conversation for
a change (having the time...in those days) and being shown other
parts of the rez.*

*Also the blessing and honor of being allowed to visit I'itoy's
cave, pick the bahi daj/saguaro fruit, visit the children's shrine.
Sitting behind the cafeteria singing with Pete and the children,
watching the sunset every evening.*

*Then, of course, there was my first (devastating!!!) experience
with a group of children out there where it took over 20 minutes
to go around the circle and get everyone's name! It's amazing I
ever returned!"*

Cricket is the mother of two of our participants.

*The first time our oldest daughter went to help out at the
summer camp for the Tohono O'odham Indian children, it had a
life changing impact on her. I still remember picking her up at
the airport after her 3 to 4 weeks away from home and the first
words out of her mouth were: "I'm not the same person I was before." As the days and weeks unfolded after this, I saw how true
her words were.*

*She spoke about how simply the Indians lived on the reserva-
tion. They didn't have all the things---and things to do---that we
took for granted. She wanted to continue living that way at
home. So to begin with, she stopped sleeping in her bed, in her
very nice bedroom. She set up a simple camping cot on the small
screened in porch we had. She stopped going out with her friends
when they went to the mall for things to buy. She found more important things to do with her time. When school was starting up
again in the fall she would not buy new clothes if she needed
something. She would only let me take her to thrift stores to find
what she could use.*

*I asked her why she was so adamant about these changes in
her way of living and she simply said, "I don't ever want to lose
what I gained on the reservation. They have something I never*

understood before." Although she also saw sadness and despair in the lives of some people there, she knew she was not on the reservation just to help them. They had helped her to see life in a new way.

Stark simplicity, doing without, can open our eyes to many things. It does not have to deprive us of living well. With the right understanding, it can add a wealth of richness to our lives and to the world around us.

Nika currently lives in Tarifa, Spain with her family. She owns and operates an English school.

I began my Truck of Love experience with poison ivy, which I had acquired in Georgia in the hot summer month before leaving for California to join Pete and Sue Fullerton. Unsure of what to expect, I joined a group of teenagers in a van and we began our trip to the Tohono O'odham Indian Reservation in Arizona.

Upon arrival, I was greeted by the smell of desert and mesquite trees. I saw large, expectant, hiding eyes in the faces of the children and young adults that gathered around the van. I was immediately aware that my open, confident smile was the luxurious result of years of comfort, of immediate gratification each time I felt hungry or in want of a hug. Of countless social situations in which I understood I was a privileged white American, who would graduate from high school, go to college, and have employment offered to me.

As I got to know some of the young people, one stood out to me. He was just a boy, but he looked angry around the edges, but in a way that was way past caring anymore. He made little eye contact, and may have been influenced by substances. In a way I couldn't define, I felt he was walking a line somewhere inside him, travelling a path illustrated to him by the life he was a spectator to, in which theft and violence were the grammar, the study, the homework.

One day, I sat, accompanied by this boy, on a bench in what little shade we could find, stuffy in the hot blanket of desert air around us. A golden puppy wandered up to where we were sitting, bringing its babyish qualities of soft fur and tumbled ears to us. My young friend grabbed a marker from his jeans' pocket and drew a gang symbol on its forehead, large, black, and garish. Had any baby been born there that hadn't been punished in the same way? Whether visible or implied, the reservation had been labeled, and this boy simply brought the truth to the surface. Innocence couldn't survive well there, nor could trust. Fear could. If we, the white, middle-class Americans, wanted to, we could trace the undercurrents of anger through the gang deaths of cousins, connect-the-dots to the alcoholism, to the nights vulnerable, restless youths began trying drugs and relaxed into its' escape, and continue going further back, to when their nomadic, peaceful existence was robbed them, when boundaries were established, and a lifestyle of harmony with the natural landscape shifted to become a cage imposed by a far-away government. I shouldn't have been shocked, therefore, that the youths of my age cared so little for puppies and horses, who milled around them with visible hunger and jutting bones. We went to visit the 'lake' in the area. It was a drought year. I saw what seemed dozens of dead horses strewn around the lake 'shores'. We viewed it from a high mountain, with the blue sky stretching baby clouds across our view. I felt I was seeing the history of the Native Americans below me. Searching for the last opportunity for hope, yet abandoned by a nation, without water, without resources, without sympathy.

The humorless rations awarded the Tohono O´odham after the political and geographical shifts ("We didn't cross the border, the border crossed us,") [The Tohono O'odham land stretches from the reservation in southern Arizona across the border into Mexico.] enforced a vicious cycle in which poverty, low levels of education, and therefore low job prospects, caused desperation, abandonment, anger, and revenge. These sharp feelings were abstract concepts to me, yet were their daily bread, and alcohol and drugs were their antidotes.

One cooler morning we gathered in the church. Pete sang "Day By Day." I sang a song, "I will Carry You," to some of the kids. The song says, "I will carry you when your strength runs dry, when you lose your will to try." My young friend asked me to sing it again. I did. He was kind to ask me to sing it again. I appreciated that he didn't pretend to smile, but he listened, and listened again.

I loved the people that surrounded me there. I loved the directors who sacrificed their summers. I loved the teens who felt they could still smile. I loved the teens who accepted me, despite the obvious reasons for hating me. And I loved the teens who didn't accept me.

That summer we peeled many, many potatoes. We cleaned out the outdoor bathrooms. We slept under a sky so vast and so full of stars they had to contain the spirits of many Tohono generations. We played basketball in the heat waves, and watched the monsoon rain clouds approach, release lightning, and weep until cleansed of feeling.

When I returned the second summer, I went to greet "friends" from the previous year… One chose to ignore my greeting… I gently touched his hand for a split second, hoping he would turn and acknowledge me. He angrily rubbed his hand where I had touched it, and spit on the ground.

I met many Tohono people who could still smile, but who told me stories that upset me. Two brothers, who tried every day to remember the tribal traditions and instill the ancient truths in the education of the young.

I was greatly changed by my experience there, and I hoped that by being there I was helping, or atoning for my ancestors' sins to them. This hope felt gratifying in some way, and allowed me to feel good about myself. One night under the stars I listened to one girl's anger and resentment… I offered phrase after hopeful phrase, feeling I had some role to play; the one who reaches out to pull someone out of the dark. She scolded me, scoffed at my hope, and told me the truth. She wouldn't let me feel better—it wasn't right. I couldn't swoop in like an angel of glory and leave feeling I'd done something good. I needed to visit hell, and acknowledge it, recognize it… but not leave thinking I'd helped. I shouldn't be afforded that… after all, it wasn't about me. The sobs that shook me after her angry speech were the strongest I've ever felt. I knew she was right. I was overwhelmed by the helplessness of her world. She knew who had been abused since they were 5, who had been killed, who had committed suicide, who had succumbed to alcoholism.

I think she may have apologized the next day. I don't remember that part well, because it was only a formality. Her scolding had been true, her generosity only a sign that she wanted to help me, when I'd come to help her.

Despite these darker accounts, I witnessed generosity and strength on the Res. I only went for two summers, before I needed to use the summer to work, but I know that the camp continued until the stronger, healed Tohono elders could take over, carrying what had always been their torch. From what I know, their story is of victory, of finding the way through the Tohono maze and reaching the truth, and I continue to hope and pray that education, including their tribal histories, is reversing the cycles I witnessed there.

The Truck of Love made a huge difference in the lives of the Tohono O'odham, but that is their story to tell. I didn't. However, I am deeply and profoundly grateful to both the Tohono O'odham and to the Truck of Love for making a difference in mine. When I returned, I was a different person. At 18 and entering college, I chose to only own a few pairs of jeans and a few only-white t-shirts. No makeup. The basic necessities. Anything more seemed a slap-in-the-face to the reality that so many others in the world live. I questioned whether I needed simple luxuries like soap, home decorations, a pillow... I saw the world in the clearest way I ever have... as though my eyes had finally opened to the excess that surrounded me. Supermarkets shocked me. I decided to stop looking in mirrors and focus my time on my inner spirit, my smile to others, and to develop a more acute awareness of the kindness and suffering of any person I came into contact with... For this and more, I can thank the Tohono O'odham, to whom I travelled, so they could save me.

Geneva is a wife and mother living in Peach Tree City, Georgia.

The summer I spent traveling down to the Indian reservation is one that is set apart from any other summer of my life.

I remember the extreme heat in the back of the van, the smiles of my fellow camp workers, and the anticipation of moments of service and love.

Though the Indians spoke our language, they were a people of quietness. I remember one particular day that I tried to understand what Jeffery was thinking, what he was feeling. He told me it was a cloudy day... He said he had no troubles on cloudy days.

Other times he simply put his headphones on me to tell me what he was feeling. I would listen to the sobering sounds and ... Feel connection.... Feel hope for him.

I led a music track for some of the smaller kids. I taught them songs but mostly I looked into their eager faces and felt humbled by their admiration.

I sat between Pete and Nika in the sweat lodge. I've never wanted to be so silent. The silence is what I needed to take from this people. The realization that, with a God as big as He is, that if I could just be smaller and quieter among so much beauty, I could touch Him.

The sunset and stars were so magnificent I would ache inside.

Thank you for the opportunity to learn through you guys what it means to love.

Hedy is currently wife, mother, and an E Learning developer in Lake Tahoe, California.

Truck of Love was the first family I ever felt I really belonged to . . . it was coming home to a group of people who gathered out of a sense of caring for other people and for each other; out of love. Growing up in suburbia, I always had everything I needed, and usually had access to anything I wanted. What I lacked and ached for was a sense of community, a sense of purpose, one that TOL had in abundance. It was amazing, like nothing I could ever put into words. I remember my brother asking smugly what I had learned in my time away, and all I could do was shake my head sadly and say "just . . . about myself, and who I am," because there was no way to communicate it. What I knew in my heart, but could not describe with my teenage words, was that it was more wonderful and more powerful than anything I had ever known before.

The things that TOL do are relatively simple, but the meaning behind it all is a profound sense of love of others and love of each other. The van rides, meals together, camaraderie and team work, and simple time together singing songs, writing poetry and watching sunsets, all wove together to create a beautiful tapestry of family. Most aptly put, it was like coming home.

So many times over the last couple of decades, I have sought to recapture the beauty of that homecoming experience, and that glow of excitement, to bring it to bear on "real life." In a sense it is so powerful because it is set apart from everyday life, but it is also the foundation of how I understand what is good and holy in our world and in my life.

My second summer at the TOL camp in PisinMo'o, I worked in the craft room, where counselors would bring rotating groups of campers throughout the day. It was a brand new experience for me: being in charge of planning, coordinating, and teaching activities to a whole camp of kids. While it was a lot of fun, it was also a bigger project than I had ever taken on before; so while the satisfaction of the kids' fun and laughter were great, the project management was . . . stressful. Several days into camp, we had already discovered that we had forgotten to bring our main stock of paper, which was of course key to most of the activities I was planning. Some construction paper arrived in the mail from a friend back home that same day without any prompting, which was amazing . . . but a different story. It was about 130 degrees in the craft room that day, and I was totally stressed out that there was a roomful of fidgety seven year olds staring expectantly at me, and somehow my project was off-track, or had changed, and was nowhere near ready to go. I could feel my frustration rising. In a fog of my usual impatience with myself and the day, I started to rush into handing out parts of the project, as a counselor looked on, wearing a look that said she was about to ask how they could help. I'm sure the answer would have been an exasperated one. Suddenly, two people appeared in the doorway that changed the rest of the class and the day. Two O'odham camp counselors, my friends from the previous year at camp, walked in casually and understood the situation without words. They immediately stepped into the project, taking over handing out paper and scissors, helping me make teaching decisions I didn't even know I hadn't made yet. It was the coolest experience. At first, I didn't even recognize one of them, but I knew as soon as they started working with me that they just understood my frustration and how to make everything better. Camp and the friends I made there . . . are just magical like that.

Tim has become a dentist. He was the lone male present the day Pete fell off Window Rock.

The first few summers spent on the Reservation were the most magical of my life. It felt like we were so far removed from home and there was little resemblance to where I grew up. Summers in PisinMo'o are best described as extreme. Extreme heat, extreme emotions, extreme fun. From the time we arrived at the village until the time we left was full of work. It takes a lot of people moving a lot of things to make a summer camp happen in the middle of the Sonoran Desert. There were arts and crafts, sports, games and cultural leadership training. All of this had to be transported by van or created in the evenings when we were not playing with children or doing other chores.

The O'odham were also generous enough to show us pieces of their culture. We would be up at 5 am to pick bahidaj, or travel far into the desert to cut wood for a sweat lodge. There were times I would feel so tired I wanted to take a break and recover. Then I would think about the children and how much it meant to them that we were there. We had three weeks to give them a summer to remember. So much of what we did was focused outwards, trying to provide a safe and fun environment for the children. It required energy, creativity, and most of all, flexibility. In the 10 years I was involved with camp it was held at four different locations, three within the PisinMo'o village. We worked with what we had and what was working at the time.

The best memories and friends in my life come from those summers. Some of my favorite memories are the early mornings and late nights, sunset singing, relaxing weekends in Topawa, hiking Baboquivari and Organ Pipe, sleeping outside at night waiting for a cool breeze, summer rains, water balloon fights, and chores. Chores, chores, and chores.

I was travelling with a family member one summer on my way back to college. We detoured through Tucson to visit Pete in the hospital and drove out to the Reservation. They were shocked by the amount of poverty and asked if the focus of our camp was to help the poor. I never saw it that way. It was never presented as a "poor" place. I asked my friend Evonne about this, and how she felt growing up on the Reservation. Her response was amaz-

252

ing: *"I have always seen it as very rich. Rich in culture and tradition. We are very wealthy."*

I never realized the gift that volunteering with the Truck of Love would end up being to myself. Those trips allowed me to develop a different perspective on life, always looking for ways to give.

Some of my best friends in my life today are people I met on Truck of Love trips. I can go a couple of years without talking to a fellow Truck of Lover and pick up right where we left off. We get it. The call for social justice does not diminish over time and the values I learned while working with the Truck of Love are at my core. My summers with the Truck of Love helped shape the person I have become and have given me direction when, at times, I felt I was lost. I was influenced for my current profession by a fellow Truck of Lover, Mike. He described to me how he chose his path to become a doctor. He was so inspiring. This could be said of most Truck of Lovers. Their energy is contagious and always makes me want to do more to help others.

I asked Tim for his memories of the day Pete fell from the mountain:

My second year of camp had been just as magical as the first. We had completed leadership training and the first week of camp was behind us. Traditionally the weekend between the first and second weeks of camp was spent at a retreat in Topawa, a quiet village south of Sells. It was a way the group could relax and regroup before the final week of camp. We normally spent one of the days hiking Baboqivari Mountain, which always turned out to be a rejuvenating and spiritual experience.

That year we were unable to hike Baboquivari due to recent fires in the area. We found a spot to hike and have a picnic south of Topawa and about 15 miles north of the Mexican border. The group had been hiking about 30 minutes and found a great place to relax and climb around on the rocks.

Pete and I had climbed up to a cave and were talking when the group was called to lunch. I climbed down to a small landing and jumped across a gulley to where the group was meeting. I turned and was watching Pete climb down, his body to the rock and his back facing me. He was letting himself down to the same landing I had just leapt off of when he missed a foothold. He had been planning to transfer his weight to his feet and had already let go with his hands. It left him awkward with his momentum on a roll. He stumbled off balance, was able to turn himself around, and then he fell...

He fell uninhibited about 35 feet and the first thing he touched was a solid rock face. He hit hard with his right foot and continued falling. The impact was so impressive he started somersaulting as he continued downwards, crashing through bushes, off rocks, through branches, all at the mercy of gravity. The only thing I remember, other than the sounds of impact, was Cathy shrieking, "My God he's still falling!" He finally came to a stop facedown at the bottom of the gulley.

People were into action immediately. I jumped over someone as I worked my way down towards Pete. After what felt like minutes we finally got down to him. It did not look good. He could only grunt initially. He was in so much pain but he was alive. His right leg was broken above the ankle at just less than 90 degrees with uneven bone sticking through his sock. His head was lacerated. He later told me he knew he had to sacrifice something if he was going to survive and decided midflight it would be his right leg.

Cathy left immediately to get help. She hiked the 30 minutes back to the cars to drive another 30 minutes to call for help. Seventeen years later she still has coffee stains on the ceiling of her 4 Runner from her frantic drive through the desert towards Sells.

Pete's right leg was bleeding heavily. We used our shirts as compresses to try and slow it down. Pete was in so much pain we did whatever we could to help him be more comfortable. We cut off his belt with the lid of a can. We removed rocks from underneath him that were poking into his body. We sang to him to keep his spirit up. Pete, being Pete, would sing with us between labored breaths. We encouraged him and prayed with him until finally help arrived.

EMT's hiked to where we were and assessed the situation. They secured Pete to a stretcher but would not be able to carry him out due to the difficulty of the hike. They called a helicopter and then another. The helicopters would not be able to land where we were due to high, narrow cliffs on both sides of us and lack of a landing zone. The only option was for the helicopter to hover above the cliffs, lower a basket, and somehow slide Pete into that basket. They tried once and it did not go well. They were unable to hold the basket steady enough due to high winds. It was too dangerous. I remember both helicopters landing near the cars and people discussing what to try next.

As is typical of her during the summer months in the Sonoran Desert, Mother Nature decided for us. She sent two monsoons to converge on our spot. Time was up. Out of options, they would try the "slide" maneuver one more time. If it was unsuccessful we would be exposed to the two mega storms bearing down on our spot.

It worked. They were able to successfully slide Pete off the mountain and secure his stretcher to the basket. I remember everyone hugging and cheering as Pete was lifted above us, dark monsoon clouds above him, towards the other waiting helicopter and finally the hospital. We spent about 6 hours on the mountain that day before they were finally able to get him out.

They told us that we saved Pete's life that day. It would not have taken long for him to bleed to death had we not placed t-shirt after t-shirt over the open break in his leg. I don't know what kind of first aid training any of us had up to that point, I just know that cooler heads prevailed and there was a sense of positive energy that kept us going.

That experience on the mountain changed our lives. Pete had his right foot amputated several months later. I still get nervous when I see someone standing too close to a ledge. More importantly, it showed how strong a group of people working together can be. A common goal, proper intentions and positive energy can create miracles.

We originally met Gloria where she lived in Tenochtitlan, she is currently a wife, mother, and teacher in Southern California.

I am so grateful that Truck of Love came in to my life. I grew up without a father and my mom had to provide for her 5 children. Going out or driving to places was not an option. The Truck of Love took me places, but more than anything was a gateway to bringing out the compassion, love, and kindness that my mom had always inculcated in me. I recall when we used to go to the

255

dump and give the workers food. I vividly recall the dust particles on the air and the dirty faces and hands of the workers, but more than anything I recall their bright smiles and gestures of hope and thankfulness. I loved going there. Going to the beach, parks, and to places I would have never gone.

Truck of Love was the reason I jumped out of bed during summer and fall break. I ran to church every morning to ask if "the Americans" had arrived. This was my first time exposure to different cultures and races. I loved seeing who was coming and how different they were. I wanted to know them as best as I could with the little English I spoke.

I could not wait to go to places, assist at summer school, listen to Pete's songs and guitar playing, and to enjoy the moment. I felt I was my true self in every possible way. I have always been somewhat adventurous, love music, arts and crafts, and teaching!! I did all these things with Truck of Love.

I recall when I did not want to go into the ocean because I was frightened because one of the two times I went with my family I was stuck in a sand hole, did not know how to swim, and panicked when no one came to get me out. Pete noticed I would not go and he picked me up and carried me on his shoulders into the ocean. It meant freedom to me as he walked me into the deepest of the ocean that I had ever been. He was confident and his confidence made me feel strong and secure. I was the happiest kid on earth! The memory still brings me to tears because no one else, not even my father, who I met when I was 10, had done anything like that for me. Fortunately, Pete and Truck of Love brought hope and freedom to my life. It was not only the freedom I felt, but that kids in neighboring communities felt as we arrived bringing not only things, but sometimes advice and counsel to their homes. I will never forget walking into a stranger's house. Pete's caring empathy was easily heard in his kind questioning and tact when responding to parents. I cannot really recall the exact questions, but I do remember how Pete's reassurance of hope and aid coming their way brightened up their faces. Another time we visited a neighboring community, further than La Divina, and we took toys to give away to the children. It was like a chant of giggles, laughs, and amazement as they selected their toys. Some of these kids were barefooted and had worn out clothes, but were highly spirited at all times even before they saw *all the treasures that we brought them. I could not help but enjoy seeing this and talking to them. That joy and the desire to help stays with me to this day.*

I also reminisce about summer school; I enjoyed listening to songs, assisting in English class as well as arts and crafts, and translating as best I could. I felt productive and helpful as I kindly assisted kids doing art work. I recall we did a butterfly out of a paper plate and decorated it with paint. In English class, I learned through songs, by translating, and struggling with English. People still asked me where did I learn and I always say it was because of Truck of Love and summer school. I learned in the most perfect environment anyone can learn: visiting places, with caring leaders, like Sue and Pete, kind members of Truck of Love, and by helping others. It could not be any more perfect and memorable.

I recall I always hoped there would be a space for me in the van, especially when going to Avenida Revolucion to feed the homeless and Marias and their little children. I loved telling them, "See you at 1:00 in the restaurant. There will be free food!" They were so thankful. At 1:00 the restaurant was packed, loud, and full of joyful conversations. We got in contact with people who were daily on the street that felt lonely and needed signs of hope; Truck of Love and all of us gave them that. At the same time, Truck of Love empowered my sense of social justice. Now that I teach I not only focus on what to teach, but on my students and their family needs. I think of my students as if they were my own kids; although they might have their fits I counsel them and give them an opportunity, understanding that I know very little about them and that they need my help regardless of what their lives are like..

I have so many fun memories as well. I recall when I went for the first time to Parque Morelos, the biggest park in Tijuana. We fit as many kids as we could in the van; kind of like cheaper by the dozen!! The kids ran once the van doors opened into the vast open grass area. It was huge and I had not ever seen so much grass and open space. We had brought a big air ball, as big as a person, and we played with it by sending it down a hill and running it over the kids.

Amanda is a wife, mother, and teacher.

When you asked about stories and what all I learned in Arizona, my first response was 'EVERYTHING'.

I can begin with a story. It's one about my first interaction with an O'odham child, and frankly, my first interaction with any child in quite a number of previous years. I'd been in college for a couple of years and my whole world was me, friends, classes, work, studying. Somehow I'd chosen (it was a simple "yes" moment and just felt right) to fly on an airplane for the first time and be picked up by a complete stranger and driven several miles into the desert to this place where some summer camp would happen.. Not just any summer camp though, one that [I had been told] was truly amazing and "made a difference."

This child was only three at most, alone on the volleyball court and looking at me. The first words I heard him say, also directed at me, were words I hadn't heard spoken from a child at all, let alone that young.

"Hey you (four letter curse word after four letter word and on and on).'

It was a whole string of expletives that I hadn't used ever; delivered especially with that low, angry tone, and it was coming from a baby. This was my first "culture shock" moment, to be followed by many.

I didn't know what to do, but I knew I didn't want to turn my back on him (what message would that send?). At the time I felt so lonely and scared, I had thought I was going out to "learn and play with kids."

My mind raced as I thought, "What should I do?"

I did the only thing I knew how to do and it worked. I crouched down, opened my arms and then surprisingly so, welcomed a child, one I'd never seen before, into a big, tight hug. Immediately, my heart knew that what had just happened was positive, loving, and enough. His smile was proof.

My heart said yes 10 years in a row. I gave so much and grew so much as a result. I learned how to:

Be open and have compassion for all, regardless of details

Give, to the point of mental and physical exhaustion

Be neutral, how to not choose sides/ listen to and understand all sides

Not feel responsible for everything, how to be a team member and trust others. Appreciate what I have and not compare to what "could be."

Be in the present moment without having to explain past experience or future goals

Be accepted for who I am, exactly how that's showing up right now.

Show true love and respect for the person who is "right in front of my face"

Accept emotional support

Understand the power of positivity

Be human and be humble.....

Embrace exhaustion, mental, emotional and physical - how to be aware that "this is how I'm feeling" and "how I'm feeling is absolutely okay."....

Be aware of previously held assumptions - whoever is "better/less than, smarter/dumber, richer/poorer, beautiful/ugly, capable/"just" there....

Accept that all people, especially all children, are the same, with the same needs.

Embrace the power of a group, with a general purpose and routine, and pure intent.

See the power in the beauty of nature, music and simply being, with self and others.

How to be aware of my thoughts and their effect on me and my actions.

And one of the most amazing things I learned from Truck of Love is how to make myself vulnerable - how to share honestly and openly in a group without a script or a planned response, without any masks or boundaries, or fear. I'm so full of love and gratitude for this life and Truck of Love. Together, we've made me, and a whole lotta others, better!

Monica spends much of her time being a wife and mother of two young sons.

I was such a young naive girl when I went on these trips. They taught me so much. Culture shock was the most prominent for me. I was overwhelmed with how much love I felt from the group & how locals joined in and what beautiful times we had. I also flash on it still in raising my kids.

I thank TOL and these trips for always keeping me aware of my blessings.

I remember how in love with the whole experience I was. I was heart- broken when Sue wouldn't let me return a third time. (I was so young minded and spent time with local boys)I guess my naive heart is what I remember, but my open HEART too. I still love that way.

I remember taking huge pots of beans to feed people who lived at the dump, singing at an old-folks home, walking down the street behind our Church fascinated by the difference in the way of life. My young mind was opened by all the experiences. Home made fresh tortillas off the press w/ PB & jelly! - super delicious. I still value the experience of not showering for weeks at a time. I recall waking up to "Back in the Saddle Again." And liking it. The strongest emotion I remember is the UNITY I felt within our group that was built by the common experience.

Bryan now lives and works in Tucson, Arizona. He and his brother, Gary, were two of the first group of O'odham teens who came to Hidden Villa for leadership training.

In the spring of 1988, I was asked to be a part of a small group of Tohono O'odham youth who would be traveling to California in the summer to attend a leadership camp in the hills of the San Francisco Bay Area. This trip was to be sponsored by the Truck of Love group who had previously held a summer camp in PisinMo'o, Arizona in 1987. When the Franciscan Sisters who were stationed in PisinMo'o asked me to be a part of this group, I was so excited to accept as I had grown fond of the Truck of Love group and was an active member of the Catholic church in and around my community, I accepted their offer almost immediate-

ly. I felt honored and humbled that my participation in the summer camp in 1987 led me to be a part of this wonderful opportunity to grow and learn more about leadership.

In June of 1988, I, along with Evonne Wilson, Wilma Lewis, Alton Calabaza and my brother Gary flew to San Jose from Tucson where we met Pete and Sue Fullerton and their group at the airport. Landing in San Jose, I was overwhelmed with the difference in the geography as I was so used to the desert southwest...everything was so green and the temperature was cool, around 75 degrees compared to 100+ here in Arizona. The Truck of Love made us feel so welcome when we arrived in the Bay Area and I've never felt so blessed to be part of such a wonderful group!

The next few days, we headed out to Hidden Villa Ranch in Los Altos Hills where we were to attend the Community Leadership Training. As we loaded up to head to Hidden Villa, I was nervous and a little scared because everything was happening so fast and I was in a "strange" land, I wanted to stay with Pete and Sue at their house for the whole summer! When we arrived at Hidden Villa, we were greeted by Susan Stanaway, the Executive Director of Hidden Villa Summer Camp and some of the camp counselors who we were going to be spending the next two weeks with, I was a nervous wreck! After getting comfortable and getting to know some of the staff, Pete and Sue said their goodbyes and the 5 of us began our two week Leadership Training.

The first night in Hollow Oak (our Leadership Camp site), I had a hard time going to sleep because we were to be sleeping under these huge trees and I was not used to that. During the two-week training, I got to know all of our fellow trainees and the counselors; we had a great time doing outdoorsy stuff like playing games in the horse pen, hiking around the campsite, singing and conversations around campfires, eating under a massive oak tree in our campsite, chores every single morning and every evening such as feeding the chickens, horses, pigs, cows, etc. And there were a lot of hugs everywhere! There was also time for fun like arts and crafts, hikes, storytelling, volleyball games, swimming and tons of outdoor fun! One of the most challenging parts of the training was when we went on a 3 day hike from Big Basin to the ocean at the end of our 2 week training, the preparation and the hike itself was physically, emotionally and mentally challenging for me, I had never done that in my life. We were driven to the spot where we were to start our hike the next morning and had supper under the stars. Sleeping under the stars and being afraid of critters stealing our food was fun! The hike was brutal...my legs hurt, my backpack was heavy, I was tired from lack of sleep but the counselors and fellow trainees encouraged us along the way and respected us if we were tired, they were a great bunch of folks whom I still think of to this day. When we got to the ocean, we did our traditional blessing with the ocean as the water is sacred to my people. My great aunt, who is an elder, told us to make sure that we do our blessing when we got to the ocean and we made sure we did it, in respect our elders and our culture. The hike was hard because the first part of the hike was going uphill and it was brutal on my legs and my back from the heavy backpack. The last part of the hike was better because we were descending from the Basin to the ocean...I liked that part because it wasn't so bad. The last night of our hike we slept on the beach and it was the most beautiful and serene feeling ever! I fell asleep to the sounds of the waves hitting the shore and night birds in the trees...a memory I hold dear to this day. All in all, I had a great time the first time I went to Hidden Villa. I felt a sense of belonging, acceptance, love, friendship and inclusion with everything and everyone there...I miss it very much. I continued to go to Hidden Villa every summer until 1992 when I graduated from high school and moved to the city and attended Pima Community College. I am forever grateful to the Truck of Love and Frank and Josephine Duveneck who started Hidden Villa Summer Camp in the early years, for allowing me, my brother and my friends to experience such a different but rewarding way to learn, trust, love and lead. I dedicate this piece of my memories of Hidden Villa and the Truck of Love to my brother Gary and my friend Alton Calabaza, may they continue to rest in eternal peace.

Carlos, husband and father, lives and works in Tijuana, Mexico. He helped us perfect the beans that became a staple in the dump.

I remember being in touch with the Truck of Love for the first time when I was peeking through the side road kitchen door because I heard singing inside and people speaking in English. I was about 14 years old when this happened. One of the group members invited me to join in a play inside the church where I played that I was dying, I don't remember what the play was about. I remember helping build a house for the lady who lived in the house on the corner. I remember we used to go to the orphanage of the sisters of mother Teresa. Going to "casa de la cuna" and to the old people's house. The best part was going to the dump. Before we went there we cooked that big pot of beans with cinnamon and potatoes that people used to love so much. (Maybe they were just really hungry.) Preparing these beans always made me feel good, eating them with people in the dump made me feel special. Casa del inmigrante (House of the immigrant) was always full of stories from guys deported from the U.S. and trying to get back. One of my favorite places was where we were doing summer school in the dump.

I was always fascinated by the language and the people of the US. I started learning English when I was about 10 years old, selling gum on Revolution Avenue. So to hear Americans in my Colonia was intriguing. I thought I wanted to know what you were doing in Tijuana. I was a friendly boy and you were really nice. So after being invited to come in I felt you were the kind of people I wanted to be around, this would allow me to help others.

Before you came I was a loner in the colonia, I didn't have many friends or didn't try to look for friends. You can imagine the impact the Truck of Love had in what's now my life. My kids (Luz Elena, Valeria Libertad and Luis Alberto) they all love when I tell them about the time I was with you and wish they also would get to do something like this.

I started selling gum because I wanted to help my mom, we didn't have much not even food items like milk or cereal. I wanted to buy me things also even when all I could think of would be buying candy or playing video games in the arcade.

263

I used to go out Friday like at 7 p.m. right after getting back from school at 5 p.m. I would first go buy a couple of boxes of gum and then hit the streets in Revolution Avenue up and down from 1st street to 11th. I would have my good days when clients would buy the complete box and then I could go home early, these of course were all US citizens. I had a few regulars. Normally I would keep selling until 6 a.m. the next day when the first bus started the first route. The first word I learned in English was "Gum" or "three for a quarter." I felt really important and full of pride when I learned how to say "chewing gum." I got hooked on English after that!!!

Scott is a husband, father, farrier, song writer, and musician in California. He and his wife Mandy founded Truck of Love South.

I love to recall the time we made a shower out of a pallet, tarp, garden hose, and a milk carton out back behind the kitchen in Ptown.

The words of the Simple Song are the most profound story I've lived through Truck of Love. It's set the tone for my life and my family and I am mucho hugely grateful for you, the gardeners, who planted the Simple Song seed in my simple little mind.

If you want to live life free, take your time go slowly
Do few things but do them well, simple things are holy
If you want to live life free, take your time go slowly
Small beginnings greater ends, heartfelt works grow purely
Day by day, stone by stone, build your secret slowly
Day by day, you'll grow too; you'll know heaven's glory
(Adapted from a Donovan song)